Academic Inquiry 1

Academic Inquiry 1

Sentences and Paragraphs

Marcia Kim
Jennifer MacDonald

SERIES EDITOR Scott Roy Douglas

OXFORD
UNIVERSITY PRESS

Oxford University Press is a department of the University of Oxford.
It furthers the University's objective of excellence in research, scholarship,
and education by publishing worldwide. Oxford is a registered trade mark of
Oxford University Press in the UK and in certain other countries.

Published in Canada by
Oxford University Press
8 Sampson Mews, Suite 204,
Don Mills, Ontario M3C 0H5 Canada

www.oupcanada.com

Library and Archives Canada Cataloguing in Publication
Kim, Marcia, author
Sentences and paragraphs / Marcia Kim, Jennifer
MacDonald ; series editor, Scott Roy Douglas.

(Academic inquiry ; 1)
Includes index.
ISBN 978-0-19-902539-8 (softcover)

1. Report writing.   2. English language–Sentences.
3. English language–Paragraphs.   4. English language–
Rhetoric.   I. MacDonald, Jennifer, 1980-, author   II. Title.
III. Series: Academic inquiry (Series) ; 1

LB2369.K56 2017   808'.042   C2017-907185-8

Cover images: © iStock/Geber86 (Top); © iStock/Rawpixel (Bottom)
Cover design: Laurie McGregor
Interior design: Laurie McGregor

Oxford University Press is committed to our environment.
Wherever possible, our books are printed on paper which comes from
responsible sources.

Printed and bound in Canada

1 2 3 4 — 21 20 19 18

To Mom and Dad
—Marcia

For R.
—Jennifer

SCOPE and SEQUENCE

		1	2	3	4	5	6
		Earth and Life Science	Technology	Engineering	Health Sciences	Sociology	Business
	Topic	Weather and the Natural World	Robotics	Structural Engineering	Kinesiology	Trends in Society	Business Practices
Exploring Ideas	**Introduction: Activating Background Knowledge**	Creating a Mind Map	Understanding Wikipedia	Starting a Discussion	Conducting a Survey	Using a Pyramid of Perspectives	Using a Chart
	Fostering Inquiry	Writing an Inquiry Question	Using the Five Senses	Inquiring into Categories and Characteristics	Expressing an Opinion	Inquiring about Changes and Trends	Inquiring into Business Practices
	Structure	Explanatory Paragraph	Descriptive Paragraph	Definition Paragraph	Opinion Paragraph	Graphic-Description Paragraph	Report
	Language Tip	Using Connectors of Sequence	Using Connectors of Location	Using Connectors of Additional Information or Examples	Using Connectors of Contrast	Using Connectors of Summary and Conclusion	Using Connectors of Importance
Academic Reading	**Vocabulary Skill**	Using a Dictionary	Forming Adjectives	Forming Nouns	Forming Verbs	Recognizing Latin and Greek Loanwords	Recognizing Collocation
	Academic Word List	6 Word Families from the Academic Word List in Each Unit					
	Mid-frequency Vocabulary	6 Word Families up to the 4K Frequency Level in Each Unit					
	Pre-reading	Skimming	Making Predictions with Visuals	Identifying Keywords	Using a Glossary	Generating Questions	Using the KWL Method
	Reading	"Thunder-storms"	"Spar Aerospace: An Arm from Earth to Space"	"Transportation Structures"	"Ben Johnson"	"The Greying of Canada"	"Booster Juice: Business in a Blender"
	Critical Thinking	Asking "Why?"	Evaluating Sources for Credibility	Stepping outside Your Box	Examining Evidence	Differentiating between Fact and Opinion	Playing the Contrarian

		1 Weather and the Natural World	2 Robotics	3 Structural Engineering	4 Kinesiology	5 Trends in Society	6 Business Practices
Process Fundamentals	**Topic**						
	Brainstorming and Outlining	Mind Mapping	Listing	Reverse Thinking	Five Points of View	Pyramid of Perspectives	Working in Groups
	Before You Write	Finding Information Online	Evaluating Websites	Asking Questions— the 5Ws + H	Taking Notes	Predicting Vocabulary	Reflecting on Your Topic
	Content Skill	Using Textbooks	Exploring Online Newspaper Articles	Using Magazine Articles	Using a Report	Using Information from a Blog Post	Using Survey Data and Reports
	Preventing Plagiarism	Not Submitting Another Person's Work	Working from Memory	Changing Words and Sentence Structure	Taking Notes	Acknowledging Your Source	Checking against the Original
	Paragraphing Skill	Understanding the Essential Elements of a Paragraph	Writing a Topic Sentence	Supporting Your Topic Sentence	Writing a Concluding Sentence	Organizing Paragraphs	Using Headings and Subheadings
	Language Skill	Making Generalizations	Using Comparatives and Superlatives	Defining	Expressing Opinions	Using the Language of Changes and Trends	Using the Language of Reports
Writing Fundamentals	**Composition Skill**	Drafting	Self-Editing	Proofreading	Using Checklists	Asking for Peer Review	Incorporating Feedback
	Writing Skill	Ensuring Flow	Avoiding Sentence Fragments	Avoiding Run-On Sentences	Avoiding Repetition	Achieving Cohesion Using Pronouns	Varying Sentence Structure
	Sentence and Grammar Skill	Writing Simple Sentences with the Simple Present and Present Continuous	Using Correct Adjective Word Order	Understanding Compound Sentences and Complex Sentences	Using Parallel Structure	Using Simple Present, Simple Past, and Present Perfect	Using Noun Phrases
Unit Outcome	**Writing Assignment**	Explanatory Paragraph	Descriptive Paragraph	Definition Paragraph	Opinion Paragraph	Graphic-Description Paragraph	Report
	Evaluation	Explanatory Paragraph Rubric	Descriptive Paragraph Rubric	Definition Paragraph Rubric	Opinion Paragraph Rubric	Graphic-Description Paragraph Rubric	Report Rubric
	Unit Review	Self-Assessment and Vocabulary Checklists					
	Learning Strategy	Understanding Assignments	Using Compensation Strategies	Using Memorization Strategies	Making Inferences	Using Affective Strategies	Using Social Learning Strategies

Contents

UNIT 1 EARTH AND LIFE SCIENCE
Weather and the Natural World

UNIT 2 TECHNOLOGY
Robotics   43

UNIT (3) ENGINEERING
Structural Engineering   83

UNIT 4 HEALTH SCIENCES
Kinesiology 127

UNIT 5 SOCIOLOGY
Trends in Society 169

UNIT 6 BUSINESS
Business Practices 215

Note to Instructors

Taking an inquiry-based approach, this series fosters academic writing skills that contribute to student success in post-secondary studies. Each unit is based on an academic discipline and opens with an introduction to theme-related content that prepares students to think about ideas within that discipline. At the heart of each unit, students develop personalized Unit Inquiry Questions to guide their study; these questions are inspired by each student's personal interest and curiosity. The process promotes higher-order thinking skills, encourages student curiosity, and resists simple yes or no answers. The Unit Inquiry Questions put an active learner-centred focus on content and prime students for dynamic engagement with unit materials, concepts, and skills.

Student writing skills are developed using a language-through-content approach to composition instruction, with each unit focused on one rhetorical writing pattern and one academic discipline. At the core of each unit is an authentic reading, such as an excerpt from an undergraduate textbook that students might typically encounter in a post-secondary setting. These readings provide a springboard for the inclusion of informative content in student writing and promote effective writing skills. Within each of the core academic readings, students are exposed to key vocabulary from the Academic Word List (AWL) along with pertinent mid-frequency vocabulary (MFV); these words are introduced to students in pre-reading activities and recycled throughout the unit to foster a greater depth and breadth of lexical usage in student writing.

Additionally, the rich contextual framework within each unit provides an opportunity for the recycling of skills and the spiralling of concepts. Each unit also emphasizes the fundamentals of the writing process as well as key composition and grammar skills, according to the demands of the unit content and writing assignments. These fundamentals are supported by special skills boxes focusing on thinking critically, developing learning strategies, and preventing plagiarism. Furthermore, all the process and writing fundamentals are accompanied by focused activities, opportunities for meaningful writing practice, and multiple writing models to provide comprehensible input to students as they gather ideas to answer their Unit Inquiry Questions and complete their own writing projects.

The final writing assignment in each unit is based on students' personalized Unit Inquiry Questions and the rhetorical pattern explored in the unit. Numerous opportunities for controlled writing output are provided throughout the unit until the final assignment is written as a culmination of the language and content knowledge gained throughout the unit. The final writing assignment is supported with evaluation and review activities to reinforce student learning and mastery of the unit outcomes.

Robustly supporting the content in the student books, the *Academic Inquiry* companion website (teacher's resource) is a rich source of supplementary materials. Online, teachers can find teaching notes, pacing guides, adaptable practice materials for each unit's learning objectives, answer keys, additional sample writing models, editing activities, and printable versions of the evaluation rubrics. Teachers will also find extension activities in the form of genre-based academic writing tasks (such as journal entries, lab reports, and case studies) and integrated tasks (such as surveys, short presentations, and posters). Finally, teachers have access to writing prompts suitable for timed exam purposes. Teachers can contact their local Oxford University Press sales and editorial representative for access to the password-protected teacher's resource.

Note to Students

Writing for academic purposes can seem like a difficult task; however, it doesn't have to be impossible. *Academic Inquiry* breaks down the task of academic writing into manageable parts. Each unit has carefully structured activities. You develop your academic writing skills step by step until you have the confidence to handle academic writing tasks on your own.

This textbook series takes an inquiry-based approach to learning. Each unit focuses on a core academic discipline, and you are encouraged to decide for yourself what specific area within that discipline you want to write about. This approach puts you in control of your learning. You find answers to your own questions. You develop your own writing topics.

Each unit opens with an opportunity to explore ideas connected to a topic within a specific academic discipline. Then you develop a question about that topic. It is a meaningful question based on your own curiosity. Throughout the unit, you have opportunities to find answers to this question—your Unit Inquiry Question.

Next, you work on expanding your vocabulary. New vocabulary supports your ability to express your ideas effectively and precisely. The new vocabulary is introduced in the context of academic readings, similar to those found in college and university settings. These readings also help you find ideas for your writing.

After you have read and responded to the readings in each unit, you have the opportunity to explore the unit topic in greater detail. You brainstorm and develop your chosen writing topic. You consider ways to prevent plagiarism. You make connections to your Unit Inquiry Question. You cover the structure and elements of quality academic writing, as well as critical thinking skills, learning strategies, vocabulary, and grammar points.

The key to developing these skills is extensive writing practice. Throughout each unit, you revisit and revise your own writing on a number of occasions. You see examples of good academic writing. You have the opportunity to review and rework your Unit Inquiry Question. You then complete the final unit assignment related to your Unit Inquiry Question. The end of each unit includes a writing rubric and self-assessment checklist connected to what you have learned in that unit. These tools help promote your understanding of the elements of effective academic writing.

The *Academic Inquiry* series guides you through the academic writing process. In each unit, you explore academic writing skills one at a time within the context of an academic discipline. In doing so, you will find the process of academic writing to be much less challenging. This style of writing is about communicating your ideas, which takes hard work and practice. However, developing the ability to express yourself clearly and effectively makes all that hard work and practice worthwhile. *Academic Inquiry* will empower you to use your skills and knowledge of the process in your future college and university studies.

Acknowledgements

The authors would like to acknowledge everyone at Oxford University Press who helped with this series and contributed to its publication. In particular, the authors thank the editorial team for their insightful suggestions and tireless dedication to excellence in English language teaching materials.

Oxford University Press Canada would like to express appreciation to the instructors and coordinators who graciously offered feedback on *Academic Inquiry* at various stages of the developmental process. Their feedback was instrumental in helping to shape and refine the book.

Carolyn Ambrose-Miller, Niagara College
Mélanie Barrière, Université de Sherbrooke
Erminia Bossio, Sheridan College
Devon Boucher, Thompson Rivers University
Kim Cechetto, Fanshawe College
Dara Cowper, Centennial College
Susan A. Curtis, University of British Columbia
Jason Doucette, Saint Mary's University
Cynthia Eden, University of Guelph
Giacomo Folinazzo, Niagara College
Sean Henderson, Wilfrid Laurier University
Gilmour Jope, University of the Fraser Valley
Barbara Kanellakos, Dalhousie University
Kristibeth Kelly, Fanshawe College

Vasie Kelos, Seneca College
Daryaneh Lane, University of Waterloo
Fiona Lucchini, Bow Valley College (retired)
Jonathon McCallum, Mohawk College
Angela Meyer Sterzik, Fanshawe College
Kristopher Mitchell, Dalhousie University
Anne Mullen, Université Laval
Thomas O'Hare, Université de Montrèal
Sophie Paish, Dalhousie University
Cyndy Reimer, Douglas College
Shawna Shulman, York University
Ardiss Stutters, Okanagan College
Elham Tavallaei, Centennial College
Jason Toole, Wilfrid Laurier University

UNIT 1

Earth and Life Science

Weather and the Natural World

EXPLORING IDEAS

Introduction

A sandstorm moves over the desert in Morocco.

A snow plow removes snow from the highway near Montréal, Québec during a storm.

Activity A | The photographs above show two kinds of extreme weather that happen in different parts of the world: a sandstorm in Morocco and a snowstorm in Montréal. Discuss the following questions with a partner or small group.

1. What do you know about extreme weather?
2. Is there extreme weather in another country you're familiar with? Describe it.
3. What are the dangers associated with the extreme weather there?
4. What do you do to prepare for extreme weather?

Activity B | A mind map is a diagram that shows connections between ideas. It is easy to create a mind map. First, draw a circle in the middle of your paper and write your main topic in it. Then think of ideas that are related to your main topic and write them in circles around your main topic. Continue thinking of ideas and how they connect to each other. Draw lines to show the connections.

Make a mind map to explore ideas related to weather and climate. Create your mind map on a big piece of paper and save it. You will use it in other activities in this unit. Here is an example of a mind map that has been started for the main topic Climate:

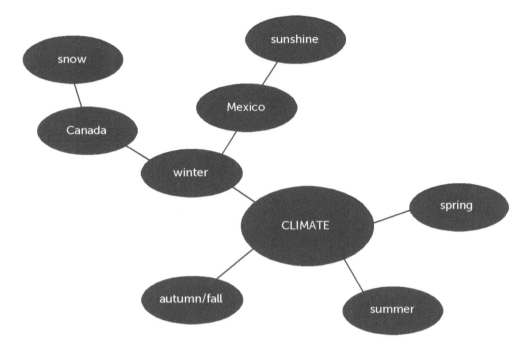

There are no specific rules to follow on how you generate your ideas, draw the circles, or make connections. Write down whatever comes to mind. You can think of examples or experiences you have had that are related to weather, climate, or the natural world. The more ideas you write down, the more ideas you have to choose from.

Activity C | With a partner, ask each other questions about the ideas you included in your mind map related to weather and climate. Take notes during your discussion. Are any of your ideas related to extreme weather?

Fostering Inquiry

Writing an Inquiry Question

Do you know what the word *inquiry* means? An inquiry is a formal investigation. An inquiry question is a question that will help you think about a topic and lead you to discover more information related to it. Creating an inquiry question will help guide your learning.

How do you make up an inquiry question? First, think about what interests you. What is something you are curious about? Is there a topic that you would like to know more about? Do not be afraid to explore a subject that is completely new to you. Your inquiry question is a chance to learn something new about a topic you find interesting.

What are the characteristics of a good inquiry question? A good inquiry question

- makes you want to explore a topic and learn more about it;
- leads to more questions; and
- asks you to think critically about your topic.

Examples

Does it hail in the winter? is a yes/no question or closed question. It is not an inquiry question. The answer is either *yes* or *no*. This question does not provoke you to think deeply about your topic.

What is weather? is a very general question. It is not necessary to research this question; the answer is in the dictionary.

How does hail form? is an inquiry question because it asks about a process and when you begin your inquiry into how hail forms, you will encounter information about hail that you may not have considered before. In your research, you may also find the answers to some related closed questions such as *Is hail dangerous?* or *Does it hail in the winter?*

How can severe weather be predicted? is another example of an inquiry question. This inquiry question is engaging—it makes you think about the topic in different ways. It also makes you think reflectively about the weather people in different parts of the world experience and the effect it has on them.

Activity A | What do you want to know more about in relation to the natural world, weather, or climate? For example:

- How does a tornado form?
- What causes a monsoon?
- Why is it so cold in Antarctica?

1. Write two or three questions you are curious about on the topic of weather, climate, or the natural world.
2. When you are finished, compare your questions with a partner or small group.
3. Choose one question to be your inquiry question for this unit. It does not have to be the same question as your partner or group.

4. Write your inquiry question in the space provided. Look back at this question as you work through the unit. This is your Unit Inquiry Question.

My Unit Inquiry Question:

_____

_____

_____

 Activity B | Writing Task: Freewriting | Freewriting can help you think of ideas related to your inquiry question and topic.

- Take out a piece of paper and a pen, or open a new Word document on your computer.
- Set a timer for five minutes and start writing about the topic you've chosen for your inquiry question. You can write anything that you think of related to your topic.
- Don't look up words and information in the dictionary or online when you are freewriting. Just let your thoughts and ideas come to you and write them down. The important thing is to not stop writing until five minutes have passed.
- When you've finished, read your text aloud. Are there any interesting ideas in your text that you would like to research in this unit?

Structure

Explanatory Paragraph

Purpose

The most important aspect of any text is its purpose. *Purpose* refers to the reason a text was written. The purpose of a newspaper article, for example, is different from the purpose of a novel. A newspaper article is written to inform, while a novel is written to entertain or to make people think about a certain issue.

Activity A | With a partner or small group, discuss the purpose of the following texts:

1. an email to your parents;
2. an email to the professor of a course you're taking;
3. a newspaper article about problems with the city's government; and
4. an essay on a university exam.

The purpose of an explanatory paragraph is to explain why or how something happens. Very often, in an explanatory paragraph you explain a process. You do this by identifying and explaining the steps or stages of the process. For example, your paragraph may explain the three steps involved in how a tornado is formed.

Audience

Remember that every text you write has an audience. The word *audience* refers to the person or people who will read the text. Depending on your audience, you may change how you write a text.

The audience for an explanatory paragraph could be an instructor or the general public. Sometimes people with specialized knowledge, such as students, researchers, or scientists, write texts about the subjects that they are experts in. The goal of these texts is to explain something complex in simple language so that a non-expert can understand. An example of this could be an article in the newspaper or on a website.

Activity B | With a partner or small group, read the short explanatory paragraph below on how a fruit tree grows. Then answer the questions that follow.

How Does a Fruit Tree Grow?

A fruit tree grows from a small seed into a large plant. A tree begins its life as a seed. A seed comes from the fruit of a tree. First, the fruit falls to the ground. The flesh of the fruit disappears and the seed remains. Then, if the seed has earth, air, light, and water, it grows into a seedling. A seedling is a small, young tree. It has roots that go into the earth and leaves that reach toward the sky. The seedling takes food from the earth through its roots. It also takes food from the air and sun through its leaves. The seedling continues to grow until it is an adult tree. Then it begins to produce flowers. The flowers turn into fruit. The fruit has seeds inside. Finally, when the fruit falls to the ground, the seeds enter the earth and a new tree begins. That is how a large adult fruit tree grows from a small seed.

1. What is being explained in this paragraph?
2. What are the steps in this explanation?
3. What words or phrases show the different steps?
4. Is there anything special about the first and last sentences?

Structure of an Explanatory Paragraph

An explanatory paragraph answers *why* or *how*. An explanatory paragraph begins with a topic sentence that states in a general way what you will explain in your paragraph.

When you write an explanatory paragraph, you break a long explanation into smaller stages or steps. This makes it easier for your reader to understand. Present the steps in a logical order. This is usually chronological order (the order that the steps happen in). Use connecting phrases to link the steps together.

Language Tip

Using Connectors of Sequence

You can use connectors of sequence to link sentences together in the correct order. These phrases usually appear at the beginning of a sentence, and are followed by a comma.

To begin,	Third,	Next,	Following this,
First,	Finally,	After this,	At this point,
Second,	Then,	Afterwards,	

For more on connectors, see the Language Tip box in each unit of this book.

Activity C | In Activity B on page 6, you read a short explanatory paragraph about how a fruit tree grows. You identified the words or phrases that show different steps. Read the paragraph again, but this time change or add connectors of sequence if possible. Choose from the connectors of sequence in the box above. Then compare your answers with a partner or small group.

Note that sometimes your explanatory paragraph will contain words or terms that your reader might not understand. You may have to include simple definitions in your paragraph. The last sentence in your explanatory paragraph is a concluding sentence. It should remind the reader what they have just learned about.

Figure 1.1 shows an outline of an explanatory paragraph. The first sentence is the topic sentence and the sentences that follow make up the main body of the paragraph. They explain the process in steps or stages. The final sentence is the concluding sentence.

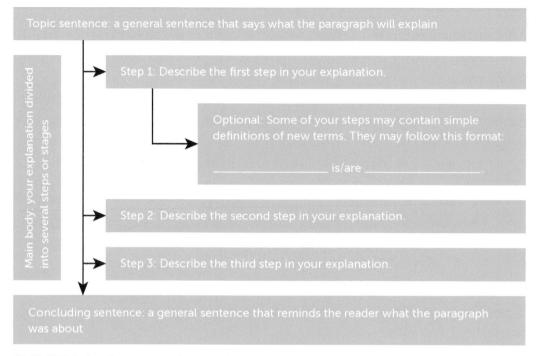

FIGURE 1.1   Structure of an explanatory paragraph

Activity D | Below you will find an example of an explanatory paragraph. It contains a topic sentence, steps in the explanation, and a concluding sentence, all linked by connectors of sequence. Read the paragraph carefully and answer the questions that follow the paragraph.

How Rain Is Formed

Rain is caused by the water inside clouds. All clouds are made of small water droplets. Most droplets inside clouds are only 0.02 millimetres in diameter. This is very small. Small droplets must grow to be heavy enough to fall to the earth. First, the water droplets start moving around inside a cloud. Both air and water droplets move and shake together. If a cloud is cold, sometimes there are ice crystals in the cloud too. Then, the droplets hit each other and blend together into larger raindrops. This is called *coalescence*. Ice crystals can also come together into snowflakes through coalescence. Next, the raindrops continue to grow until they have a diameter of between 0.5 and 2.0 millimetres. Finally, the raindrops or snowflakes are big enough to fall to the ground. When snowflakes leave the cloud, they may melt into raindrops, depending on the temperature. These water droplets fall from the cloud to the earth as rain. To sum up, droplets grow to become raindrops or snowflakes and then fall to the ground.

1. What is the <u>purpose</u> of this paragraph?
2. Who is the audience of this paragraph: experts or non-experts? How do you know this?
3. What is the topic sentence of this paragraph?
4. Are any terms defined in this paragraph? Find and underline the definitions.
5. This explanatory paragraph gives the steps in how rain is formed. Find and number these steps in the text.

Activity E | Think of something interesting or special that happens in the natural world, something that you are familiar with. Imagine explaining this process to someone. Complete the top box in the following outline and then fill in each of the rest of the boxes with one sentence. (You can add a few more steps if you have to.)

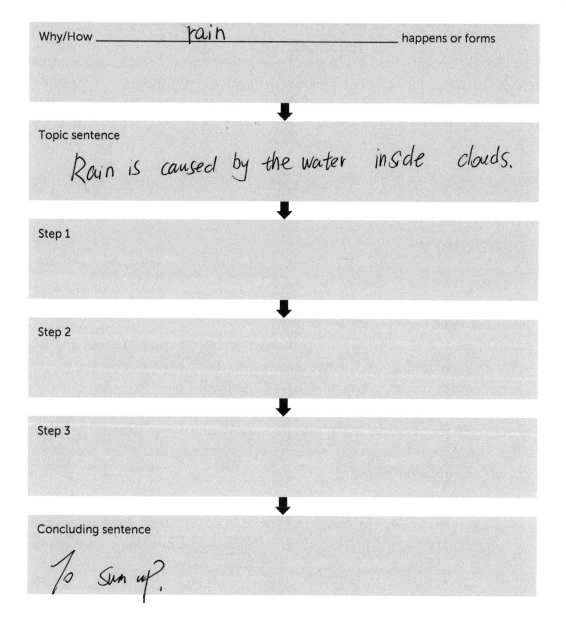

Why/How _____ rain _____ happens or forms

Topic sentence

Rain is caused by the water inside clouds.

Step 1

Step 2

Step 3

Concluding sentence

To Sum up.

Activity F | Exchange your outline with a partner. Read your partner's sentences and provide feedback, using the following questions to guide you.

1. Does this explanation include several steps or stages necessary for something to happen?
2. Does the topic sentence state in a general way what the paragraph will explain?
3. Are the steps or reasons organized in a logical order?
4. Are there any terms that need defining in this paragraph?
5. Is there enough detail in the explanation to understand why or how the event happens?
6. Is the language appropriate for a non-expert audience?
7. What do you like most about these sentences?
8. Could these sentences be expanded into a paragraph?
9. How would you improve these sentences?

Activity G | Revisit your Unit Inquiry Question on page 5. What information or new ideas have you thought of or discussed that will help you answer your question? Share your ideas with a partner or small group. At this point, you may consider revising your Unit Inquiry Question.

ACADEMIC READING

Vocabulary

Vocabulary Skill: Using a Dictionary

One of the most useful tools for improving your academic writing skills is a good dictionary. A dictionary entry contains valuable information about a word. Depending on your dictionary, it may include the definition, pronunciation, part of speech, how the word is used, synonyms, and antonyms.

Knowing as much as possible about the word may help you improve the precision and variety in your writing. It may also help you improve your spelling. It doesn't matter whether you have an electronic or a paper dictionary. When choosing a dictionary, consider the following:

- Dictionaries that have translations can be helpful. However, as your English vocabulary increases and you start writing with more specialized vocabulary, you will find that the translations in your dictionary may not be accurate. If you want to write fluently in English, you should use an English-only dictionary as much as possible.

- An electronic dictionary with audio pronunciation is helpful. However, both electronic and print dictionaries generally have the pronunciation of each word spelled out using the International Phonetic Alphabet (IPA). If you learn how to use the IPA, you will be able to figure out the pronunciation of any word. This is helpful not only for speaking, but for writing with a natural-sounding rhythm.
- Some words have several meanings and may be used as different parts of speech. The entry for each word should clearly indicate which meanings go with each part of speech. Your dictionary should also give clear examples for all the meanings.

Activity A | Label the definition, pronunciation, part of speech, and example sentences in this dictionary entry for *thunderstorm*.

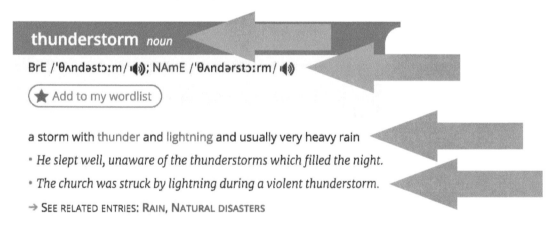

Vocabulary Preview: The Academic Word List

The Academic Word List (AWL) is a tool to help improve your academic reading, writing, listening, and speaking in English. It is a list of more than 500 of the words most commonly used in academic books, articles, and lectures. If you know the words on this list, it will help you better understand what you read and hear. They will also help you improve your speaking and writing.

Activity B | The following AWL words are taken from the academic reading "Thunderstorms," on pages 14–16. The definitions of the words are provided. Read the words and their definitions and choose the correct word to complete the sentences that follow. You might have to change the form of the word to fit the sentence.

intense (adj.): very great or strong
source (n.): a place, person, or thing that you get something from
mature (adj.): fully developed
eventually (adv.): at the end of a period of time or a series of events
release (v.): to set free
expand (v.): to become greater in size

1. Environment Canada is the ___Source___ for most Canadian weather forecasts.

2. Researchers will ___release___ genetically modified mosquitoes to decrease the number of wild mosquitoes in problem areas.

3. The ___intense___ summer heat makes it almost unbearable to be outside.

4. Ice floes in the Arctic Ocean are disappearing; however, the Antarctic sea ice is ___expanding___.

5. The weather in Calgary is unpredictable. This morning the rain turned to ice, then ___eventually___ to snow.

6. ___Mature___ elm trees have long weeping branches and can grow up to 30 metres tall.

Vocabulary Preview: Mid-frequency Vocabulary

Many students focus only on definitions when learning English vocabulary. However, it's also important to think about word frequency. Word frequency refers to how often certain words are used in speaking and writing. For example, the most common 2000 word families in English are called *high-frequency vocabulary*. These word families make up around 80 percent of most texts, so they are important to know. Once you've learned these words, you can start to focus on *mid-frequency vocabulary*. These are words that are less common than high-frequency vocabulary, but important as you read more difficult texts or want to speak about more complex ideas.

Activity C | Read each sentence and match the bolded word to its definition below. Write the letter on the line provided.

Sentences

1. ___f___ After three days of rain, the river rose **rapidly**.

2. ___e___ The thick fog **surrounding** us kept us from finding our way back to the road.

3. ___c___ The **attractive** forces within a thundercloud pull molecules together.

4. ___d___ The **peak** of the tornado season in southern Saskatchewan is June and July.

5. ___b___ **Extreme** pressure under the volcano can cause it to erupt.

6. ___a___ The hailstorm was terribly **destructive**. It broke windows and dented vehicles.

Definitions

a. causing great damage
b. great
c. relating to forces that pull things toward each other
d. the point when something is best, most successful, strongest, etc.
e. all around someone or something
f. very quickly

Reading

The following reading, "Thunderstorms," is an excerpt from the textbook *Science Power 10*. This textbook is used in high school science classes in Nova Scotia, Canada.

Skimming

Skimming is a way of reading. When skimming a text, read it very quickly, paying attention to words or ideas that are repeated throughout the text. You should also look at the title, headings, and any photos or graphics. While skimming, if there is a word you don't understand, just skip it. You don't use a dictionary when you are skimming a text. Skimming is a helpful pre-reading strategy when you receive a new text.

Try to get a general idea of what the text is about from the repeated words and ideas, title, headings, and visuals. This will help you better understand the text when you go on to read it more slowly in detail.

Activity A | Think of a thunderstorm that you've experienced in real life or seen on TV or in a movie. With a partner or small group, brainstorm a list of words associated with thunderstorms.

Activity B | Skim the reading below. Pay special attention to the illustrations (Figures 1.3 and 1.4). What aspects of thunderstorms do you think this text is going to be about?

Activity C | Now read the text. In the margins of the reading, number the steps or stages of the formation of a thunderstorm. How many stages are there? Compare your answer with a partner.

READING

Thunderstorms

1   Thunderstorms can be quite **destructive**. They bring lightning and strong gusting winds. They also bring torrential[1] rains that can cause flash floods. Thunderstorms can form "out of the blue" in a very short time. They form from cumulus[2] clouds that continue to grow and develop into cumulonimbus[3] clouds. So the conditions that create thunderstorms are much the same as the conditions that create cumulus clouds. Only a small percentage of cumulus clouds ever develop into thunderstorms, however.

2   Meteorologists usually describe the development of a thunderstorm in three stages. The first stage is the formation of a cumulus cloud. A cumulus cloud forms when warm air rises upward **rapidly**. This may happen because very warm ground is heated quickly by the sun and starts the process of convection.[4] A cold front[5] can also cause a cumulus cloud to form. Often, in fact, many cumulus clouds form in a line along a cold front.

3   How does the small, fluffy cumulus cloud develop into a cumulonimbus, or storm cloud? As shown in Figure 1.2, a large amount of warm, moist air must be available to feed the cumulus cloud. In the second stage of thunderstorm

---

[1] falling in large amounts

[2] a type of thick white cloud

[3] a high mass of thick cloud with a flat base, often seen during thunderstorms

[4] the process in which heat moves through a gas or a liquid as the hotter part rises and the cooler, heavier part sinks

[5] the line where a mass of cold air meets a mass of warm air

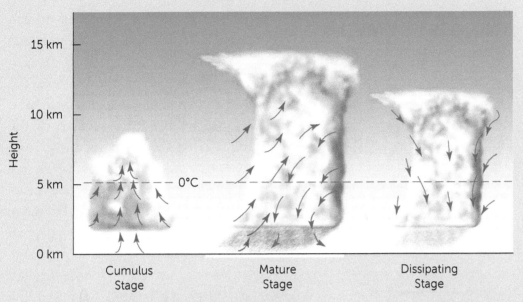

FIGURE 1.2 The formation of a thunderstorm

development, more hot air rises up into the cloud and condenses. The condensation[6] **releases** latent energy.[7] The latent energy becomes thermal energy.[8] Still warmer than the **surrounding** air, the warm air continues to rise. This creates an updraft that pulls in more air from below.

4   Soon so many cloud droplets are rising and colliding in the turbulence that the top drops below freezing. Ice crystals form. The process of coalescence[9] speeds up. Then rain begins. The rain cools the air and pulls it along. This creates a downdraft. At the **peak** of a thunderstorm, rain and a downdraft of cool air are at the leading edge of the cloud. An updraft of warm, moist air is at the trailing edge. The top of the cloud reaches the top of the troposphere.[10] The strong winds are blowing, usually out of the west. These winds blow the top of the cloud forward, forming the familiar anvil[11] shape. If the updrafts and turbulence in this stage are strong enough, hail can form.

5   It is during the second, or **mature**, stage that the thundercloud produces lightning. The **extreme** turbulence in the cloud causes ice crystals, snow particles, and water droplets to collide with great force. This strips electrons from some

rain   _hail_   _Snow_

---

[6] the process of a gas changing into a liquid

[7] the energy that exists in something but is not being used (also called *potential energy*)

[8] the heat-related energy that exists in something

[9] the act or process of coming together to form one larger group, substance, etc.

[10] the lowest layer of the earth's atmosphere, between the surface of the earth and about 6–10 kilometres above the surface

[11] a metal tool that is cone-shaped, meaning its top is larger than its bottom

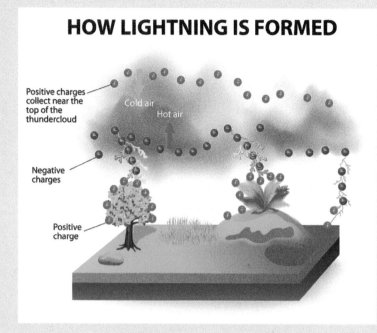

HOW LIGHTNING IS FORMED

Positive charges collect near the top of the thundercloud

Cold air

Hot air

Negative charges

Positive charge

FIGURE 1.3   A lightning bolt lights up the night sky. The collision of ice and snow particles in a cloud creates the energy source.

particles and leaves them on others. Positively charged particles accumulate at the top of the cloud. Negatively charged particles accumulate at the bottom. The negative bottom of the cloud drives negative charges away from the surface of the ground, leaving the surface of the ground positively charged. As the amount of charge separation increases, the **attractive** forces intensify between the positive and negative charges. **Eventually**, the attraction is so great that a tremendous electrical discharge occurs. The charged particles race through the air, creating a flash of lightning. The energy of the collisions of the charged particles is so great that the temperature of this thin strand of air rises to over 30,000 degrees Celsius—five times hotter than the surface of the sun. Due to the **intense** heat, the air **expands** with a tremendous force. It collides with the surrounding air particles. The collisions of air particles continue outward from the lightning bolt. This forms the sound wave that we hear as thunder.

6   Eventually the rain and the downdraft of cool air cool off the updraft of warm, moist air—the **source** of energy for the storm. This is the third stage of a thunderstorm: the dissipating stage. The rain continues until the supply of moisture runs out. Then the storm is over.

Source: Grace, E., Mustoe, F., Ivanco, J., Gue, D., Brown, E., Edwards, L., & Bello, R. (2000). *Sciencepower 10* (Atlantic ed., pp. 502–503). Toronto, ON: McGraw-Hill Ryerson.

Activity D | Discuss the following questions with a partner or small group.

1. In your own words, explain the stages of a thunderstorm's development.
2. What causes thunder and lightning?
3. Which parts of a thunderstorm do you think are most dangerous to humans?
4. Have you ever experienced a thunderstorm as described in the article? Do you remember anvil-shaped clouds, rain, thunder, lightning, and maybe hail?
5. What do you know about thunderstorms that you did not know before?

Activity E | Writing Task: Diagram Description | Look at Figure 1.2 on page 15. Write three sentences that describe what happens in Stage 1 of a thunderstorm, three sentences that describe what happens in Stage 2, and two sentences that describe what happens in Stage 3.

If you reuse any of the key vocabulary from the reading, make sure that you make the sentences your own. Be careful if you use any new vocabulary from the text. After you have written your sentences, check that they all have a subject and a verb, and begin with a capital letter and end with a period.

Stage 1	Stage 2	Stage 3
1. The warm ground is heated quickly by the sun.	4. Hot air rises up into the cloud and condenses.	7.
2. Starts the process of oven convection.	5. Still warmer than the sur surrounding air, the warm air continues to rise.	8.
3. Warm air rises upward rapidly	6. Creating an updraft that pulls in more air from below	

Activity F | Compare your sentences with the Unit 1 sample sentences in Appendix 2, then answer the following questions.

1. Does each of your sentences have a subject and a verb?
2. Does each of your sentences begin with a capital letter and end with a period?
3. Have you used any new nouns from the article? Are they used correctly in your sentences?
4. Have you used any new adjectives from the article? Are they used correctly in your sentences?
5. Have you used any new verbs from the article? Are they used correctly in your sentences?
6. How do the ideas in the sample sentences compare with the ideas in your sentences?

Critical Thinking

Asking "Why?"

Thunderstorms seem to develop very quickly, but as you've read, they don't happen without a reason. A calm day can turn into a thunderstorm if the conditions are right. The process leading from a blue sky to thunder and lightning can be broken down into several steps or stages.

Think of some other natural events: tides, forest fires, a full moon, tornadoes, and so on. Why do these things happen? What are the conditions in the atmosphere or natural environment that cause these events to take place? Can you look at these processes and break them down into stages or steps?

Asking *why* is a critical thinking skill that can be applied to all topics. For example, in Unit 2, you will read about robotics. When you begin thinking about an inquiry question related to robotics, you might ask why robots are designed to have "human-like" features.

PROCESS FUNDAMENTALS

Brainstorming and Outlining

Brainstorming is a technique for generating a lot of ideas about a topic quickly. It is often the first step in the writing process. When you brainstorm, you write down all your ideas about your topic. All ideas are good ideas when brainstorming.

When you brainstorm, don't write full sentences; just write phrases or words. Brainstorming allows you to see how your ideas relate and connect to each other. There are many different ways to brainstorm. One technique is mind mapping.

Mind Mapping

Mind mapping is a common brainstorming technique to start the writing process. A mind map shows how your ideas relate to each other. Draw a circle and write your main topic in it, and then write ideas that are related to your main topic in circles around your main topic. Continue thinking of ideas and how they connect to each other. Show the connections between ideas by drawing lines between circles. Remember that there is no correct way to generate ideas, draw the circles, or make connections.

Activity A | Look at the mind map you created in Activity B of the *Exploring Ideas* section on page 2, and then discussed with a partner. See if you can add more circles with ideas, examples, or thoughts. Then show your mind map to the same partner. Tell your partner how your ideas connect.

Activity B | Look at the example of the mind map below. It is on the topic of storms. Use the terms *blizzard*, *cyclone*, *wind*, *sleet*, *shuts down air travel*, and whatever other words and phrases you can think of to add more circles to the mind map. Share your mind map with a partner and discuss your ideas.

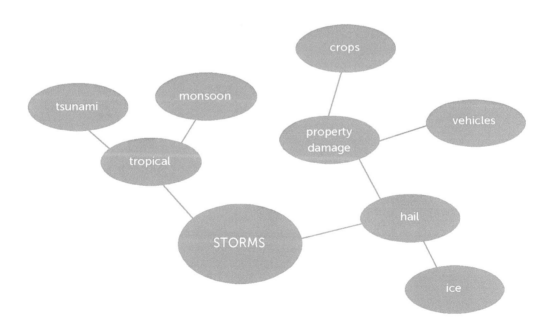

Activity C | Create a mind map for your Unit Inquiry Question. Include as many ideas as possible.

Outlining

An outline is a plan that can help you organize your writing. An outline will help you see if you have the necessary parts to write a good paragraph. Follow these steps to create an outline:

1. First of all, write the five main headings down the left side: Topic sentence, Supporting idea 1, Supporting idea 2, Supporting idea 3, and Concluding sentence.
2. Next, look at the mind map you made for your inquiry question. What is your main idea? What do you want to say about this topic? Write this down under the topic sentence heading.
3. Finally, look at your mind map again and begin filling in ideas under the rest of the headings. As you decide on your supporting ideas, you can also write down specific examples that will support them.

Topic sentence	• main idea—what the paragraph is about • controlling idea—what you want say about the topic
Supporting idea 1	(include examples and details)
Supporting idea 2	(include examples and details)
Supporting idea 3	(include examples and details)
Concluding sentence	summary of main points

Outlining is part of the planning stage of writing. At this point, you are planning and brainstorming ideas, so don't worry if your outline is messy. After you complete your outline, you can see if your ideas relate to each other and if you have enough examples and details to support your main points.

Look at this example of a basic outline for an academic paragraph.

Topic sentence: Write a topic sentence that contains the **main idea** (what the paragraph is about) and the **controlling idea** (what you want say about the topic). It is usually the first sentence.

Fog forms in different ways.

Supporting idea 1: After the topic sentence, write the first supporting idea. Support this idea with **examples and details**.

The first way is through infrared cooling. Seasonal changes cause infrared cooling. For example, the ground absorbs heat in the summer. When fall comes, the moist air and the cooler air create fog. This type of fog is the most common. It is called radiation fog.

Supporting idea 2: Write the second supporting idea. Support this idea with **examples and details**.

The second way is through advection. Advection creates fog from wind. Wind blows warm air over a cool surface. This fog is usually thicker and stays around longer.

Supporting idea 3: Write the third supporting idea. Support this idea with **examples and details**.

Fog also forms over oceans and lakes. Sea smoke is an example. It forms when cool air moves across a warm surface like land or a body of water.

Concluding sentence: Summarize your main points in the concluding sentence. It is usually the last sentence in the paragraph.

All in all, fog can form whenever the ground and air have a temperature difference.

FIGURE 1.4 Basic outline for an academic paragraph on the topic of fog

Activity D | Look at the mind map you developed for your Unit Inquiry Question in Activity A. Create an outline for a paragraph based on your mind map. As you complete more tasks in this unit, you can use your outline to add more ideas and details to support your topic.

Before You Write

Finding Information Online

Before you write, you will need to find information to support your main idea. The Internet contains a wealth of information that you can use. Once you have decided on your topic and identified necessary keywords (words that will help you find information), you can use different search terms to help you narrow down your search. For example, when your search term is *wind*, your result will be a list of links to pages that contain the word *wind*.

You can also use search term operators, such as AND, OR, a minus sign, and quotation marks. When you search wind AND rain, you will get pages that contain both *wind* and *rain*. If you search wind OR rain, you will get pages that have either *wind* or *rain*. If you search wind -rain, you will get pages with *wind* but not *rain*. If you use quotation marks around your search term (for example, "wind and rain"), your results will include pages that contain that exact group of words.

Activity A | Look at the search terms in Columns A and B. Decide if these searches will return the same result. Discuss your answers with a partner.

Column A	Column B	Same Result? (yes or no)
storm	hurricane	
storm AND hurricane	hurricane AND storm	
storm OR hurricane	storm OR storm OR hurricane	
storm AND hurricane	"storm and hurricane"	
-storm hurricane	storm -hurricane	

Note: Different search engines will return different results. However, they all use these same basic search term operators.

Activity B | The fewer searches you have to do, the more efficient you are. With a partner, discuss strategies for efficiently finding information online. What combinations of search terms would you use for the topics below?

1. naming conventions for typhoons
2. hurricanes other than Hurricane Katrina
3. the differences between cyclones, tornadoes, and monsoons
4. how beavers build dams
5. types of clouds

Activity C | Identify the most important words in the Unit Inquiry Question you wrote on page 5 and do an online search using different combinations of words and search term operators. What results do you get when you change the search term operators? Discuss your findings with a partner.

Content Skill

Using Textbooks

You will use different sources of information in your academic career: online encyclopedias, government websites, and newspapers are just a few examples. Which resources you use depends on your assignment and your topic.

When you are looking for supporting details to include in a writing assignment, textbooks can be a great source of information. They cover a subject well and often include diagrams, pictures, charts, and graphs, which may be useful for your assignments.

Understanding the features of textbooks may help you use them more effectively in your research. You will be able to find information on your own and easily. This is a skill you can use in all your college or university courses.

Activity A | Look at one of your current textbooks. Which of the features below does your textbook have?

a. ☐ Table of Contents
b. ☐ Appendix
c. ☐ Index
d. ☐ Glossary
e. ☐ A message from the authors (might be called "Note to Students" or "How to Use this Book")
f. ☐ Special Features
g. ☐ Web Activities

Activity B | Pick three different features from the list above. With a partner, prepare an explanation of the purpose of each feature for another pair of students.

Activity C | **Writing Task: Explanatory Sentences** | In order to write an explanatory paragraph about the causes of hurricanes, you would likely search science textbooks for information. The following reading about hurricanes comes from the science textbook *SCIENCEPOWER 10*. Read the text carefully. As you read, try to identify the steps that lead to the creation of a hurricane. When you've finished reading, jot down the steps, then close your book and write five sentences for your paragraph: one topic sentence, three sentences that could be developed into supporting ideas, and one concluding sentence.

Hurricanes

1   A hurricane can be described as a gigantic, 500-kilometre-wide, whirling, roving thunderstorm. Where does all this energy come from?

2   A hurricane gets its energy from the thermal energy of warm, tropical, ocean water. Trade winds blow warm ocean water toward the west. They cause the water to "pile up" when it approaches a continent. This deep, warm water is what fuels hurricanes. Meteorologists have found that the water temperature must be at least 26 degrees Celsius, to a depth of at least 60 metres, for a hurricane to develop fully and be sustained. In the Atlantic Ocean, waters reach this temperature in the late summer. As a result, most of the hurricanes in this region occur in August, September, and October. Hurricanes are called typhoons in the West Pacific. They are called tropical cyclones in the Indian Ocean.

3   Hurricanes do not occur directly over the equator. The reason is that the Coriolis effect is absent directly over the equator. The Coriolis effect is needed to give hurricanes their spin.
Thus, the following conditions are necessary to generate a hurricane:

- the conditions needed to develop a thunderstorm;
- deep, warm, ocean water for energy to keep the thunderstorm going; and
- the Coriolis effect to give it spin.

4   Most hurricanes that affect North America start as waves of disturbances in the trade winds over the Atlantic Ocean, west of the African coast. These easterly waves are the source of several unorganized thunderstorms. In order for the thunderstorms to grow tall enough and strong enough to develop into a hurricane, there must be little or no wind shear. That is, the winds at the top of the cloud must be similar in strength and direction to the winds at sea level. Wind shear could tear apart the clouds and prevent their growth. The warm, moist air rises until it cools enough to condense and form clouds. As it condenses, it releases latent energy. The latent energy keeps the air warm so that it rises higher and higher. The warm ocean water provides an almost endless supply of water vapour. The water vapour continuously adds energy to the growing storms.

5   As the storms grow stronger, the updrafts draw air inward. They help to pull several thunderclouds together. The Coriolis effect helps them organize and begin to rotate. When wind speeds within the storm reach about 37 kilometres per hour, the storm is classified as a tropical depression. When the wind speeds grow to 65 kilometres per hour, the classification changes to tropical storm. If the storm takes on the form shown in Figure 1.5, and the wind speeds reach 120 kilometres per hour, the storm earns the classification of hurricane.

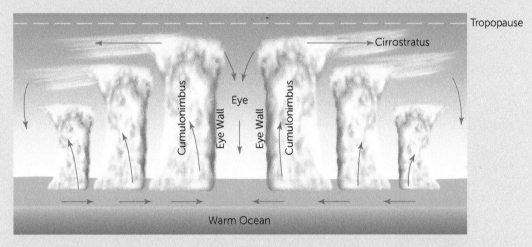

FIGURE 1.5   A hurricane is made of many cylindrical thunderstorms

6   In a hurricane, the entire system is whirling around. At the same time, strong updrafts draw air into the thunderclouds. Then some air flows back down between the clouds. The rapidly rising air creates a low-pressure zone at sea level. It creates a high-pressure zone above the clouds. As the air moves outward from the high-pressure zone, the Coriolis effect causes it to curve to the right—opposite to the direction of the hurricane's spin. The high winds and low pressure at the centre of a hurricane draw the ocean surface upward. This ridge of sea water is called the *storm surge*. It may be as high as 5.5 metres. In the middle of the hurricane, there is a calm clear central zone called the *eye*. The eye averages about 30 kilometres wide. Sometimes tropical birds become trapped in the eye. They must move with the hurricane until it dissipates.

Source: Adapted from Grace, E., Mustoe, F., Ivanco, J., Gue, D., Brown, E., Edwards, L., & Bello, R. (2000). *SCIENCEPOWER 10* (Atlantic ed., pp. 507–509). Toronto, ON: McGraw-Hill Ryerson.

Not Submitting Another Person's Work

To plagiarize is to take someone else's work or ideas and pass them off as your own. Plagiarism is a very serious offence in academic settings. It is an example of academic dishonesty and is considered cheating. You may be suspended or even expelled from the university or college.

Plagiarism is complicated. Many students are confused about it. The best way to answer any questions you have about plagiarism is to ask your instructor.

Consider these two examples:

A student has to write an essay for one of his classes in university. The student's older brother took the same class last year and still has his essay. The student gets a copy of the essay from his brother, changes the name and date on the title page, and hands it in to his instructor as if it were his own assignment.

The same student has to give a presentation for a class, but he was busy with other assignments. He asks his brother for a presentation he prepared for a different class. The student gives the presentation in his class as if he were the one who prepared it.

In both of these examples, the student is plagiarizing. He is using another person's work and passing it off as his own. Even if his brother gives him permission to use his work, this is still considered plagiarism.

Paragraphing Skill

Understanding the Essential Elements of a Paragraph

Paragraphs discuss one main idea and contain several sentences. There are many ways to structure a paragraph. Earlier in the unit, you saw that the basic structure of an academic paragraph includes a topic sentence, supporting sentences, and a concluding sentence.

Activity A | The first three sentences of this paragraph are in the correct order. The rest are in the wrong order. Figure out the correct order and write the number in front of the sentence.

---

(1) Hail forms in thunderclouds. (2) Hailstones start as small drops of water. (3) Strong rising winds or updrafts carry these small drops of water high into the clouds. (_____) Some hailstones that fall to the ground can be as large as baseballs. (_____) Each hailstone grows as more water freezes to it. (_____) These hailstones fall to the ground. (_____) Soon, the hailstones become too heavy for the rising winds. (_____) In sum, hailstones begin as water, and then freeze and slowly grow so big they fall to the ground. (_____) The drops of water freeze and form hailstones. (_____) While some hailstones hit the ground, others melt as they fall.

Activity B | Compare the order of the sentences with a partner. Discuss why you chose the order you did.

Activity C | Make sentences with each of the following groups of words. You will need to add prepositions, articles, punctuation, capital letters, and/or conjunctions. You may also have to conjugate the verb.

1. parts / Alberta / Saskatchewan / Manitoba / experience / frequent / hailstorms
2. Alberta / get / approximately / 60 / days / hail / year / southern
3. worst / months / hail / be / July / August
4. hail / come / late-afternoon / thunderstorms

Imagine that the sentences you just created make up the body of a paragraph. Which of the following would be the best topic sentence for that paragraph? Why?

a. Hailstorms occur most frequently on the prairies.
b. Hailstones have a variety of characteristics.
c. Hailstorms are destructive.

Activity D | Make sentences with each of the following groups of words. You will need to add prepositions, articles, punctuation, capital letters, and/or conjunctions. You may also have to conjugate the verb.

1. hail / flatten / crops / young / plants
2. large / hailstones / dent / cars / break / windshields
3. hail / damage / property / roofs / fences
4. insurance companies / be / busy / after / major / hailstorm

Which of the following sentences would be the best topic sentence for a paragraph that contained the four supporting sentences you just created?

    a. Heavy hail drops to the ground quickly.
    b. Hail causes a lot of damage every year.
    c. If you have hail damage, contact your insurance company immediately.

Language Skill

Making Generalizations

In explanatory paragraphs and other types of academic writing, you will often make generalizations.

Example
Thunderstorms are more dangerous than ordinary rainstorms.

This sentence is not describing one thunderstorm or one rainstorm, but referring in general to *all* thunderstorms and *all* rainstorms. Generalizations are made about nouns: people, places, things, or ideas. When making generalizations in your writing, it is important to pay attention to the structure you use for nouns.

Count nouns are nouns that you can count. You can have one, two, five, or ten of these things. These nouns have both a singular and plural form.

Activity A | Look at the underlined nouns in the sentences below. These are all count nouns. Some of these sentences are correct (marked with ✓) and some are incorrect (marked with ✗). What do you observe about the sentences below? Can you figure out the grammatical rule? What form must count nouns be in when making generalizations? Discuss with a partner or small group. Then compare your answer with the answer in the Answer Key that your instructor gives you.

✓   Thunderstorms are more dangerous than ordinary rainstorms.
✓   A thunderstorm is more dangerous than an ordinary rainstorm.
✗   The thunderstorm is more dangerous than the ordinary rainstorm.
✗   Thunderstorm is more dangerous than ordinary rainstorm.
✓   Raindrops must have a minimum diameter of 0.5 millimetres to fall to the ground.
✓   A raindrop must have a minimum diameter of 0.5 millimetres to fall to the ground.
✗   The raindrop must have a minimum diameter of 0.5 millimetres to fall to the ground.
✗   Raindrop must have a minimum diameter of 0.5 mm to fall to the ground.

Activity B | Read the generalizations below. Each sentence has one mistake. Find the mistake and correct it.

1. Thunderstorm can sometimes cause heavy rain.
2. Elephants eat a diet of twigs, leaves, and the plants.
3. A volcanoes erupts because of pressure inside the Earth.
4. Canada's climate is too cold for the scorpions.
5. Birds often build their homes in a tall trees.

As you saw, you can use count nouns when you are talking about precise numbers of things. However, some nouns cannot be counted precisely. These are non-count nouns.

Non-count nouns cannot be counted and do not have a plural form. For example, *sand* is a non-count noun, so write

Sand is made of material such as weathered rocks.

Do not write

✗ Sands is made of material such as weathered rocks.

Another non-count noun is *equipment*. Write

✓ Equipment in the lab should always be checked before using it.

It is incorrect to write

✗ Equipments in the lab should always be checked before using it.

When making generalizations about non-count nouns, use the noun without any article. It is incorrect to use the definite article *the* or the indefinite articles *a* or *an*.

Examples
✓ Water is necessary for any plant to grow.
✗ The water is necessary for any plant to grow.
✗ A water is necessary for any plant to grow.

Activity C | Write one generalizing sentence about each of the nouns below.

1. tree
2. water
3. oxygen
4. dog
5. spider
6. education
7. cellphone
8. technology
9. snowflake
10. research

WRITING FUNDAMENTALS

Composition Skill

Drafting

Drafting is an important stage of the writing process. Once you have decided on your topic and have collected information to use, you can start writing a draft. A draft is a rough, early version of a piece of writing. A first draft is the basis for your final draft. When it's done, you will likely see that you need to improve. A first draft shows where you could add more information or where you need to change ideas.

It is common to write multiple drafts of an assignment. You may have a first draft, a second draft, and a final draft. It is a good idea to give yourself enough time to work through all your drafts before you have to hand in your final assignment. For some students, it is a challenge to start writing the first draft. The thing to keep in mind is that your first draft won't be perfect. Once you start writing, you might be surprised at how your ideas start to flow.

When you write your first draft, you put your ideas into sentences without stopping to edit your sentences. Also, don't stop to look up the perfect word in your dictionary or worry about grammar or punctuation. After you have finished writing your first draft, leave it for a day. When you return to it, read it to see what areas need more work. When you finish writing your first draft, you should go on to the next stage of the writing process—the second draft.

Activity A | Writing Task: First Draft | Look at the outline you wrote on page 21 and use it to write a first draft of an explanatory paragraph based on your Unit Inquiry Question.

Activity B | Discuss your first draft with a partner. Ask your partner if your topic sentence, supporting ideas, examples, and concluding sentence are clear. Ask your partner for suggestions about how you can better develop your ideas. Your partner will do the same.

Writing Skill

Ensuring Flow

Good writing flows. This means that each paragraph is made of sentences that are connected, not disconnected. The ideas in one sentence move smoothly to the ideas in the next. This makes the text easy to read and understand.

In many texts, each sentence will have some connection to the ideas in the sentence that came directly before it. To better understand how this happens, it's helpful to know what the theme of each sentence is.

Any sentence can be broken down into *theme* (what the sentence is about or the topic of the sentence) and *rheme* (the comment or what is said about the theme). In English, the theme is generally at the beginning of a sentence.

The second stage of a thunderstorm	occurs when thunder and lightning are produced.
theme	*rheme*
Mosquitoes	are eaten by animals such as bats and birds.
theme	*rheme*

In some sentences, an *adjunct* can appear before the theme. This could be a phrase or clause starting with an adjective, preposition, or adverb. It is usually separated from the rest of the sentence by a comma.

In the wild,	a black bear	can live up to 30 years.
adjunct	*theme*	*rheme*
Every autumn,	many trees	lose their leaves.
adjunct	*theme*	*rheme*

In some paragraphs, several sentences share the same theme.

Thunderstorms can be quite destructive. **They** bring lightning and strong gusting winds. **They** also bring torrential rains that can cause flash floods. **Thunderstorms** can form "out of the blue" in a very short time.

However, in many paragraphs, the theme of one sentence is part of the rheme of the sentence that came before it.

The condensation releases **latent energy. The latent energy** becomes thermal energy.

Pronouns and synonyms are sometimes used to avoid repetition when the rheme from one sentence flows into the theme in the next.

Mosquitoes **are eaten by animals such as bats and birds. These animals** are then eaten by mammals higher up the food chain.

You should try to have variety in your writing. Some sentences should share the same theme as the sentence before them and some sentences should share the same rheme as the sentence before them.

Thunderstorms can be quite destructive. **They** bring lightning and strong **gusting winds. These winds** can cause damage to houses and buildings.

Activity A | Look at the following diagram that shows the life cycle of the silkworm.

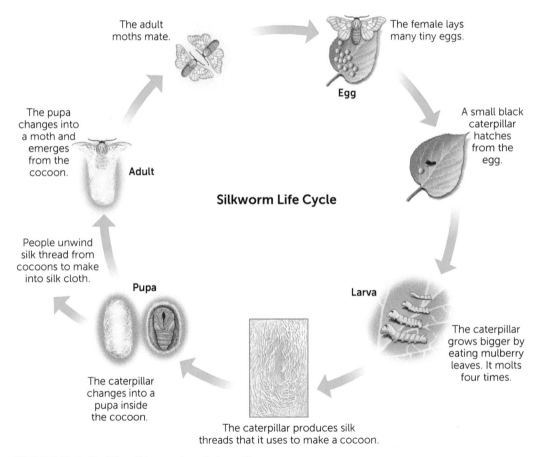

The adult moths mate.

The female lays many tiny eggs.

Egg

A small black caterpillar hatches from the egg.

The pupa changes into a moth and emerges from the cocoon.

Adult

Silkworm Life Cycle

People unwind silk thread from cocoons to make into silk cloth.

Pupa

Larva

The caterpillar changes into a pupa inside the cocoon.

The caterpillar grows bigger by eating mulberry leaves. It molts four times.

The caterpillar produces silk threads that it uses to make a cocoon.

FIGURE 1.6   The life cycle of the silkworm

The two sentences below describe different stages in the life cycle of the silkworm. For each sentence given, write two additional sentences using information from the diagram. The first sentence you write should have the same theme as the given sentence. In the second sentence you write, the theme of your sentence should be connected to the rheme of the given sentence.

1. The leaves of the mulberry plant are where the silkworms lay their eggs. *[handwritten above: pronoun]*

   The adult _____

   _____

2. The caterpillar uses silk threads to create a cocoon. *[handwritten: These + [N.P]]*

   The caterpillar produces silk threads, these are used to create a *[handwritten at right: Cocoon,]*

   _____

Activity B | Once you have completed Activity A, trade sentences with a partner. Look at the theme in each of the sentences your partner has written. In the first sentence of each pair, is the theme the same as the theme in the given sentence? In the second sentence of each pair, is the theme connected to the rheme in the given sentence? Has your partner used pronouns or synonyms to connect with the rheme in the given sentence?

Sentence and Grammar Skill

Writing Simple Sentences with the Simple Present and Present Continuous

Simple Sentences

Simple sentences express a single idea. They have only one clause, which means they contain a subject and a verb. Sometimes simple sentences also have modifiers like adverbs or prepositional phrases.

The lightning bolt strikes suddenly.
    subject   *verb*   *adverb*

Simple sentences can also have two subjects or two verbs. They are called compound subjects and compound verbs. When you use two subjects or two verbs, you do not have to use a comma.

The **thunder** and **lightning** scares the dog.
         compound subject

The lightning bolt **strikes** suddenly and **flashes** in the sky.
         compound verb   *prepositional phrase*

In academic writing, everything is built on simple sentences. Simple sentences can be used to summarize key points and to get the reader's attention. Using a variety of sentence types will make your writing more interesting to read.

Activity A | The sentences below are grammatically correct, but they can be revised. The sentences contain unnecessary repetition. Rewrite them using the information on page 33 and identify the type of simple sentence you wrote (e.g., compound subject or compound verb). Then compare your rewritten sentences with those of a partner.

1. Wind damages crops and hail damages them too.
2. Dark clouds move across the sky and then the dark clouds cover the sun.
3. Bees pollinate plants and bees produce honey also.

Simple Present

Every sentence must have a verb. A verb is a word that expresses an action or state (the way something is). Verbs can be conjugated in many different tenses. The simple present verb form is used to describe

- a habit, routine, or repeated action

  Frank rakes the leaves in his yard every fall.
  The sun rises every morning and sets every evening.
  Snow falls in winter in Canada.

- a fact or something that is always true

  Water boils at 100 degrees Celsius.
  Movement of the Earth's tectonic plates causes earthquakes.
  Thunder is loud.

When the subject of a simple present verb is in the third person singular (*he, she,* or *it,* or can be substituted by *he, she,* or *it*) there is an -s on the end of the verb.

Affirmative

Subject	Verb
I	work
You	work
He/She/It	work**s**
We	work
They	work

Verbs such as *be* and *have* are different.

Subject	Verb	
I	am	interested in studying meteorology.
You	are	wet from the rainstorm.
He/She/It	**is**	in the backyard.
We	are	scared of the heavy rain.
They	are	cumulus clouds.

Subject	Verb	
I	have	a weather app in my phone.
You	have	a good understanding of the process.
He/She/It	**has**	a fear of thunderstorms.
We	have	hailstorms in the prairies.
They	have	a way to predict the weather.

Negative

In the negative, an auxiliary verb (*do*) needs to be added. In the third person singular, there is an -es on the auxiliary verb *do*, making it *does*.

Subject	Auxiliary Verb	Negation	Main Verb
I	do	not	work.
You	do	not	explain.
He/She/It	do**es**	not	forget.
We	do	not	copy.
They	do	not	understand.

It is a common mistake to forget the -*s* in the third person singular. When you are proofreading a text you have written, check every sentence carefully. If the subject is *he*, *she*, or *it*, make sure you have not forgotten the -*s* on the end of the verb.

Activity B | Read the following sentences. Find the verb in each sentence and underline it. Find the subject of each sentence and highlight it. Add an -*s* if necessary to the main verb or auxiliary verb.

1. My brother and I read books at the library every weekend.
2. She never knows when to stop working.
3. Studying for exams require a lot of concentration.

4. My classmates meet to speak English every day after class.

5. The dog run around the park on Saturdays.

Some verbs have a spelling change in the third person singular when adding the -*s*. To know which verbs have a spelling change, you should look at the ending of the verb.

If the verb ends in	Change to	Examples
-*o*	-*oes*	They g**o**. It g**oes**.
-*s*	-*ses*	They pas**s** the ball. She pas**ses** the ball.
-*ch*	-*ches*	They wat**ch** birds. She wat**ches** birds.
-*z*	-*zes*	They buz**z**. It buz**zes**.
-*sh*	-*shes*	I wa**sh** the equipment. He wa**shes** the equipment.
-*x*	-*xes*	I mi**x** the chemicals. She mi**xes** the chemicals.
[consonant] + *y*	-*ies*	I stud**y**. He stud**ies**. I fl**y**. She fl**ies**.

Activity C | Read the following text carefully. Find and correct five mistakes related to the simple present.

A black bear's yearly routine is always the same. In the summer when the weather is warm, it finds and eat~~s~~ a lot of food. A bear enjoys plants, fruit, and smaller animals. A black bear t~~r~~ys *tries* to eat as much food as possible in the summer. In the autumn, a female bear have *has* babies. In the winter, a female bear and her babies find~~s~~ a place to hibernate, or sleep all winter. In the spring, when the weather becomes warm, all bears come~~s~~ out of hibernation. They return to live in the forest.

Activity D | Choose one piece of writing you have done for this unit. Find the verb in each sentence. If it is in the simple present, underline it. Find the subject and circle it. For each subject, decide whether it is in the third person. If the subject is in the third person singular, look at the simple present verb. Is there an -*s* on the end of the main verb or auxiliary verb?

Present Continuous

The present continuous is used to describe an activity that is happening at the moment of speaking. It is happening now. For the present continuous, you use an auxiliary verb and add -ing to the main verb.

✳ Don't forget the auxiliary

Subject	Auxiliary Verb	Main Verb
I	am	work**ing**.
You	are	work**ing**.
He/She/It	is	work**ing**.
We	are	work**ing**.
They	are	work**ing**.

In the negative, add *not* after the auxiliary verb:

I am not working.

You are not working carefully.

The students are not working tomorrow.

Activity E | Look at the following pairs of sentences. They are all grammatically correct. Discuss the difference in meaning with a partner.

1. a. Typhoons come from the Pacific.
   b. Typhoon Allan is coming from the Pacific.

2. a. Grizzly bears hibernate in the winter.
   b. The grizzly bears are climbing the ridge.

3. a. Freezing rain often creates slippery road conditions.
   b. The freezing rain in Toronto is causing accidents on Highway 401.

4. a. Water boils at 100 degrees Celsius.
   b. The water is boiling on the stove.

5. a. Hurricanes are destructive.
   b. Hurricane Katrina caused millions of dollars in damage.

Activity F | Complete the sentences by conjugating the verbs provided. Use the simple present or the present continuous.

1. Bears _____ (hibernate) for six to seven months every year.

2. The Ganges Delta ___*experienced*___ (experience) heavy rainfall this winter.

3. He _____ (not, leave) the house in bad weather.

4. Moose ___*eat*___ (eat) plants. They are herbivores.

5. I can't sleep because the storm _____ (howl).

Understanding Assignments

Before you begin any assignment, make sure you understand the assignment and all the requirements. What are you expected to do to complete the assignment successfully?

Suppose your assignment is to write an explanatory paragraph. First, read the assignment and highlight important information such as the due date, how to submit it to your instructor, and formatting requirements.

Second, decide on a topic. If you have trouble coming up with a topic, brainstorm ideas and discuss them with your instructor.

Third, identify the purpose and audience. Considering the purpose and audience may help you decide how complex your paragraph should be.

Next, begin to gather information. Textbooks are a good place to start your research. Once you have the information you need, create an outline for your explanatory paragraph, then write a first draft. Ask a classmate to read your draft and give you feedback on the order of information and whether the connectors link your ideas logically. Consider the feedback and revise your paragraph as necessary.

Finally, double-check the assignment description and make sure your assignment is complete before handing it in.

UNIT OUTCOME

Writing Assignment: Explanatory Paragraph

Write an explanatory paragraph of 100 to 200 words on a topic related to weather. (Your instructor may give you an alternative length.) You may write on a topic based on your Unit Inquiry Question, develop another topic of your choosing connected to weather, or choose one of the following topics:

- What are the characteristics of the Northern Lights?
- What are chinooks and how do they occur?
- What is freezing rain and how does it form?

Use the skills you have developed in this unit to complete the assignment. Follow the steps below to practise each of the new skills you have learned to write a well-developed explanatory paragraph.

1. **Brainstorm and find information**: Look back at the freewriting you did in the *Fostering Inquiry* section. Use a mind map to brainstorm some more ideas related to the topic you want to explore in answering your Unit Inquiry Question. Information related to your Unit Inquiry Question may be found in the readings and other topic-related information in this unit. You may also find information in a textbook or on the Internet.

2. **Outline**: List your topic, your chosen inquiry question, and the working title of your paragraph.

   Topic: _____

   Inquiry Question: _____

   Paragraph Title: _____

   Use the template below to create an outline for your paragraph. See the outline on page 20 for more detail about the body of the paragraph.

Topic Sentence

Topic sentence that states what the paragraph will explain:

Main Body (Supporting Ideas)

Step 1 or supporting idea 1 (1–3 sentences):

Step 2 or supporting idea 2 (1–3 sentences):

Step 3 or supporting idea 3 (1–3 sentences):

Concluding Sentence

Concluding sentence to remind your reader what the paragraph is about:

3. **Write a first draft**: Write a first draft of your paragraph. Use AWL and mid-frequency vocabulary from this unit if possible.

4. **Self-check**: Wait a day, then check your first draft. Remember to check the following:
   - Check that your explanatory paragraph has a topic sentence, main body (sentences explaining the sequence of steps or giving the supporting ideas), and a concluding sentence.
   - Check that each sentence has at least one subject and one verb.
   - When you have made generalizations, check that count and non-count nouns are used correctly.
   - Check that you have used connectors of sequence appropriately.
   - If you have used AWL and mid-frequency vocabulary from this unit, make sure you have used them correctly.
   - Check for flow. Make sure some of your sentences have the same theme as the previous sentence, and some have the same rheme as the previous sentence.

5. **Revise**: Revise your first draft.

6. **Compose final draft**: Write a final draft of your explanatory paragraph.

7. **Proofread**: Check the final draft of your paragraph for any small errors you may have missed. In particular, look for spelling errors, typos, and punctuation mistakes.

Evaluation: Explanatory Paragraph Rubric

Use the following rubric to evaluate your essay. In which areas do you need to improve most?

E = **Emerging**: frequent difficulty using unit skills; needs a lot more work
D = **Developing**: some difficulty using unit skills; some improvement still required
S = **Satisfactory**: able to use unit skills most of the time; meets average expectations for this level
O = **Outstanding**: exceptional use of unit skills; exceeds expectations for this level

Skill	E	D	S	O
The explanatory paragraph has a topic sentence, sentences explaining the different steps or stages, and a concluding sentence that connects to the topic.				
AWL and mid-frequency vocabulary items from this unit are used when appropriate.				
Any generalizations in the text are made using the plural form of count nouns or with an indefinite article before a count noun.				
The paragraph uses connectors of sequence to link ideas together smoothly.				
The paragraph flows well with sentences that share either the theme or the rheme of the previous sentence.				
The paragraph includes grammatically correct simple sentences in the simple present and the present continuous.				

Unit Review

Activity A | What do you know about the topic of weather, climate, or the natural world that you did not know before you started this unit? Discuss with a partner or small group. Be prepared to report what you learned to the class.

Activity B | Look back at the Unit Inquiry Question you developed at the start of this unit and discuss it with a partner or small group. Then share your answers with the class. Use the following questions to help you:

1. What information did you find in this unit that helped you answer your question?
2. How would you answer your question now?

Activity C | Use the following checklist to review the skills you have learned in this unit. First decide which 10 skills you think are the most important. Circle the number beside each of these 10 skills. If you learned a skill in this unit that isn't listed below, write it in the blank row at the end of the checklist. Then put a check mark in the box beside those points you feel you have learned. Be prepared to discuss your choices with the class.

Self-Assessment Checklist	
☐	1. I can talk about weather, climate, and the natural world based on what I've read in this unit.
☐	2. I can develop an inquiry question to guide my learning.

☐	3. I can use connectors of sequence to join my sentences together.
☐	4. I can use a dictionary to learn valuable information about a word.
☐	5. I can use AWL and mid-frequency vocabulary from this unit in my writing.
☐	6. I can ask "why" to engage critically with the texts I read.
☐	7. I can use a mind map to develop my ideas before writing.
☐	8. I can create an outline with key ideas before writing a paragraph.
☐	9. I can search online and use textbooks to find information on a topic.
☐	10. I can avoid plagiarism by never submitting someone else's work.
☐	11. I can write grammatically correct sentences when making generalizations using count and non-count nouns.
☐	12. I can create drafts of my text before I write the final draft.
☐	13. I can make my sentences flow by connecting the theme of each sentence to either the theme or rheme of the sentence that comes before it.
☐	14. I can write grammatically correct simple sentences containing a noun and a verb.
☐	15. I can write grammatically correct sentences in the simple present and present continuous, remembering the final -s on third person singular verbs in the simple present.
☐	16. I can analyze assignment requirements before I begin to work.
☐	17. I can write a well-structured explanatory paragraph that contains a topic sentence, supporting sentences, and a concluding sentence.
☐	18.

Activity D | Put a check mark in the box beside the vocabulary items from this unit that you feel confident using in your writing.

Vocabulary Checklist

☐	attractive (adj.) `2000`		☐	mature (adj.) `AWL`
☐	destructive (adj.) `3000`		☐	peak (n.) `3000`
☐	eventually (adv.) `AWL`		☐	rapidly (adv.) `2000`
☐	expand (v.) `AWL`		☐	release (v.) `AWL`
☐	extreme (adj.) `2000`		☐	source (n.) `AWL`

UNIT 2 — Robotics

Technology

EXPLORING IDEAS

Introduction

1. Drone

2. Paro

3. Ludwig

Activity A | Discuss the following questions with a partner or small group.

1. What do you know about robotics? Is it a subject that interests you?
2. Where have you seen or heard of robots being used?
3. What kinds of robots can you identify in the photographs above?
4. What jobs do you think they might do?
5. What do you know about how robots work?

You can use the Internet to learn more about a topic. One commonly known Internet site that stores much information is Wikipedia, a kind of free Internet encyclopedia. It is available in multiple languages. It is a tool that you can use when you are just beginning to learn about a topic.

Activity B | Wikipedia could be a good place to find background information as you are starting to learn about a topic. An interesting feature of Wikipedia is that the public can update information, so the information is always changing. However, since you don't know who is updating the information, you should not rely on Wikipedia as your only source of information. Wikipedia contributors list references at the bottom of every Wikipedia entry. These references may be helpful for learning about a topic.

If you have access to the Internet, find the Wikipedia page for hitchBOT. If you don't have access to the Internet, see the screenshot below of the hitchBOT page from Wikipedia. Skim the information and write down five interesting statements you see there in your own words.

hitchBOT

From Wikipedia, the free encyclopedia

hitchBOT was a Canadian "hitchhiking robot" created by David Harris Smith of McMaster University and Frauke Zeller of Ryerson University.[1] It gained international attention for successfully hitchhiking across Canada and in Europe, but in 2015 an attempt to hitchhike across the United States ended shortly after it began when the robot was destroyed by vandals in Philadelphia, Pennsylvania.[2]

hitchBOT displayed at an exhibition

> **Contents** [hide]
> 1 Description
> 2 Travels
> 3 Destruction
> 4 Legacy
> 5 Other social experiment robots
> 6 References

Description [edit]

The robot had a cylindrical body composed mainly from a plastic bucket, with two flexible "arms" and two flexible "legs" attached to the torso. The top section of the cylindrical body was transparent, containing a screen which displayed eyes and a mouth, making the robot approximately humanoid in external appearance, but gender-neutral.[2]

The robot was able to carry on basic conversation and talk about facts, and was designed to be a robotic travelling companion while in the vehicle of the driver who picked it up. It had a GPS device and a 3G connection, which allowed researchers to track its location. It was equipped with a camera, which took photographs periodically to document its journeys. It was powered either by solar power or by cigarette lighter sockets in cars.[2]

The robot was not able to walk – it completed its "hitchhiking" journeys by "asking" to be carried by those who picked it up.

It was created as a social experiment. The robot's "hitchhiking" was reported by the press in many countries.[2]

_____

_____

_____

_____

_____

Activity C | With a partner, discuss what you read about hitchBOT in Activity B. What kind of robot is hitchBOT? What is his job? What do you know about how hitchBOT works? Read your partner the five statements you wrote about hitchBOT. Which of your statements are the same as your partner's? Which ones are different?

Activity D | The three sentences below each describe one Canadian robot. Read the sentences and match each description to the correct photograph. Write the number of the sentence next to the photograph. Check your answers with a partner.

1. This robot looks like a giant insect with really long arms. It is used for space exploration.
2. This robot is shaped like a pancake. It vacuums the floor.
3. This robot looks like a person. It has a body, two arms, and two legs. The head is clear and has a screen with eyes and a mouth.

_____ *a. Bobsweep*   _____ *b. hitchBOT*   _____ *c. Dexter*

Activity E | Writing Task: Descriptive Sentences | Choose one of the robots pictured in the *Introduction* section and write five sentences describing what it looks like, what you think it sounds like, and how it might feel if you touched it. Discuss your sentences with a partner. Can you add more descriptive language to your sentences?

Fostering Inquiry

Using the Five Senses

When you are asked to describe something, you may be curious about many different kinds of details. For example, you might want to know more about how something looks, tastes, feels, smells, or sounds. When writing descriptively, consider the five senses described below.

Sight   You might be curious about what something looks like. To satisfy that curiosity, you might explore the colour, size, or shape of the object you are inquiring about. For example, if you are investigating household robots like the Roomba vacuum cleaner, you might want to examine how the size, shape, and other design features make it an effective appliance. You might ask *How does the size and shape of the Roomba make it an effective household appliance?* You might also be curious about what you see in relation to how the Roomba moves. You might ask *How quickly does it move across the floor?* or *What does it look like when it moves across the floor?*

Taste   You may also want to know more about what something tastes like. You are probably familiar with the five basic tastes: sweet, sour, bitter, salty, and umami. Depending on your object of inquiry, you might be curious about taste. When describing robotics, you are unlikely to describe how they would taste!

Touch   You may want to know more about what something feels like. As you are exploring this sense, you may need to guess what your object of inquiry feels like based on what it looks like. For example, if your object of inquiry is the therapy robot Paro the robot seal, you might ask *What is Paro made of?* When you want to know what something feels like or why it feels that way, consider the texture or the temperature.

Smell   You may want to know more about what something smells like. As you are exploring this sense, you might be curious about what causes your object of inquiry to give off certain smells. For example, if you are inquiring into scented household products—such as a room freshener or scented candle—you might ask *How is the smell produced?* or *What kinds of chemicals are used?*

Hearing   You may be curious about the sounds your object of inquiry makes. To learn more about these sounds, you might investigate what produces the sound or why the inventor chose that sound. For example, Paro the robot seal sounds exactly like a baby seal and many humanoid robots sound like real people. You might ask *What makes the robot sound lifelike?*

Activity A | What do you want to know more about in relation to technology and robotics? For example:

- What does the inside of a humanoid robot look like?
- What makes that "whirring" sound in drones?
- How are robotic therapy pets designed to look, sound, and feel real?

1. Write two or three questions you are curious about on the topic of technology and robotics.
2. When you are finished, compare your questions with a partner or small group.
3. Choose one question to be your inquiry question for this unit. It does not have to be the same question as your partner or group.

4. Write your inquiry question in the space provided. Look back at this question as you work through the unit. This is your Unit Inquiry Question.

My Unit Inquiry Question:

_____

_____

_____

Activity B | Writing Task: Freewriting | Write for at least five minutes on the topic of your Unit Inquiry Question. Do not stop writing during this time. After five minutes, read what you have written and circle two or three ideas that you would like to explore further to answer your Unit Inquiry Question.

Structure

Descriptive Paragraph

Purpose

The purpose of a descriptive paragraph is to describe a person, place, or thing. The goal of a descriptive paragraph is to appeal to the reader's senses. Your words paint a picture of the person, place, or thing so that the reader can visualize what you are describing.

Activity A | With a partner or small group, discuss the purpose and goal of the following text types:

1. a movie review
2. a blog about a restaurant
3. a holiday destination brochure
4. a description of a used item
5. a poster advertising an event at your university

Audience

The audience for a descriptive paragraph could be your instructor—if the paragraph is a class assignment. Descriptive writing is also used in a variety of disciplines—advertising, art, literature, and engineering are a few examples. The audience for descriptive writing could also be the general public. An example of this is a description of a product for marketing purposes or a description of a character in a novel or play.

Activity B | Look back to the list of texts in Activity A and discuss with a partner or small group who each text would appeal to. In other words, what audience is the text written for? Discuss how the writer might make the item appealing to that audience.

Structure of a Descriptive Paragraph

Descriptive paragraphs have a similar structure to other types of paragraphs. A descriptive paragraph begins with a topic sentence. The topic sentence tells your reader what you are going to describe. You can include an adjective in your topic sentence. Depending on what you are describing in your paragraph, decide which senses you want to appeal to. This will help you organize your descriptive paragraph.

Once you have decided on two or three senses, write one to three sentences for each sense you want to appeal to in your reader. Remember that you want to write your description by engaging as many of the reader's senses as possible. Think about how you can evoke (or call to mind) images or feelings in your reader. You can do this by using words that evoke images of what you are describing. Try to use precise adjectives to help your reader imagine the object you are describing. For example, rather than writing *Paro is an interesting robot*, you can write *Paro has black eyes and a black nose*. Finally, write a concluding sentence. This is a general sentence, reminding the reader what your paragraph was about.

Language Tip

Using Connectors of Location

If you are describing a place, you can use connectors of location. Connectors of location give information about where and how things are located in relation to each other. For example, in the following sentence, the connector of location *above* indicates where the control lever is in relation to the power switch:

The control lever is above the power switch.

there	here	beyond	in the front (of)
in the back (of)	next to	adjacent to	under
above	opposite		

Examples

There was a grassy field **in the back of** the schoolyard. **Beyond** the field was a vast parking lot surrounding a modern shopping mall. **In front of** the shopping mall was a row of tents set up for a special sale. **Under** the tents was a wide variety of discounted, slightly damaged merchandise sold by clerks from a number of stores.

As you saw in Unit 1, connectors can appear in different places in the sentence. Usually, the connector comes at the beginning of the sentence, but it is possible to put it in the middle or at the end of the sentence. It depends on the connector and what you are emphasizing in your sentence.

Examples

Opposite the school is the park.
The school is **opposite** the park.

Activity C | Figure 2.1 shows an outline for a descriptive paragraph. The first sentence is the topic sentence. The next three to six sentences describe your object of inquiry (what you are describing). The last sentence is the concluding sentence.

With a partner, read each part of the outline and discuss the following questions:

1. Is it necessary to include an adjective in the topic sentence?
2. How can you appeal to your reader's senses in your description?
3. What is the purpose of the concluding sentence?

Topic sentence: a general sentence that states what you will describe in your paragraph

Descriptive point 1: One to three sentences that appeal to the first sense.

Descriptive point 2: One to three sentences that appeal to the second sense.

Descriptive point 3: One to three sentences that appeal to the third sense.

Concluding sentence: a general sentence that reminds your reader what the paragraph was about

FIGURE 2.1 Structure of a descriptive paragraph

Activity D | On the next page you will find an example of a descriptive paragraph. Read the paragraph carefully and notice how the writer describes his first robot. Answer the questions that follow the paragraph.

My First Robot

When I was nine years old, my uncle Jim gave me my first robot for my birthday. It was shaped like a human but with a smooth-edged rectangular box for a body, and a clear blue plastic dome for the head. The chest was shiny like chrome, even though it was made of plastic, too. On each side of the chest was an arm that could swing. At the end of each arm was a pincer-shaped hand, kind of like a crab's claw. Underneath the chest were two short red plastic legs, one longer than the other, with a stubby flat foot at the end of each. The robot's head was transparent blue. You could look down into the body, and see the metal gears, springs, tiny cogs, pins, and screws joining the legs to the tiny wind-up motor mechanisms inside. On the robot's right side was a thin but strong shiny silver piece of steel that connected the robot's torso to a small round white plastic knob. The knob had small grooves all the way around it that made it easy to grip and twist. You could only twist it to the right, but it would go around more than a dozen times, each time making a short, satisfying, creaking sound, winding a spring inside. When you finished winding up the robot, you could let it go on the floor, and the feet would move around in a little circle, like the robot was riding a bike. It made a clicking sound when it walked. Sometimes it would wobble and wander in this direction and that, all the time making a kind of buzzing and whirring sound as the spring inside unwound. Sometimes it would fall over and roll from side to side as it kicked its legs, looking like it was trying to stand up again. Of course, the robot was small enough to fit in the palm of my hand, or put in my pocket, so I took it just about everywhere. I will never forget my first robot.

1. What is the main idea of this paragraph?
2. How is this descriptive paragraph organized?
3. Which senses does the paragraph appeal to? Do you think the writer does a good job? Explain.
4. What adjectives are used in the descriptive paragraph?
5. Which connectors of location are used to paint a picture of the robot being described?

Activity E | Think of a robot or another device you can describe. Fill in the sections of the following outline with a topic sentence, descriptive sentences, and a concluding sentence.

Topic Sentence

A general sentence that states what you will describe in your paragraph.

Main Body (Supporting Ideas)

Descriptive point 1: One to three sentences that appeal to the first sense.

Descriptive point 2: One to three sentences that appeal to the second sense.

Descriptive point 3: One to three sentences that appeal to the third sense.

Concluding Sentence

a general sentence that reminds your reader what the paragraph was about

Activity F | Exchange your outline with a partner. Read your partner's sentences and provide feedback, using the following questions to guide you. Did your partner include a topic sentence, descriptive supporting sentences that appeal to the senses, and a concluding sentence? How can your partner improve his or her outline? Give your partner two or three more ideas that he or she can add to the outline.

Activity G | Revisit your Unit Inquiry Question on page 48. What information or new ideas have you thought of or discussed that will help you answer your question? Share your ideas with a partner or small group. At this point, you may consider revising your Unit Inquiry Question.

ACADEMIC READING

Vocabulary

Vocabulary Skill: Forming Adjectives

Adjectives are words that describe or modify nouns, such as *tall*, *short*, *heavy*, and *silver*.

Examples

The **robotic** cat is **fluffy**.

The WowWee **balancing** plastic robot is available in **black** or **white**.

Activity A | Look at these photographs of robots. What adjectives would you use to describe them? Brainstorm as many adjectives as you can think of for each robot. Then compare your lists of adjectives with a partner.

_____

_____

_____

_____

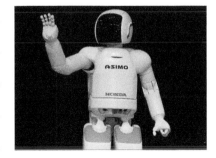

_____

_____

_____

_____

Many adjectives are created by adding a prefix or a suffix to a noun or verb. The chart below contains some common suffixes used to form adjectives.

Suffixes	Examples
-able, -ible	responsible, manageable
-ful	helpful, playful
-like	lifelike, birdlike
-al	mechanical, logical
-ic	economic, energetic
-ly	lovely, friendly
-y	bony, stony

Activity B | Add as many adjectives as you can think of to the chart on page 54. Then show your list to a partner. How many different adjectives did you and your partner add to your charts?

Activity C | Negative prefixes, such as *-in*, *-un*, *-il*, and *-im*, can be added to many adjectives to create an adjective with the opposite meaning. Write the opposite of each adjective. The first two are done for you.

1. friendly _____*unfriendly*_____

2. tolerant _____*intolerant*_____

3. visible _____

4. correct _____

5. sensitive _____

6. helpful _____

7. believable _____

8. common _____

9. legal _____

10. logical _____

11. legible _____

Activity D | Writing Task: Descriptive Sentences | Look back at Activity A on page 53. Using some of the adjectives you brainstormed for that activity, write a sentence for each of the robots pictured. Compare your sentences with a partner. What adjectives did your partner use to describe the robots? Did you use any of the same adjectives? What different adjectives did you and your partner use?

Vocabulary Preview: The Academic Word List

Activity E | The following AWL words are taken from the academic reading "Spar Aerospace: An Arm from Earth to Space," on pages 58–59. The definitions of the words are provided. Read the words and their definitions and choose the correct word to complete the sentences that follow. You might have to change the form of the word to fit the sentence.

capable (adj.): having the abilities necessary for doing something
conceive (v.): to form an idea or a plan in your mind
device (n.): an object or a piece of equipment that has been designed to do a particular job
indicate (v.): to show that something is true or exists
version (n.): a form of something that is slightly different from an earlier form or from other forms of the same thing
visible (adj.): that can be seen

1. The Canada wordmark was clearly _____ on the side of the Canadarm.

2. Robots with artificial intelligence may one day be _____ of destroying humans.

3. A telerobot is a remote-controlled _____ operated from a distance.

4. Salman Khan _____ of the idea of his online educational network, Khan Academy, while he was tutoring his cousins in math.

5. The latest _____ of the solar powered car won first place.

6. The flashing red light _____ that the robot is on and functioning.

Vocabulary Preview: Mid-frequency Vocabulary

Activity F | Read each sentence and match the bolded word to its definition below. Write the letter on the line provided.

Sentences

1. _____ The young girl likes reading about space **explorers**.

2. _____ There are various theories of how the **universe** began.

3. _____ The satellite made in Alberta is going to **launch** into space on Saturday.

4. _____ Jupiter is the largest **planet** in the solar system.

5. _____ One of the greatest scientific **endeavours** is the MESSENGER spacecraft launched by NASA in 2004.

6. _____ He looked at the International Space Station with his **telescope**.

Definitions

    a. an attempt to do something new or difficult
    b. all of space and everything in it including Earth, planets, and stars
    c. a large round object in outer space that revolves around a star
    d. a thing that looks like a tube and is used to make objects in the distance appear bigger
    e. send something into space
    f. a person who travels to unknown places to learn more about them

Reading

The following reading, "Spar Aerospace: An Arm from Earth to Space," is an excerpt from the textbook *Breakthrough! Canada's Greatest Inventions and Innovations.* This textbook describes many Canadian inventions and innovations.

Making Predictions with Visuals

One helpful pre-reading strategy is examining the visuals that accompany a text to make predictions about the content of the reading or the point of view of the author. In university textbooks, you may find diagrams, charts, or graphs that summarize information. Visuals can have various functions. For example, in a textbook, a chart may summarize the contents of a chapter. Photographs can illustrate or show examples of what the text is about.

Activity A | Look at the photographs that accompany the reading and discuss the following questions with a partner or small group. What information about the reading do you get from the photographs? Why is it helpful to review visuals in a text before reading it? In other words, what information about the text can you get from the visuals? Thinking about it differently, if the chapter did not have visuals, what would be more difficult or different for you as the reader?

Activity B | In the reading, parts of the Canadarm are compared to parts of the human body, such as the hand, arm, and shoulder. Look at the photographs of the Canadarm and write down other things that the Canadarm reminds you of. What do you think it is made of? What special features does it have? What do you think the Canadarm was used for? After you have written down your ideas, share them with a partner.

Activity C | Read the text and check your answers for Activity B above against the information given in the article. Discuss with a partner.

READING

Spar Aerospace: An Arm from Earth to Space

1   Millions of people around the world watched the television coverage of the American spaceship *Endeavour* being **launched** from Cape Canaveral, Florida, on May 16, 2011. This was the beginning of the final trip for that shuttle.[1] It carried six crew members, one of whom was a young American-Canadian named Drew Feustel, embarking[2] on his second flight beyond the bounds of our **planet**. Two years earlier, he had been one of the courageous astronauts[3] who made repairs to Hubble; the big space **telescope** that, since its launch in April 1990, has been helping human beings see and learn about the **universe** that continues to expand before us.

2   On those missions, Feustel was able to do his work because of a uniquely Canadian invention specifically built for the rocket he rode. It is a unique, unbelievably complex machine. It was **conceived** in Canada, built here, and now that the shuttle programs are over, will be placed in museums for all to see. Canadians call it Canadarm.

3   Canadarms were standard equipment on shuttles, and a more complex **version** was installed on the International Space Station. Both the station and the shuttles that were used to build and service it have helped advance our knowledge of the universe. The early **explorers** found new lands; the space programs new worlds. Canadians have been partners in making this possible. Some of our contributions are widely known; others recognized by few. But of them all, the amazing Canadarm is in a class by itself.

4   The arm made for space shuttles is like the human one. There is a "shoulder," a "wrist," an

---

[1] a spacecraft designed to be used, for example, for travelling between Earth and a space station

[2] to get onto a ship or aircraft; begin

[3] a person who is trained to travel in a spacecraft

"elbow," and a "hand." A tiny motor, the size of a coffee cup, drives each joint. However, unlike the human arm, this one is "15 metres long and **capable** of manoeuvring payloads[4] about the size of a bus." Because of the extreme temperatures in space, tiny electrical heaters are concealed inside the two long booms that are most **visible** to anyone looking at the Canadarm. The arm has to move freely in different directions: up and down, sidewise, and in a circular motion. The "hand" is the most different from the human one, but it still has to be able to clutch objects, such as communications satellites that have to be taken from or returned to the payload bay. The "hand" is really three snare wires that are capable of grappling an object. In order for this capture manoeuvre to work, each satellite to

be retrieved had a kind of hook built onto its outer surface. Then, the "hand" of the Canadarm could grab the object in question and place it where needed.

5   Today, as we look at photographs of the Canadarm in space, we tend to focus on its "arm" section rather than on other parts such as the "shoulder" of the **device**. The long extension that we see is white and gold and it often seems to glisten in the sunlight, particularly when viewed against the velvet blackness of space. Prominently emblazoned on the white external coating is the wordmark "Canada." It was obviously put there to **indicate** the country of origin of the space crane[5]— and most Canadians have a true sense of pride when they see it.

6   A few of the facts about the Canadarm reflect just what had been achieved. "Weighing less than 480 kilograms, Canadarm can lift over 30,000 kilograms—up to 266,000 kilograms in the weightlessness of space . . . using less electricity than a tea kettle." The machine was a technical marvel and has been problem-free. It has been employed hundreds of times, often by Canadian astronauts.

Source: Melady, J. (2013). *Breakthrough!: Canada's greatest inventions and innovations* (pp. 128–133). Toronto, ON: Dundurn Press.

---

[4] equipment or goods carried by a vehicle

[5] a machine used to lift heavy items

Activity D | Discuss the following questions with a partner or small group.

1. In your own words, describe the Canadarm.
2. What is significant about it?
3. Which feature or characteristic about the Canadarm is most interesting to you? Why?
4. Are you interested in space? What new information from the article did you learn?
5. What do you know about the Canadarm that you did not know before? Use some of the words from the article in your discussion.

Activity E | Writing Task: Descriptive Sentences | Choose one of the photographs below and write three to five sentences about the Canadian invention pictured. You can be creative in writing your descriptive sentences. Don't limit yourself to describing exactly what you see in the picture. To get started, ask yourself these questions:

- What does it look like?
- What special features does it have? How do they work?
- What is it used for? Who might use it? How?
- What does it look like, sound like, or act like when it's being used?

Try to include some of the new vocabulary words introduced in this unit. Then read your sentences to a partner. After you have each taken a turn, look at your sentences together and decide how you can make them even more appealing to the senses. Can you add adjectives or more sentences to your descriptions?

Activity F | After you have finalized your sentences in Activity E, exchange your sentences with a partner. Choose your partner's best sentence and explain what makes it a good descriptive sentence. Then go to Appendix 2 and compare your sentences with those on pages 257–258. The key vocabulary items from this unit are bolded in the sample sentences. Which words from this unit did you use in your sentences? Which words from this unit did your partner use in his or her sentences? Which senses did each of your partner's sentences appeal to?

Critical Thinking

Evaluating Sources for Credibility

As a college or university student, you will encounter many different sources of information. You need to be able to decide whether the sources you use in your assignments are credible (reliable). It might seem overwhelming to evaluate all your sources, but the following questions and suggestions will help you break the task down so that it is manageable.

1. **Who** wrote the text? If you cannot find the name of the author (or organization) who wrote it, continue searching for one that does list the author.
2. **Where** does the information come from? Is the source a reliable website, such as a government or university website? If not, continue searching for a website or another source with a good reputation.
3. **How old** is it? **When** was the text written? If it was published more than five years ago, continue searching for a more current source of information.
4. Who was the text written for? University students, high school students, researchers, the general public? Notice the **tone and language** used in the text. If it is conversational, the text might be written for the general public. If it is formal and academic, the text might be written for an academic audience.
5. Is the information accurate? Are the sources cited (named)? If there is bias (an opinion that supports only one side) in the text, continue searching for a source that is not biased.
6. Does the article have spelling or grammar mistakes?

PROCESS FUNDAMENTALS

Brainstorming and Outlining

Listing

Listing is a brainstorming technique. When listing, make a list of words or phrases about a topic. After writing down your ideas, look at your list and then cross out any words that are not related to your specific topic of inquiry. From there, decide which ideas you would like to develop into a paragraph.

Activity A | Look at the brainstorming list below on the topic of robots. What can you add to the list? Consider, for example, types of robots, jobs that robots do, where robots are used, and who uses robots. When you have written as many ideas as you can think of, share your list with a partner. Discuss what each of you wrote and cross out any words that are not related to your topic.

ROBOTS	
assemble cars	expensive
toys	military
companionship	robots replace humans

Activity B | Look back to the Unit Inquiry Question you wrote on page 48. What other ideas or questions come to mind? For example, if your topic is humanoid robots, you might be curious about what they look like or what they sound like; your Unit Inquiry Question might be *What are the characteristics of a humanoid robot?* To generate ideas, you can think of what humanoid robots look like, what they sound like, or what they feel like to touch. Brainstorm by creating a list with as many words, phrases, or ideas as possible that are related to the topic of your inquiry question.

Here is an example of a listing brainstorm for humanoid robots:

human	resemble	walk	tricks	head
arms	mouth	legs	metallic	programmable
lifelike	command	speak	greeting	controversial
complex human tasks	cold	technologically advanced	application	smooth
household	expensive	voice		

Look at the list of words and phrases you've brainstormed about your Unit Inquiry Question. Put similar words and ideas into groups and cross out any unnecessary, repetitive, or irrelevant words and ideas from your list.

- What groups did you come up with?
- Which words did you cross out?
- How did you decide what groups to make and which words to cross out?

Discuss with a partner how you arrived at your brainstormed lists. Your goal is to share your decision-making process with your partner. This is an important part of brainstorming. Here are some questions you and your partner can ask each other: *Why did you cross out this word? Why did you keep this word? Why did you group these words together?*

Outlining

Activity C | Writing Task: Descriptive Paragraph Outline |

Create an outline for a descriptive paragraph based on your listing brainstorm in Activity B. As you complete more tasks in this unit, you can use your outline to add more ideas and details to support your topic. Refer to the descriptive paragraph outline on page 50 to help guide you.

Here is an example of an outline that a student has started. Notice the words from the listing brainstorm in Activity B. This outline is not yet complete. What else needs to be done?

Example

Outline for inquiry question *What are the characteristics of a humanoid robot?*

Topic sentence—A humanoid robot seems human.

Description 1: head, arms, legs, mouth, lifelike

Description 2: speak, command, voice, greeting

Description 3: cold, metallic, smooth

Before You Write

Evaluating Websites

When you start researching information for your assignments, you will use a variety of websites. There are many kinds of websites. Some of them, such as university websites, are reliable; others, like personal blogs, are not. If you use information from websites in your assignments, you need to evaluate the quality and reliability of the website. Here are some tips that might help you:

1. Consider the author, source, and the date of publication. Are references included? If so, where does the author's information come from? Is the name of the author listed?

2. If the information on the website has spelling or grammar errors, this is a sign that it is not reliable. Also, you should always check that the information is accurate and up to date. If the information is old and has not been updated, this is a sign that the website is not reliable.

3. If the website does not include information about its creator (authors or organization) and about how they are qualified to write about the topic, this is a sign that the website is not reliable.

4. If the website does not look like it was professionally produced, this is a sign that the website may not be reliable.

5. Consider the intended audience. For example, is the information written for experts or the general public? Adults or teenagers? Make sure that any information you use from websites is level-appropriate for your task.

If you have any doubts about the quality and reliability of a website, you can ask your instructor or librarian for help. For further information, see the Critical Thinking Skills box on page 61.

Activity A | With a partner or small group, discuss the criteria for evaluating websites. Do you use these or any other criteria to evaluate websites? Can you think of one or two more criteria that you could use to evaluate the credibility of websites?

Activity B | If you have access to the Internet, go to the Government of Canada website at https://www.canada.ca/en.html and search "Canadarm." If not, look at the screen shot on the next page. Quickly evaluate the website and the information it provides about the Canadarm. What do you think? Consider these:

1. Is this a reliable website? Why or why not?
2. Would you use information from the Government of Canada website for your assignments?
3. What useful information from this website could you use in an assignment?

Share your ideas with a partner or small group.

Canadarm, Canada's most famous robotic and technological achievement, made its space debut on the Space Shuttle <u>Columbia (STS-2)</u> on November 13, 1981. The design and building of the arm, also known as the Shuttle Remote Manipulator System, marked the beginning of Canada's close collaboration with the National Aeronautics and Space Administration (NASA) in human space flight–a sterling example of successful international cooperation in space.

The Shuttle's Canadarm wrapped up 30 years of successful operations when it was retired along with the Space Shuttle program after mission STS-135, which marked the robotic arm's 90th flight. The arm's legacy lives on, though, since it established Canada's international reputation for robotics innovation and know-how and generated the <u>family of Canadian robotics</u> on board the <u>International Space Station</u> (ISS), as well as <u>future generations to come</u>. Its excellent performance record has inspired several generations of scientists and engineers as they develop new technologies for industry, medicine, and other applications.

Canadian Space Technology to Help Sick Children

Exhibit for Canada's National Space Icon: the Canadarm

The Government of Canada is proud to welcome one of our greatest technological contributions to international space exploration: the original Canadarm flown on the Space Shuttle Endeavour. Visit the Canadarm at the <u>Canada Aviation and Space Museum</u> in Ottawa.

Content Skill

Exploring Online Newspaper Articles

You will use various sources of information to complete your assignments. Articles from peer-reviewed journals, chapters from university textbooks, and reports are just a few examples. Which resources you use depends on your assignment and your topic.

Online newspaper articles are another possible source. Newspapers can be a great source of information when you are looking for supporting details to include in a writing assignment. The information is usually current and concisely summarized, and the articles often include photographs that illustrate significant aspects of the story. The other benefit of using newspaper articles is that they often feature current stories about a popular topic or issue.

Where can you find newspaper articles? The following is a list of generally reliable news sites:

- *The Globe and Mail* is a daily Canadian newspaper. It is printed in six cities in Canada and has an estimated readership of two million. The main office is in Toronto. It was founded in 1844. The website includes links to News, Opinion, Sports, Life, and Arts among other topics. There are also links to featured news stories, news highlights, and the most popular news stories. Toward the bottom of the website, there is a list of popular news videos and photos.

- The *National Post* is a daily Canadian newspaper distributed in six provinces. It was founded in 1998. The website includes links to News, Comment, Personal Finance, Investing, Tech, and Sports among other topics. In the main part of the website are news stories with headlines and photographs.

- Thestar.com is Canada's largest online news site. The *Toronto Star* is a daily Canadian newspaper. The website includes links to Top Stories and to stories related to the Greater Toronto Area, Sports, Business, and Life and Entertainment. There is also a section for international news.

- *The Guardian* is a daily British newspaper founded in 1821. The website focuses on UK news stories related to politics, culture, education, media, and society. Toward the bottom of the website is the Spotlight, which contains a top story. Videos of stories are also available for viewing.

- *The New York Times* website focuses on American news stories. A brief summary of the story appears under each headline. Short videos of news stories are also available. The *Times* can also be read in Chinese and Spanish online by clicking the language at the top of the website. Readers can access *The New York Times International Edition* from this website.

Sources: www.globeandmail.com; www.nationalpost.com; www.thestar.com; www.theguardian.com; www.nytimes.com

Activity A | Do you read the news online? Which news sites do you go to? Do you ever buy the newspaper to read? Why or why not? Discuss your news reading habits with a partner.

Activity B | Read the news article below from thestar.com. It is about Paro the robot seal. As you read the article, notice how it differs from something you would read in a university textbook. For example, what do you notice about the format of the news article, compared to the format of a chapter in a textbook? What do you notice about the language and sentence structure? What other things do you notice? Describe in what ways they are different. Write down three things and discuss with a partner.

Meet Paro, a Furry Friend to Dementia Patients

Japanese engineer Takanori Shibata has spent years developing Paro, a robot modelled after a Canadian harp seal, which could help dementia patients around the world.

NANTO, JAPAN—In March 2002, a helicopter carried Takanori Shibata over the Gulf of St. Lawrence and deposited him on an ice floe.

1   The Japanese engineer had spent the previous nine years developing "Paro," a device designed to tackle one of the biggest public health issues of the 21st century: dementia. On that day he was finally meeting the inspiration for his invention. "Mehhrrrr!" cried the baby seal. Very cute, the engineer thought, as his video recorder captured the moment.

2   Thirteen years later, that adorable seal cry has been programmed into 3500 Paro devices deployed to more than 30 countries. So what exactly is Paro? It looks like the Canadian baby seal Shibata met on that ice floe. For many patients coping with dementia, Paro has become an unexpected source of relief.

3   Paro is astonishingly lifelike, thanks to artificial[6] intelligence. The seal looks at people

Motonari Tagawa for the Toronto Star

Robots such as Paro the harp seal can have a soothing effect on people suffering from dementia. The lifelike Paro looks at you when you're talking and can recognize its own name.

---

[6] not real

Weighing five and a half pounds, Paro is covered with sensors that allow it to detect temperature, touch (both stroking and hitting), and its own posture, so it knows when someone is lifting it.

when spoken to, cries in response to stimuli,[7] and closes its eyes when scratched under the chin. Paro can even learn its name.

4   The seal's large black eyes are oddly expressive. "I feel it's looking into my soul," says a dementia patient. "I didn't want to develop a robot that had emotional expressions," says Shibata. "I wanted to develop a robot that (made people think) the robot had emotions."

How Paro Works

5   • Body: Paro is five and a half pounds, the weight of a human baby. Paro's body is covered with sensors that allow it to detect temperature, touch, and its own posture, so it knows when someone is lifting it.

• Fur: Petting animals can have an anxiety-reducing effect. Anyone who meets Paro for the first time will find it difficult to resist stroking it. Paro's fur is antibacterial and soil-resistant.

• Face: Shibata tweaked Paro's facial dimensions many times. "If we change the ratio in this (eyes-nose) triangle, Paro can (evoke) a different feeling. In the beginning, the eyes were small. They got larger and then I made them smaller again."

• Nose: Paro "sees" with its black button nose, which contains two light sensors that help it detect light. When the lights come on, Paro knows it's time to play. When they go off, Paro knows to go to sleep.

• Mouth: Paro's battery can be recharged with a device shaped like a pacifier. Paro has been programmed with sounds recorded from a real baby harp seal and it coos in response to stimuli.

• Ears: Paro's ears have microphones. It is capable of both speech recognition (it can recognize its name) and sound localization (so Paro knows where to look when spoken to).

• Joints: Paro has seven joints that allow it to mimic the basic movements of a seal: it "crawls," blinks, and looks right and left.

Source: Yang. J. (2015, October 5). Meet Paro, a furry friend to dementia patients. *Thestar.com*. Retrieved from http://www.thestar.com/news/insight/2015/10/05/meet-paro-a-furry-friend-to-dementia-patients.html

---

[7] something that produces a reaction in a human, an animal, or a plant

Activity C | Writing Task: Descriptive Paragraph | Write a short descriptive paragraph about Paro the robot seal. Use some of the information about Paro from the news article. The topic sentence and concluding sentence are provided for you.

Topic sentence: Paro is a therapy robot seal that looks and sounds like a real baby seal.

Sentence 1: _____

_____

Sentence 2: _____

_____

Sentence 3: _____

_____

Sentence 4: _____

_____

Sentence 5: _____

_____

Concluding sentence: The realistic features of Paro the robot seal bring comfort and happiness to patients.

Preventing Plagiarism

Working from Memory

As a college or university student, you have to write papers and other assignments for your classes. Once you know your topic, you need to gather information from different sources. Regardless of what sources you use, you have to put the information in your own words. When you read something, it is very difficult to put it in your own words immediately, especially if it is sitting in front of you. If you want to put something in your own words, wait a few hours between the time you read it and when you write it down.

If you are reading about a complex topic, you might be very tempted to copy the words from your sources straight into your paper. Instead, put the book away and wait for two hours before you try to write. Then write as much as you can from memory. Once you are finished, you can check the original source again for details and accuracy, but don't change the way you wrote your sentences. Keep your writing in your own voice.

You can use a similar approach when you are collaborating with classmates. It is very useful to discuss ideas with other people who are doing the same assignment or reading the same material. Of course you can't copy exactly what they say. After you meet with them, you need to wait a couple of hours before writing down what you remember. This will help make sure that you are using your own words, not someone else's. Remember, it is always your responsibility to make sure you have not copied anyone else, and that no one else has copied you.

Paragraphing Skill

Writing a Topic Sentence

A paragraph contains several sentences. In Unit 1, you saw that a paragraph typically contains a topic sentence and it is usually the first sentence in a paragraph. It is the most important sentence and the most general because it gives the main idea of the paragraph. A topic sentence in a descriptive paragraph helps readers know what you will be describing.

A topic sentence has two parts: the topic and controlling idea. The topic tells the reader what the paragraph is about. The controlling idea restricts what you will discuss about the topic.

Write the topic of the paragraph first and then the controlling idea.

Paro the robot seal is popular with senior citizens.
    topic   *controlling idea*

Activity A | Read these topic sentences. Underline the topic and highlight the controlling idea.

1. Robots are used extensively in manufacturing.
2. Robots have replaced many assembly line jobs in factories around the world.
3. White collar jobs are the next type of employment that will be heavily impacted by robots.

4. Household robots will become more common in the next 10 years for three reasons.
5. The military is investigating how to apply robotic technology in their forces.
6. Therapy robots are being used in seniors' homes for companionship.
7. Robots should be used for tasks that are too dangerous or too monotonous for humans.

Activity B | Writing Task: Topic Sentences | Go back to the three photographs in the *Exploring Ideas* section on page 44 and write a descriptive topic sentence for each photograph. Each of your topic sentences should include a topic and controlling idea. Compare your descriptive topic sentences with a partner. How do they differ?

Activity C | The paragraph below describes a robot called bObsweep. The paragraph is missing its topic sentence. Read the paragraph and write a topic sentence on the line. Discuss your topic sentence with a partner.

---

bObsweep

_____

_____

_____ It was designed by Canadian researchers to clean household floors. bObsweep has a circular shape and is approximately 35 centimetres wide and 11.5 centimetres high. It weighs almost nine pounds and comes in different colours. It has a large dustbin and powerful brushes. As part of its sanitizing function, it uses special sensors that can detect if floors need to be disinfected. It is an intelligent robot that knows when the floors are clean and will return to its recharging dock when it is finished or when the battery needs to be recharged. bObsweep is great for homes that have pets or people with allergies. It is also a must-have appliance for busy families with children because it can be programmed to clean the floor after everyone has gone to bed. bObsweep is a household appliance that cleans floors and gives families more time to spend together.

Source: http://www.bobsweep.com/

Language Skill

Using Comparatives and Superlatives

In a descriptive paragraph, using comparatives and superlatives will strengthen your descriptions. Comparatives and superlatives are forms of adjectives. You use a comparative when you are comparing two things. You use a superlative when you are comparing three or more things. A comparative is usually formed with *-er* and a superlative is usually formed with *-est*.

Examples
Paro the robot baby seal is **cuter** than the teddy bear.
Drones are becoming **smaller** all the time.
Already, the **smallest** is less than three millimetres wide.
The KUKA KR 1000 is the world's **largest** robot.

See the chart below for the general rules for forming comparatives and superlatives. Note that there are exceptions to these rules, which you will learn as you progress in your study of English.

	Adjective	Comparative	Superlative
one-syllable adjective	*small*	add *-er*	add *-est*
		smaller	*smallest*
	adjective ends with an *-e* *cute*	add *-r*	add *-st*
		cuter	*cutest*
	adjective ends with vowel + a consonant:	double the consonant and add *-er*	double the consonant and add *-est*
	big, hot, sad	*bigger, hotter, sadder*	*biggest, hottest, saddest*
two-syllable adjective that ends with a -y	*happy, heavy, cloudy*	change the y to i and add *-er*	change the y to i and add *-est*
		happier, heavier, cloudier	*happiest, heaviest, cloudiest*
adjective with two or more syllables	*beautiful, important, expensive*	more + adjective + than	the + most + adjective
		more beautiful than, more important than, more expensive than	*the most beautiful, the most important, the most expensive*

When you form a sentence using comparatives, you need to add *than* after the adjective because you are comparing two things.

Paro is **cuter than** the teddy bear.

When you form a sentence using a superlative, you need to add *the* in front of the adjective.

Paro is **the cutest** therapy robot on the market.

The word *the* signals that the item being described is the top among all things it is being compared to.

Activity A | Choose photographs of three different robots pictured in the unit and write comparative and superlative adjective sentences about them. Compare your sentences with a partner.

Activity B | Discuss the following topics and questions in small groups. Whenever possible, use comparative and superlative adjectives in your responses.

1. Some retirement homes have programs where the patients are visited by therapy dogs. Others are experimenting with robot pets like Paro. Which do you think is more expensive? Which do you think is more effective? Which do you think the patients prefer? Which do you think the nurses and doctors prefer? Why?

2. Some doctors are being assisted by robot surgeons. Soon, robot surgeons will be able to do many routine operations. What would be the advantages of a robot surgeon compared to a real surgeon? What would be the advantages of a real surgeon compared to a robot surgeon? Which one do you think would do a better job? Which one do you think would be more expensive? Which one would be more reliable?

3. Several companies are manufacturing robotic cars, also called driverless cars. What benefits or problems can you imagine? How do you think drivers will feel about it? Do you think people will like driverless cars more than traditional cars?

Activity C | After your group discussion, write as many comparative and superlative sentences as you remember.

WRITING FUNDAMENTALS

Composition Skill

Self-Editing

Self-editing is an important step in the writing process. Some people like to check their spelling and grammar while they are writing their paragraph, but this can slow you down and make you lose sight of your main topic. When you get to the end of your paragraph, ask yourself these questions:

- Are my topic and concluding sentences complete and accurate?
- Are my supporting details organized logically?
- Is my paragraph coherent (easy to understand)?
- Do the details directly and clearly support and develop my main idea?

Once you have taken care of those things, you can proofread to find and correct any spelling and grammar mistakes you may have made.

Activity A | Go back to the *Fostering Inquiry* section on pages 46–48 and review the information about the five senses. Considering your Unit Inquiry Question, write down the five senses and take notes for each sense in relation to your Unit Inquiry Question. Discuss your notes and ideas with a partner.

Activity B | Writing Task: First Draft | Write a first draft of a descriptive paragraph using the notes you took in Activity A. When you have finished, follow the editing steps below:

Step 1: Check that your topic sentence includes the topic and controlling idea.
Step 2: Check that the supporting sentences and details support and develop your main idea.
Step 3: Check that your description appeals to your reader's senses.
Step 4: Check that your paragraph is coherent and well organized.
Step 5: Check that your concluding sentence restates the topic sentence or summarizes the main points.

Activity C | Look at your first draft. What aspects of your paragraph need the most editing? What would you edit first? Would you change any supporting details? Why? How would you make your descriptive paragraph more appealing to your reader's senses? After you have reflected on these questions, share your reflections with a partner and discuss the self-editing process.

Writing Skill

Avoiding Sentence Fragments

A clause is a group of words that has a subject and a verb. If a clause expresses a complete idea, it is a sentence. A *sentence fragment* (or incomplete sentence) is a group of words, punctuated like a sentence, that either does not express a complete idea, or does not have a subject and a verb.

Examples

1. The Roomba vacuum cleaner is expensive. (*Sentence*)
2. The Roomba vacuum cleaner expensive. (*Sentence fragment*)

The first sentence is a complete sentence because it contains a subject (*Roomba vacuum cleaner*) and verb (*is*). The second example is a sentence fragment because it does not include a verb.

There are two types of clauses. A clause that includes a subject and verb and expresses a complete idea is called an **independent clause**.

A **dependent clause** starts with an adverb such as *after, before, while, because, since, although, unless,* or *until.* A dependent clause cannot stand by itself. It must be connected to an independent clause:

Examples

1. After the Roomba finished vacuuming, it recharged its battery.
2. The Roomba recharged its battery after it finished vacuuming.

In the examples above, a dependent clause (*after the Roomba finished vacuuming*) is connected to an independent clause (*it recharged its battery*). The dependent clause can go at the beginning or the end of the sentence.

By itself, a dependent clause is a sentence fragment.

Activity A | Read the sentences and sentence fragments below. Put an S next to the sentences and an SF next to the sentence fragments.

1. _____ Very common industrial robots.

2. _____ Since Paro, a cute, fuzzy, seal-like robot.

3. _____ Industrial and agricultural robots are becoming more popular as technology advances.

4. _____ Computer commands direct the movements of a robot.

5. _____ Because a typical industrial robot has an arm, a controller, a drive, and a sensor.

Activity B | Look back at the first draft of a descriptive paragraph that you wrote in Activity B on page 74. Check your sentences for sentence fragments. If you have sentence fragments, correct them. You can also ask a partner to check your first draft for sentence fragments.

Sentence and Grammar Skill

Using Correct Adjective Word Order

An adjective describes a noun. It is possible to use several adjectives before a noun in a sentence. If you do, you will need to put them in a particular order. For example, write *a slim, young woman*, not *a young, slim woman*. Notice that a comma separates each adjective.

Adjectives can describe various types of aspects of nouns. The following word order for adjective types, while not fixed, is normally used:

opinion → size → age → shape → colour → origin → material + NOUN

opinion	beautiful, pretty, difficult
size	small, big, large, tiny
age	old, young, ancient
shape	round, square, cylindrical
colour	silver, black, red
origin	Canadian, Italian, German
material	steel, leather, cotton

Example
a beautiful, small, new, circular, silver, Japanese, steel robot

Activity A | Write three sentences using correct adjective word order to describe the three robots in the *Exploring Ideas* section on page 44. In your sentences, use a combination of two or three adjectives. Then share your sentences with a partner.

Activity B | Writing Task: Second and Final Drafts | Go back to Activity B on page 74 where you practised self-editing on the first draft of your descriptive paragraph. Looking at your self-editing notes, write a second draft of your descriptive paragraph. When you are finished, ask a partner if your descriptive sentences appeal to his or her senses. Is it possible to add a few more adjectives to your paragraph? Do this only if your partner feels that it makes your paragraph more appealing. Then, if necessary, write a final draft of your paragraph.

Using Compensation Strategies

Sometimes when you are writing, you realize you are missing something. You might be missing the right word, you're unsure of the correct grammar, or you're missing some fact or piece of information that you need. You need to compensate for whatever you are missing. That is, you have to make up for what you don't have, so that your sentence will still say what you want it to say. Compensation strategies are learning strategies that help you do this.

For example, when you can't think of the right word, one strategy is to describe what the word means. Suppose you are writing a sentence about robots and can't think of the word *automatic*. You could write "The robot performs its job without being told."

If you can't remember how to write a grammatically correct comparative sentence, you can compensate by writing the sentence in a different way. You want to write "Paro the seal robot is more realistic than the dog robot." Instead you could write "Paro resembles a seal, but the dog robot doesn't look like a real dog."

When you are missing some fact or piece of information that you need, compensate by making an educated guess. If you are writing about Canadarm and are unsure if Canada had an official space agency, you could write "The organization that operates the Canadian space program is opening a museum."

Remember, you are always free to go back and rewrite, but compensation strategies help you find a way to work around the gaps.

Source: Oxford, R. L. (1990). *Language learning strategies: What every teacher should know.* Boston, MA: Heinle & Heinle.

UNIT OUTCOME

Writing Assignment: Descriptive Paragraph

Write a descriptive paragraph of 150 to 250 words on a topic related to robotics. (Your instructor may give you an alternative length.) You may write on a topic based on your Unit Inquiry Question, develop another topic of your choosing connected to robotics, or choose one of the following topics:

- What do companion cat or dog robots look like, feel like, and sound like?
- What mechanisms do robots have to ensure child safety?
- What are the design details of an electric skateboard?

Use the skills you have developed in this unit to complete the assignment. Follow the steps below to practise each of the new skills you have learned to write a well-developed descriptive paragraph.

1. **Brainstorm and find information**: Look at the freewriting you did in the *Fostering Inquiry* section. If necessary, use the listing technique or a mind map to brainstorm some ideas related to your Unit Inquiry Question. Then do a search for information related to your Unit Inquiry Question. In addition to the readings and other topic-related information in this unit, your information sources may include a newspaper article.

2. **Outline**: List your topic, your chosen inquiry question, and the working title of your paragraph.

   Topic: _____

   Inquiry Question: _____

   Paragraph Title: _____

   Use the template below to create an outline for your paragraph. See the outline on page 50 for more detail about the body of the paragraph.

   Topic sentence that states what the paragraph will describe:

Topic Sentence

Descriptive point 1 (with details):

Main Body (Supporting Ideas)

Descriptive point 2 (with details):

Descriptive point 3 (with details):

Concluding Sentence

Concluding sentence to remind your reader what the paragraph is about:

3. **Write a first draft**: Write a first draft of your paragraph. Use AWL and mid-frequency vocabulary from this unit if possible.

4. **Self-check**: Wait a day, then check your first draft. Remember to check the following:

- Check that your descriptive paragraph has a topic sentence (topic and controlling idea), supporting ideas, and a concluding sentence.

- Check the adjectives in your paragraph. When you have used adjective suffixes, are they correct? Are they spelled correctly?

- Check the word order of the adjectives in your paragraph. When you have used multiple adjectives, are they in the correct order? Have you separated them with commas?

- Check the comparatives and superlatives in your paragraph. Are the adjectives used and spelled correctly?

- Check that your paragraph does not have any sentence fragments.
- Read current newspaper stories about your topic. Is there any additional information you can add to your paragraph?

5. **Revise**: Revise your first draft.

6. **Compose final draft**: Write a final draft of your descriptive paragraph.

7. **Proofread**: Check the final draft of your paragraph for any small errors you may have missed. In particular, look for spelling errors, typos, and punctuation mistakes.

Evaluation: Descriptive Paragraph Rubric

Use the following rubric to evaluate your essay. In which areas do you need to improve most?

E = **Emerging**: frequent difficulty using unit skills; needs a lot more work
D = **Developing**: some difficulty using unit skills; some improvement still required
S = **Satisfactory**: able to use unit skills most of the time; meets average expectations for this level
O = **Outstanding**: exceptional use of unit skills; exceeds expectations for this level

Skill	E	D	S	O
The descriptive paragraph has a topic sentence, descriptive sentences that appeal to the reader's senses, and a concluding sentence that connects to the topic.				
AWL and mid-frequency vocabulary items from this unit are used when appropriate and with few mistakes.				
Comparative and superlative sentences are written correctly.				
The paragraph uses connectors of location to describe where something is in relation to something else.				
The paragraph is free of sentence fragments.				
Affixes added to words to form adjectives are used correctly.				
When multiple adjectives are used, the word order is correct.				

Unit Review

Activity A | What do you know about the topic of robotics that you did not know before you started this unit? Discuss with a partner or small group. Be prepared to report what you learned to the class.

Activity B | Look back at the Unit Inquiry Question you developed at the start of this unit and discuss it with a partner or small group. Then share your answers with the class. Use the following questions to help you:

1. What information did you find in this unit that helped you answer your question?
2. How would you answer your question now?

Activity C | Use the following checklist to review the skills you have learned in this unit. First decide which 10 skills you think are the most important. Circle the number beside each of these 10 skills. If you learned a skill in this unit that isn't listed below, write it in the blank row at the end of the checklist. Then put a check mark in the box beside those points you feel you have learned. Be prepared to discuss your choices with the class.

Self-Assessment Checklist
☐ 1. I can talk about robotics based on what I've learned in this unit.
☐ 2. I can develop an inquiry question to guide my learning.
☐ 3. I can use Wikipedia to begin learning about a writing topic.
☐ 4. I can appeal to the five senses to make my writing more descriptive.
☐ 5. I can use connectors of location in my descriptive writing.
☐ 6. I can create adjectives by adding prefixes and suffixes to nouns, verbs, or other adjectives.
☐ 7. I can use AWL and mid-frequency vocabulary from this unit in my writing.
☐ 8. I can make predictions about the content of text using the visuals that accompany it.
☐ 9. I can evaluate sources for credibility.
☐ 10. I can use the listing technique to brainstorm ideas before writing.
☐ 11. I can use online newspapers to find information.
☐ 12. I can avoid plagiarism by working from memory.
☐ 13. I can write a topic sentence.

☐	14. I can write grammatically correct comparative and superlative sentences.
☐	15. I can edit my own work and identify areas that need the most improvement.
☐	16. I can identify and avoid sentence fragments.
☐	17. I can use compensation strategies to help myself with my writing.
☐	18. I can write a well-structured descriptive paragraph that contains a topic sentence, descriptive details, and a concluding sentence.
☐	19.

Activity D | Put a check mark in the box beside the vocabulary items from this unit that you feel confident using in your writing.

Vocabulary Checklist

☐ capable (adj.) AWL   ☐ launch (n./v.) 4000

☐ conceive (v.) AWL   ☐ planet (n.) 4000

☐ device (n.) AWL   ☐ telescope (n.) 3000

☐ explorer (n.) 4000   ☐ universe (n.) 4000

☐ endeavour (n.) 3000   ☐ version (n.) AWL

☐ indicate (v.) AWL   ☐ visible (adj.) AWL

UNIT 3

Engineering

Structural Engineering

KEY LEARNING OUTCOMES

Creating an inquiry question for exploring categories and characteristics

Finding information from magazine articles

Writing strong supporting sentences

Proofreading your writing

Writing complex and compound sentences

Writing a definition paragraph

EXPLORING IDEAS

Introduction

The Confederation Bridge (above) is located in eastern Canada and connects the province of Nova Scotia to the province of Prince Edward Island. It is a famous bridge within Canada. It is 8.9 kilometres long and is the world's longest bridge over ice-covered waters in winter.

Activity A | Look at the photos above and discuss the following questions with a partner or small group.

1. Why do you think this bridge is so famous?
2. What difficulties or challenges would have been involved in building this bridge?
3. What famous structure do you know of in Canada or in another country? What makes it famous or special?

Activity B | A discussion is a conversation that can help you to explore ideas about a topic. Two or more people can take part in the discussion. One way to start a discussion is to use something called a *prompt*. This can be, for example, a photo or even a word that everyone looks at and then comments on to begin the discussion. Using the prompts on page 85, prepare two questions for each that you could ask to begin a discussion.

Prompt #1

BUILDING

Prompt #2

Activity C | Working with a group of two to four other students, discuss the prompts in Activity B. Take turns asking each other the questions you wrote. Continue asking follow-up questions to keep the discussion going. Take notes. What direction did your discussion take after you began to ask follow-up questions?

Fostering Inquiry

Inquiring into Categories and Characteristics

Categories and characteristics guide some of the questions you can ask to learn more about something. According to the *Oxford Advanced Learner's Dictionary*, characteristics are the "typical features or qualities that something/somebody has." For example, the characteristics of a car are that it has four wheels, an engine, and it moves people from one place to another.

The word *category* means the different types or kinds of something. For example, buildings can be grouped into categories like *residential* (used for living, like a house), *commercial* (used for a business, like a store or office), and *industrial* (used to make things, like a factory). These different categories have different characteristics. A house will have bedrooms and a kitchen, while a factory would not. A store might have very large windows, while a house might not.

Thinking about categories and characteristics can guide your inquiry. For example, if you're interested in the Egyptian pyramids, you might think about the characteristics of them: what was special about their structure, the materials, the height, and the building process? Or you might inquire about different categories of pyramids. The pyramids in Egypt, pyramids in Mexico, and pyramids in Indonesia are all different categories of pyramids, with different characteristics.

The built environment refers to the parts of our world that are not natural (like mountains, rivers, and trees), but rather were built by humans. Buildings, telephone towers, cities, and farms are all examples of the built environment.

Activity A | What do you want to know more about in relation to structural engineering and the built environment? For example:

- What different types of roads are there?
- What are the characteristics of a lighthouse?
- What is the definition of a "green" building?

1. Write two or three questions you are curious about on the topic of the built environment.
2. When you are finished, compare your questions with a partner or small group.
3. Choose one question to be your inquiry question for this unit. It does not have to be the same question as your partner or group.
4. Write your inquiry question in the space provided. Look back at this question as you work through the unit. This is your Unit Inquiry Question.

My Unit Inquiry Question:

_____

_____

_____

Activity B | Writing Task: Freewriting | Write for at least five minutes on the topic of your Unit Inquiry Question. Do not stop writing during this time. After five minutes, read what you have written and circle two or three ideas that you would like to explore further to answer your Unit Inquiry Question.

Structure

Definition Paragraph

Purpose

The purpose of a definition paragraph is to define a person, place, thing, or idea. To define something means to describe who or what it is, explaining the most important characteristics that make it unique.

Audience

The audience for a definition paragraph depends on the context for which it is written. Definition paragraphs may be found in encyclopedias, textbooks, and some advanced dictionaries. The audiences for these are students or the general public. Sometimes students write definition paragraphs as part of a research paper, an exam, or for an in-class presentation. In these cases, the audience is your instructor or your classmates.

Activity A | One place you will find definition paragraphs is an encyclopedia. Have you ever used an encyclopedia? What's the difference between an encyclopedia and Wikipedia? Discuss with a partner or your class.

Activity B | With a partner or small group, read the short definition paragraph below on a type of house called a yurt. Then answer the questions that follow.

A yurt is a type of traditional home found in Central Asia. The yurt is similar to a tent. It is small and circular, with a wooden frame. The outside is made of felt or animal skins. As well, many yurts have a stove inside. This stove burns wood. Smoke escapes through a chimney, which passes through the roof. Yurts are very suitable for nomads, people with no fixed address who move around with their animals. For example, yurts can be built in two hours and then taken down quickly. The frame and felt covering can be carried on the back of a horse or yak. Yurts are a simple yet very convenient home for nomadic people.

1. What does this paragraph define?

   _____

2. What are the three supporting ideas in this paragraph?

   _____

3. What words or phrases introduce the different supporting ideas?

   _____

4. Is there anything special about the first and last sentences of this paragraph?

   _____

Structure of a Definition Paragraph

While an explanatory paragraph answers *why* or *how*, a definition paragraph answers *what*. For example, a definition paragraph might answer the question *What is concrete?* or *What is a yurt?*

The topic sentence in a definition paragraph is a simple one-sentence definition of the person, place, object, or thing to be discussed.

Your paragraph should then contain one to three supporting ideas. These ideas expand on the general definition in your topic sentence. The most common types of supporting ideas are shown in the chart below.

Type of Supporting Idea	Example Sentence
characteristic	A yurt is small and circular, with a wooden frame.
category	There are two types of yurt: traditional and modern.
synonym or comparison	A yurt is similar to a tent.
	Another word for yurt is *ger*, which comes from the Mongolian language.

Note: a negative definition is a type of comparison. It helps to define something by contrasting it with something that it is not.

A yurt is different from a house because a house cannot be moved from place to place.

A yurt is not a permanent building.

A yurt and a house are different types of buildings.

Each supporting idea in your paragraph should have one to three details to support it. Supporting details can be examples, explanations, or facts that you've found in a book or magazine or on a website.

The last sentence in your definition paragraph is a concluding sentence, which should remind readers what they have just learned about.

Figure 3.1 shows an outline of a definition paragraph.

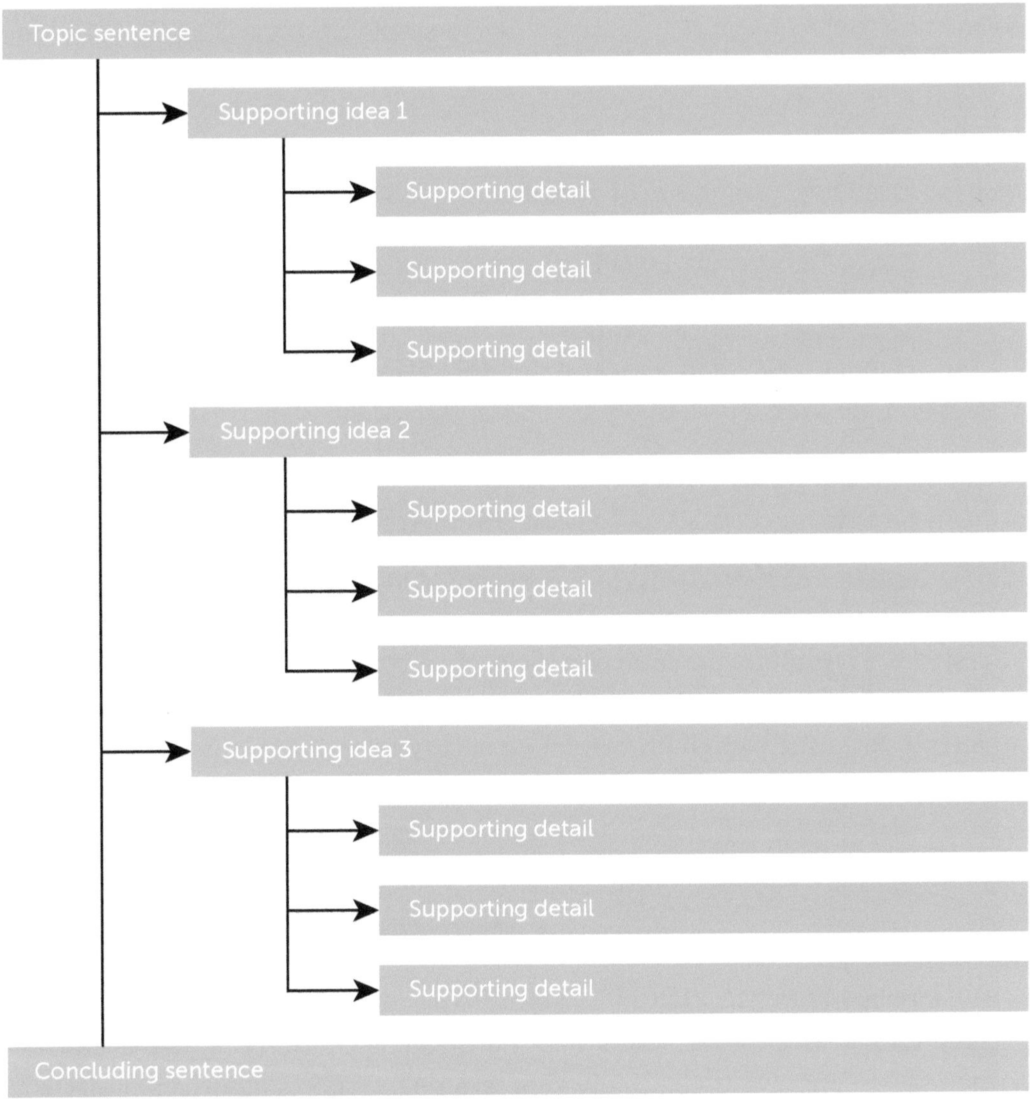

FIGURE 3.1   Structure of a definition paragraph

Language Tip

Using Connectors of Additional Information or Examples

You can use connectors to link the topic sentence, supporting ideas, detail, and concluding sentences together.

Additional Information	Examples
Also,	For example,

As well,	For instance,
In addition to this,	An example of this is _____,
Additionally,	X, such as Y,

Connectors can appear in different places in a sentence. The most common position is at the beginning of the sentence. When a connector is at the beginning of a sentence, it must be followed by a comma.

As well, many yurts have a stove inside.

The connector *also* can appear in the middle of the sentence, between the subject and the simple present verb, or after the modal verb.

Nomadic people **also** make yurts out of wool or felt.
Yurts can **also** be carried on the back of horses or yaks.

Activity C | Definition paragraphs are closely related to explanatory paragraphs, which you learned about in Unit 1. Below you will find an example of a definition paragraph. Read the paragraph carefully and pay attention to the information it contains. Answer the questions that follow the paragraph on page 91.

Intelligent Transportation Systems

Intelligent transportation systems (ITSs) are applications that use technology to improve roads and transportation. These systems can be used to improve traffic safety. One example of ITS is automatic traffic enforcement technology that helps catch drivers who break the law. This technology may include cameras to film drivers who go through red lights or who go over the speed limit. Additionally, ITSs are used to improve traffic flow. For example, on some roads the speed limit changes depending on how many cars are on the road. Also, on a road with many traffic lights, there are systems that will coordinate the light changes so a driver does not have to stop as many times. ITSs use many different technologies, such as wireless technology, computers, Bluetooth, and GPS. As well, simple technologies, such as magnetic metal loops, audio recording, and video recording are used. There are many uses of intelligent transportation systems.

1. What is the purpose of this paragraph?
2. Who is the audience of this paragraph: experts or non-experts? How do you know this?
3. What is the topic sentence of this paragraph?
4. What is the person, place, thing, or idea being defined in this paragraph? Find and underline the general definition.
5. Find and number the three supporting ideas in the text. Highlight the supporting details for each of these supporting ideas.

Activity D | Writing Task: Paragraph Outline | Think of something from the built environment that you are familiar with. Fill in the following graphic with one sentence in each box to create an outline for a short, simple definition paragraph that answers the question *What is it?*

Remember that the topic sentence should be a general one-sentence definition of the thing you are defining. Then add three supporting ideas, giving characteristics, categories, synonyms, or negative definitions. Your concluding sentence should close the paragraph.

Topic Sentence

Main Body (Supporting Ideas)

Supporting idea 1

Supporting idea 2

Supporting idea 3

Concluding Sentence

Activity E | Exchange your completed outline with a partner. Read your partner's sentences and provide feedback, using the following questions to guide you.

1. Is the topic sentence a one-sentence definition of the person, place, thing, or idea that you are defining?
2. Are the supporting ideas organized in a logical order?
3. Does this outline include one to three different supporting ideas? Are they characteristics, categories, synonyms, or negative definitions?
4. Does your concluding sentence close the paragraph appropriately?
5. Is there enough detail in the definition to understand what this person, place, thing, or idea is?
6. Is the language used appropriate for a non-expert audience?
7. What do you like most about these sentences?
8. Could these sentences be expanded into a paragraph? Would you be able to come up with one to three different details for each supporting idea? Explain.
9. How would you improve these sentences?

Activity F | Revisit your Unit Inquiry Question on page 86. What information or new ideas have you thought of or discussed that will help you answer your question? Share your ideas with a partner or small group. At this point, you may consider revising your Unit Inquiry Question.

ACADEMIC READING

Vocabulary

Vocabulary Skill: Forming Nouns

Knowing one word in a word family can help you to figure out how to form two or three other words in that family. If you know a verb or an adjective, you can often form the related noun by adding a suffix. A suffix is a series of a few letters that goes on the end of a word. See the examples below. Notice that sometimes there are spelling changes when adding a suffix.

Adjective or Verb	Suffix	Noun
happy (adj.)	-ness	happyiness → happiness
manage (v.)	-ment	management
pollute (v.)	-ion	polluteion → pollution
build (v.)	-er	builder
drain (v.)	-age	drainage

Activity A | Look at the following list of adjectives and verbs. Can you guess what the corresponding noun might be? Check your answers with a dictionary.

Adjective or Verb	Noun
drive	
hard	
short	
adjust	
construct	

Vocabulary Preview: The Academic Word List

Activity B | The following AWL words are taken from the academic reading "Transportation Structures" on pages 96–99. The definitions of the words are provided. Read the words and their definitions and choose the correct words to complete the paragraph that follows. You might have to change the form of the word to fit the sentence.

construct (v.): to build or make something such as a road, building, or machine
route (n.): a way that you follow to get from one place to another
similar (adj.): like somebody/something but not exactly the same
transportation (n.): a system for carrying people or goods from one place to another using vehicles, roads, etc.
vehicle (n.): a thing that is used for transporting people or goods from one place to another, such as a car or truck
structure (n.): a thing that is made of several parts, especially a building

The TransCanada highway is a _____ that runs from the province of Newfoundland and Labrador in eastern Canada to British Columbia in the west. It is 8030 kilometres long from coast to coast. Although _____ began in 1950, the highway did not open until 1962. Every year, millions of _____ travel on the TransCanada highway, which is one of the world's longest _____ systems. Australia's Highway 1 and the Trans-Siberian Highway are _____ road networks that stretch for thousands of kilometres. Highways, bridges, tunnels, toll stations, and ferries are some of the human-made _____ that make up the TransCanada.

Vocabulary Preview: Mid-frequency Vocabulary

Activity C | Read the words and definitions below. Then read the sentences and choose one word from the list for the blank in each sentence.

develop (v): to gradually grow or become bigger, more advanced, stronger, etc.; to make something do this

extend (v.): to make something reach something or stretch

obstacle (n.): an object that is in your way and that makes it difficult for you to move forward

slope (n.): a surface or piece of land that slopes (is higher at one end than the other)

compact (v.): to press something together firmly

path (n.): a line along which somebody/something moves; the space in front of somebody/something as they move

1. A ball will roll slowly down a gentle _____ and more quickly down a steep one.

2. Military vehicles are designed to be able to drive over most _____, such as rocks or small trees, that may be in their path.

3. An engineering student will _____ knowledge in the areas of mathematics, physics, and chemistry.

4. There is a modern, paved road for cars to drive on through the village. In the past, it was a simple walking _____ used by animals and people.

5. To make a good snowball, you must _____ the snow between your hands.

6. The soccer goalie had to fully _____ her arms to catch the ball before it entered the net.

Reading

The unit reading on pages 96–99, "Transportation Structures," is an excerpt from the textbook *Technology and Engineering*. This textbook is used in high school science classes in Canada.

Identifying Keywords

Every text has some words that are important for understanding what the text is about. These are called *keywords*. Keywords are repeated several times in the text. Keywords are often closely related to the topic of the text. Before you read a text, it is a good idea to identify the keywords and make sure you know the meaning of them. It will help improve your comprehension of the text.

Activity A | Think about the different structures related to transportation you see when you walk down a city street or drive down a country road. With a partner or small group, brainstorm a list of structures related to transportation.

Activity B | Skim the reading on pages 96–99. Pay attention to any keywords. Which five words seem to be the most repeated in the reading? Are any of these on the list of words you made for Activity A?

_____   _____

_____   _____

_____

Activity C | Now read the text. Underline the keywords as you read. Did you predict the top five keywords accurately? Write a simple definition in your own words for each of the five most common keywords you identified. Are there any other words you would add to the list? Compare your answer with a partner.

_____   _____

_____   _____

_____   _____

_____   _____

_____   _____

READING

Transportation Structures

1   **Transportation** systems depend on **constructed structures** such as railroad lines, highways and streets, waterways, and airport runways. Other constructed works help **vehicles** cross uneven terrain and rivers. These structures include bridges and tunnels. Pipelines are land transportation structures used to move liquids or gases over long distances. Let us look at some examples of these constructed works. We will discuss roadways and bridges.

Roadways

2   Roads are almost as old as civilization. People first used trails and **paths** to travel. Later, they **developed** more extensive systems. The Romans built the first engineered roads more than 2000 years ago. Their influence remained until the 1700s when modern road building started. Today's roads have their roots in the work of the Scottish engineer John McAdam. He developed a crushed-stone road built of three layers of crushed rock, laid in a 10 inch (25 centimetre)–thick ribbon. Later, this roadbed was covered with an asphalt[1]–gravel mix that is very common today. A more recent development is the concrete roadway.

3   Building a road starts with selecting and surveying the **route**. Next, the route is cleared of **obstacles** such as trees, rocks, and brush. The roadway is graded so it will drain. Drainage is important to prevent road damage from freezing and thawing. Also, a dry roadbed withstands heavy traffic better than a wet, marshy one. Another reason for grading is to keep the road's **slope** gentle. Elevation changes are described using the term *grade*.[2] Grades are expressed in percentages. A road with a five percent grade gains or loses five feet (152 centimetres) of height every 100 feet (30.5 metres) of distance. Most grades are kept below seven percent.

4   Once the roadbed is established, the layers of the road are built. See Figure 3.2. The graded dirt is **compacted**, and a layer of coarse gravel is laid. This is followed with finer gravel that is leveled and compacted. Next, the concrete or asphalt top layer is applied. Concrete roads are laid in one layer. Asphalt is generally applied in two layers: a coarse undercoat and a finer topcoat. Finally, the shoulders, or edges, of the road are prepared. The shoulders can be gravel or asphalt.

---

[1] a thick black sticky substance used especially for making the surface of roads
[2] a gradient or slope

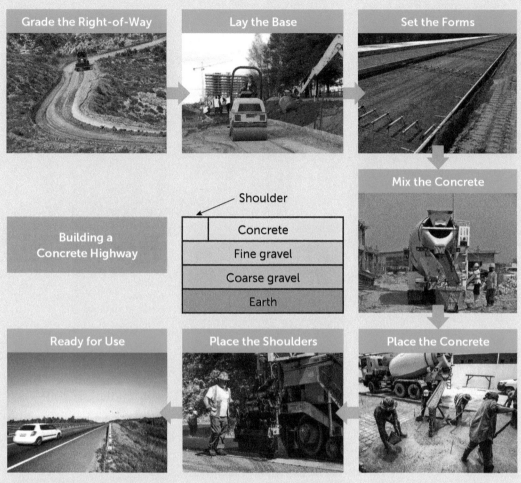

FIGURE 3.2 Road building is a step-by-step process

Bridges

5   Another constructed structure vital for transportation is the bridge. Bridges provide a path for vehicles to move over obstacles. These obstacles include marshy areas, ravines, other roads, and bodies of water. Bridges can carry a number of transportation systems. These systems include highways, railroads, canals, pipelines, and footpaths.

6   Generally, there are fixed and movable bridges. A fixed bridge does not move. Once the bridge is set in place, it stays there. Movable bridges can change their positions to accommodate traffic below them. This type of bridge is used to span ship channels and rivers. The bridge is drawn up or swung out of the way so ships can pass.

7   Bridges have two parts. See Figure 3.3. The substructure spreads the load of the bridge to the soil. The abutments[3] and the piers are parts of the substructure.

---

[3] a structure built to support the lateral pressure of an arch or span, e.g., at the ends of a bridge

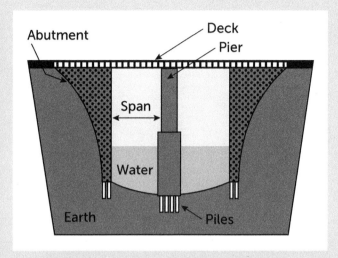

FIGURE 3.3   The parts of a bridge

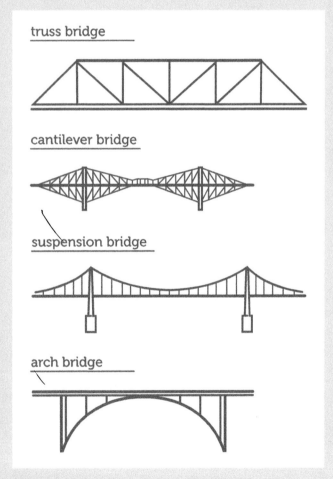

truss bridge

cantilever bridge

suspension bridge

arch bridge

FIGURE 3.4   Four types of bridges

The superstructure carries the loads of the deck to the substructure. The deck is the part used for the movement of vehicles and people across the bridge. 8   The kind of superstructure a bridge has indicates the type of bridge it is. The types of bridges are beam, truss, arch,[4] cantilever, and suspension.   *two way*

Beam bridges

heavy   long

Beam bridges use concrete or steel beams[5] to support the deck. This type of bridge is widely used when one road crosses another one. Beam bridges are very common on major highway systems.

Truss bridges

Truss bridges use small parts arranged in triangles to support the deck. These bridges can carry heavier loads over longer spans[6] than beam bridges can. Many railroad bridges are truss bridges.

Arch bridges

Arch bridges use curved members to support the deck. The arch can be above or below the deck. See

---

[4] a curved structure that supports the weight of something above it, such as a bridge or the upper part of a building

[5] a long piece of wood, metal, etc. used to support weight, especially as part of the roof in a building

[6] the width of something from one side to the other

Figure 3.4. Arch bridges are used for longer spans. One of the longest arch bridges spans more than 1650 feet (502 metres).

Cantilever bridges

Cantilever bridges use trusses[7] extending out in both directions from the support beams, similar to arms. The ends of the arms can intersect with the road leading up to the bridge or hook up to another truss unit to form a longer span. The arms transmit the load to the centre.

Suspension bridges

Suspension bridges use cable to carry the loads. A large cable is suspended from towers. From the large cable, smaller cables drop down to support the deck. Suspension bridges can span distances as great as 4000 feet (1220 metres) and longer.

Source: Adapted from Wright, R. T. (2012). *Technology and engineering* (6th ed., pp. 354–357). Tinley Park, IL: Goodheart-Willcox.

---

[7] a frame made of pieces of wood or metal used to support a roof, bridge, etc.

Activity D | Discuss the following questions with a partner or small group.

1. Where did the idea for modern roadways come from?
2. In your own words, explain the process of building a concrete highway.
3. What is the difference between a fixed and a movable bridge?
4. Vancouver's Lions Gate Bridge (pictured here) is very famous. Think about what you've read in the article. What type of bridge is the Lions Gate Bridge?
5. What do you know about transportation structures that you did not know before?

Activity E | Writing Task: Definition Sentences | Write seven sentences to answer the question *What is a bridge?* You may want to focus on the categories and characteristics of bridges. Concentrate on reusing some of the key vocabulary from the text, but also making the sentences your own. Use a dictionary to help you if you need it.

Activity F | Compare your sentences with the Unit 3 sample sentences in Appendix 2, then answer the following questions.

1. Have you written complete sentences? Does each one have a subject and a conjugated verb?
2. Does each sentence begin with a capital letter and end with a period?
3. Do your sentences include any new nouns from the reading? Are they used correctly?
4. Do your sentences include any new adjectives from the reading? Are they used correctly (including the comparative and superlative forms)?
5. Do your sentences include any new verbs from the reading? Are they used correctly?
6. Have you used any punctuation in your sentences? Is it used correctly?
7. How do the ideas in the sample sentences compare with the ideas in your sentences?

Critical Thinking

Stepping outside Your Box

Have you ever heard the expression "think outside the box"? It means to think about an issue or problem from a different point of view than the one you're used to.

When considering the built environment in our cities, different people have different boxes. An engineer may look at a bridge and think about its structures and how it was constructed. An ecologist may see all the cars travelling across the bridge and wonder how to reduce pollution by reducing the number of cars on the bridge. A teacher may consider how the lack of sidewalks on the bridge would make it unsafe for a class walking trip.

When you are thinking about a problem or question, try to determine what your "box" is and step outside it. Consider the problem from the points of view of different disciplines (areas of study) or types of people different from yourself. It may help you find a solution or come up with new creative ideas.

PROCESS FUNDAMENTALS

Brainstorming and Outlining

Reverse Thinking

Reverse thinking is a type of brainstorming. It might help you come up with ideas for your writing by making you think about things in a different way. Normally when brainstorming, you try to generate as many interesting ideas as possible related to a certain topic. With reverse thinking, do the opposite. Look at your topic and think "What would be the *least* interesting thing to write about related to this topic?" or "What am I *not* interested in writing about?" or "What do I think my classmates or instructor would already know about?" Write down all the ideas you come up with. This may sound strange, but it will help you look at your topic in a different way. It could lead you to think of some new ideas you haven't already thought of.

Once you have some ideas from reverse thinking, look at them a second time from a positive angle. Is there anything on your list that you might actually want to write about?

Activity A | Do three minutes of reverse thinking about your Unit Inquiry Question on page 86. Write down as many ideas as possible. When you've finished reverse thinking, look at what you've written from a positive angle. Did you come up with any ideas related to your Unit Inquiry Question that you might like to research and write about?

Outlining

The ideas you generated from your reverse thinking can become the supporting ideas in the definition paragraph you write about your Unit Inquiry Question.

Activity B | Create an outline for a definition paragraph based on your Unit Inquiry Question. First, write a topic sentence that responds to your question. Then use the ideas you developed using reverse thinking to create three supporting ideas for your paragraph. Add these to your outline. Remember to keep this outline in a safe place. As you complete more tasks in this unit, you may find examples, explanations, or facts that you will want to add to your outline as detail for each of your supporting ideas. Later, you can use the outline to help you write your final writing assignment.

Before You Write

Asking Questions: The 5Ws + H

The 5Ws refers to the five question words in English that begin with the letter *w*: *who*, *what*, *when*, *where*, and *why*. Though it doesn't start with *w*, the question word *how* is often included on this list.

It is important to ask questions before you begin to write. You can ask questions about your topic or the things you will write about in your paragraph. For example, if your topic is driverless cars, you could ask questions such as

- Who buys driverless cars?
- What are they made of?
- When did they become popular?
- How do they work?

You should also ask questions about the sources of information you will use in your writing, such as

- What words or phrases should I use to search for information on this topic?
- Who will be the most knowledgeable about this topic? What type of experts should I look for?
- Where will I find the most accurate information? What type of sources should I look for?
- When would the most relevant information on my topic have been written? What date should I look for on the sources I find?
- Why might some authors not present all the necessary information when writing about a certain topic? For example, could issues of advertising, money, or business influence what is mentioned in an article or on a web page?
- How will I know my information is correct and can be trusted?

Activity A | Imagine you are writing a definition paragraph on the following topics. Come up with 5W + H questions for each of these topics.

- solar-powered roadways
- wood construction
- earthquake-resistant buildings

Activity B | Using the same topics you generated 5W + H questions for in Activity A, think about the sources of information you would use to research these three topics. Come up with 5W + H questions that will help you find information.

Activity C | Think about the Unit Inquiry Question you wrote on page 86. Write some 5W + H questions about the sources of information you would use to research this topic. Then share your questions to a partner. Can your partner think of any more questions?

Content Skill

Using Magazine Articles

There are many types of magazines. Some popular magazines, such as sports or fashion magazines or magazines with fictional stories, are mostly for entertainment. Other popular magazines are meant to educate and inform their readers. These magazines may be about science, business, geography, or politics. There are also magazines that are very focused in one area. These are called trade magazines and are meant for people who work in a particular industry. Informative popular magazines and trade magazines can be a good source of information for your writing.

Activity A | Here is a list of some of the bestselling magazines in Canada. Looking at the names alone, can you determine which ones might be a good source of information for academic writing? Compare your choices with the choices of a partner.

Canadian House and Home	Canadian Gardening
Canadian Geographic	The Engineer
The Economist	Popular Science
LouLou—Canada's Shopping Magazine	Advertising Age
Psychology Today	Popular Mechanics
The Hockey News	Nature

Activity B | If you were looking for information on the topic of your Unit Inquiry Question, what type of magazine would you search for? Discuss with a partner.

Nowadays, most magazines are available in print format or online. You can find print copies of magazines at your public or university library. Both online and print format magazines usually have lots of photos and graphics, which can help you understand the text.

There are different types of magazine articles:

- News articles discuss recent news events or developments.
- Feature articles are longer than news stories and give a lot of information on one topic.
- Opinion pieces give one person's opinion or point of view on a topic.
- How-to articles present an explanation of how to do or make something.
- Reviews are short articles where writers share their thoughts on a new book, album, film, restaurant, or artwork.
- Humorous or satirical pieces are not serious. They are written to make people laugh.

Activity C | Quickly skim the online magazine article below. Look at the types of magazine articles. Which type of magazine article do you think it is? How do you know this?

Why Igloos Work

How Can You Stay Warm Inside Them?

1   You've probably seen images of igloos on television or on the Internet. It's common knowledge that these dome-shaped structures are made of compacted ice and snow and keep the people inside nice and warm. What's less commonly known is how they work so well to stay warm inside, even when the surrounding temperatures reach far below zero. It's a question worth exploring: Why are igloos so well insulated?

2   It has to do with the physical characteristics of snow. Snow is a an "incredible insulator" (Patel, 2016). Just ask animals such as bears and raccoons, who build themselves snow caves to hibernate all winter. Snow's insulation properties come from what it is made of. Though we think of snow as frozen water, it is actually 90 to 95 percent air that has been trapped in tiny ice crystals. As the air is trapped in these crystals, it can't move around, and so heat stays trapped within any snow we shape into compact blocks or walls.

3   Igloos are such great shelters not only because of this insulating characteristic of snow, but also because of their unique structure. The unique dome shape of an igloo is called a *catenoid*. On a square building with flat walls and a flat roof, if something causes stress to the roof, such as falling snow or a falling object, the roof alone must resist the stress of the object. If it is too heavy, the roof will fall

in. Catenoids spread the tension in a structure out over all the bricks that make up the roof and walls of the dome. So if there is pressure on the structure of an igloo, the roof is less likely to collapse. Snow is not a very stable building material, as it "changes over time as temperatures rise and fall" (Patel, 2016), and so the catenoid structure is what allows an igloo to stay standing.

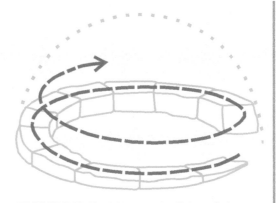

FIGURE 3.5   How to build an igloo

4   The bricks used to build an igloo should be of snow that is a few days old. It should be dense and compact, rather than the light, fine powder of new snow. The blocks should all be of the same thickness and density. The blocks should be stacked in an upwards spiral. As you build the igloo, no additional support is needed to keep the bricks from falling. The blocks should be cut at such an angle that the pressure they put on each other keeps them from falling. A well-built igloo should be able to support the weight of a human standing on the roof, without it falling in.

5   To prevent the cold wind from entering your igloo, you should build a narrow tunnel to the door. A tunnel entrance will also prevent heat loss. As igloos are so well insulated, the body heat of one person can bring the interior temperature of an igloo as high as 16 degrees Celsius, despite the fact that temperatures outside may be well below freezing.

6   The floor inside the igloo is not level. It should dip down toward the tunnel entrance and rise inside toward the sleeping area. As hot air rises and cold air falls, this means that the sleeping area will stay warm, while the cold air will move toward the door. Traditionally, animal skins are used to make the igloo door.

7   Although igloos are strong and well-insulated structures, they can be built in only a few hours if you have enough snow and a good sense of how to construct a catenoid structure.

Reference

Patel, N. V. (2016, February 10). Why igloos work: Catenoids, crystal structures, and the 61-degree melt point. *Inverse Magazine*. Retrieved from https://www.inverse.com/article/11327-why-igloos-work-catenoids-crystal-structures-and-the-61-degree-melt-point

Activity D | Writing Task: Simplified Paragraph | Imagine you were going to write a definition paragraph about igloos. Carefully read the article "Why Igloos Work," then close your book and write five sentences based on what you've read: one topic sentence, three sentences that could be developed into supporting ideas, and one concluding sentence. Trade paragraphs with a partner. How are your paragraphs similar? How are they different?

Activity E | If you had to find more information about igloos, you might turn to other magazines, either online or in print. Science or geography magazines might be the best sources for information on this topic. Read "How to Build an Igloo" below from the magazine *Popular Mechanics*. Try to find one or two more examples, explanations, or facts that you could add to each of the supporting ideas from the simplified paragraph you wrote for Activity D.

How to Build an Igloo

Northern indigenous peoples build igloos with few tools and the material at hand, eyeballing the angles. Norbert E. Yankielun, author of How to Build an Igloo and Other Snow Shelters, walks us through the process.

1   Material: In wind-packed snow, shovel a trench to facilitate cutting the first block. Using a snow knife or snow saw, cut a block 12 inches wide, 24 inches long, and 18 deep. Remove the block from the trench and repeat.

2   Foundation: Mark the centre of the igloo with a stick or ski pole, then trace a circle 6 to 10 feet in diameter. Position blocks along it, using a snow knife to mitre the ends for a tight fit.

3   Construction: Cut a ramp that starts between two blocks and extends halfway around the bottom row. Bevel the tops of the blocks along an imaginary line from the outer edge of the blocks to the igloo's centre (1). Trim snow from the bottom of the blocks in higher rows so they touch only at the corners (2), and bevel the tops along the angle of sight to the igloo's centre. Stagger the blocks.

4   Exit Strategy: Dig an exit tunnel, ideally beneath a downhill-facing wall.

5   Last Steps: Slide the top block (3) sideways through the opening, turn horizontally, and drop into place. Chink gaps between blocks with loose snow. Poke holes for ventilation.

Source: Wise, J. (2012, February 24). How to build an igloo. *Popular Mechanics*. Retrieved from http://www.popular mechanics.com/technology/design/a7555/how-to-build-an-igloo/

Changing Words and Sentence Structure

When you get information from sources such as books, websites, and articles, you may use the author's ideas and/or his or her words. To prevent plagiarism, you have to tell your reader where those ideas or words came from.

If you use an author's words exactly as they appear in the original text, you have to use quotation marks around the words to show that it is a *direct quotation*. Always include an in-text citation and reference list to tell where those words originally came from.

If you use another person's ideas but change his or her words, you don't have to use quotation marks. An in-text citation and reference list are still needed.

If you are not using a direct quotation showing the author's exact words inside quotation marks, it is important to change the author's words and sentence structure to avoid plagiarizing. There are many ways to do this. You will find yourself making more than one change to the way an author has written something when sharing that author's ideas with your reader. Here are three common ways to change an author's words and structures:

- Change word forms. Change verbs in the original sentence into nouns, or nouns into adjectives.
- Use synonyms. Substitute a word with a similar meaning.
- Reorder the sentence. Change the order of the clauses or sections in a sentence.

Example

Winter weather includes high winds and low temperatures in many parts of Canada. →

In many Canadian provinces and territories, winters are windy with sub-zero temperatures.

Paragraphing Skill

Supporting Your Topic Sentence

You know that a strong academic paragraph includes a topic sentence, supporting sentences with details, and a concluding sentence.

The topic sentence expresses the main topic of your paragraph and what you will say about it. The topic sentence is then followed by one to three supporting ideas. Each supporting idea needs detail to support it. Information about your supporting ideas and detail can come from websites, books, articles, or sometimes from your own experience.

Each supporting idea is usually one to three sentences.

Activity A | Imagine you are going to write a definition paragraph on dams. Here is the topic sentence:

A dam is a barrier built across a river to stop the flow of water.

Match the following supporting ideas with the corresponding detail.

Supporting Ideas	Details
1. Dams are built for a variety of reasons. _____	a. These dams are called hydroelectric dams. The power of the water turns giant metal wheels called *turbines*, which generates electricity.
2. Some dams are built to produce electricity. _____	b. They could be used to store water for drinking or for agriculture, or to control flooding.
3. Many dams are built by humans, although some dams are natural. _____	c. The Sanxia, or Three Gorges Dam, is a large dam located on the Yangtze River in China. It took 13 years to build and the construction cost over 24 billion dollars.
4. Large dams can be very complex and take a lot of work, power, time, and money to build. _____	d. Animals called beavers build dams on small rivers. They use sticks and mud to build their dams. These slow down the river and create new ponds.

Activity B | Share your answers with a partner. Were all your answers the same? If not, discuss why you chose the answers you did.

Activity C | A topic sentence and two supporting ideas are given in the chart on page 109. Add one detail below each of the supporting ideas. In the last column, write both a supporting idea and a corresponding detail. Use the text "All about Concrete" on page 109 to help you.

Topic Sentence: Concrete is one of the world's most common materials for building.

Supporting Idea 1	**Supporting Idea 2**	**Supporting Idea 3**
Concrete is often used in the construction of buildings.	Concrete is an excellent material for building roads.	

All about Concrete

The use of concrete dates back to the Romans in the second century BCE, who used it to create large buildings that are still standing today. It then became less popular until the mid-eighteenth century, when modern concrete was developed. Both in the past and present, concrete is widely used for many types of construction because the ingredients used to make it are available almost everywhere, it is inexpensive, it resists fire and water, and it insulates against sound. It is the main building material for houses, buildings, bridges, highways, and airports. As well, concrete doesn't require a lot of specialized knowledge to work with so it can be used in many different contexts.

How is it made? Concrete consists of cement, water, and either gravel, crushed rock, or sand. When concrete is fresh, it is soft, and it takes up to four days to fully harden. This is one of the advantages of concrete for building roads—it can be poured to fit the size and shape of any roadbed. This flexibility means it can be used for the main structures as well as decorations on houses and buildings.

Sometimes steel beam or other objects are inserted inside the concrete to make something called *reinforced concrete*, which is very strong. Reinforced concrete is used in very tall buildings, such as skyscrapers, or in structures that must withstand a lot of force, such as an ocean bridge. Concrete can be used to build very long bridges.

Activity D | Look back at your Unit Inquiry Question. Write a list of supporting ideas you might use when you write about it and where you would go to find information on those ideas. Exchange your list with a partner. Share any suggestions for supporting ideas and sources.

Language Skill

Defining

Academic writing includes a lot of definitions. Definitions give the meaning of a word, an idea, or a concept. They explain the characteristics of the word, the concept, or the idea. Dictionaries, encyclopedias, and textbooks give definitions, and much of the writing you'll do as a student does too. It is important to learn the three kinds of language available to use when you are defining something. You can describe characteristics, you can compare (or contrast), or you can indicate the category that something belongs in.

Characteristics

There are various ways to describe the characteristics or the essential features of something.

Purpose	Function	Example
to give a description	say what something **is**	A car is a small motor vehicle.
to list different parts or features	say what something **has**	A car has a metal frame, four wheels, a motor, and one to five doors.
	say what something **consists of**	A car consists of a metal frame, four wheels, a motor, and one to five doors.
	say what something **includes**	A car includes a metal frame, four wheels, a motor, and one to five doors.
to give a synonym	say what something **means**	The word *car* means small motor vehicle.
	say what something **is defined as**	A car is defined as a small motor vehicle.
to explain a function	say what something **can do**	A car can carry people or objects.

Activity A | Choose something in the built environment. Write three sentences describing its essential features or characteristics. Be careful of subject–verb agreement and the language of generalizations, as discussed in Unit 1. With a partner, read and discuss each other's sentences.

1. _____

2. _____

3. _____

Comparing

Comparisons are also helpful to include in definitions. The chart below shows some examples of the language used to compare (or contrast) two things.

Function	Example
say that something **is similar to** something else	Cement is similar to rock.
say that something **is like** something else	Cement is like rock.
say that something **is the opposite of** something else	Moving is the opposite of standing still.

Activity B | Using the same object you wrote three sentences about in Activity A, write two sentences comparing it to other things. With a partner, read and discuss each other's sentences. Has your partner used any of the comparing phrases in the chart above?

1. _____

_____

2. _____

_____

Categories

Describing categories can also be helpful in writing definitions. The chart below shows some examples of the language used to write about categories.

Function	Example
say that something **is a kind of** [*category name*]	A car is a kind of motor vehicle.
say that something **is a type of** [*category name*]	A car is a type of motor vehicle.
say that **there are** [*number*] **types/kinds** of things and then list them Note: You must use the plural if there are two or more of something.	There **are** three type**s** of cars. There **are** gas-powered, electric, and hybrid car**s**.

Activity C | Using the same object you wrote about in Activity A and Activity B, write two more sentences describing categories related to this object.

1. _____

2. _____

Activity D | Each of the following sentences contains a language error. Correct the sentence.

1. There are four kind of tunnels.

   _____

2. A table have a top and three or more legs.

   _____

3. Roadways consists of compacted earth, gravel, and asphalt.

   _____

   _____

4. Airplanes likes cars in the sky.

   _____

WRITING FUNDAMENTALS

Composition Skill

Proofreading

Proofreading is an important skill for any writer. Editing refers to making changes to the grammar, sentence structure, or vocabulary of a text, while proofreading has to do with the details of spelling, punctuation, and formatting. Before you submit an assignment, hand in an exam or test, or send an email, you should always give yourself time to proofread the text. You may find some mistakes in your text that you will then have to correct.

When you are proofreading a text, you should look for the following:

- Spelling mistakes: Be especially careful of commonly misspelled words, such as those with silent letters like *government* or *although.*
- Punctuation mistakes: Are commas (,), periods (.), apostrophes ('), and question marks (?) used correctly?
- Capitalization mistakes: Is the first word of every sentence capitalized? Are the names of all countries, nationalities, languages, months, holidays, people, and cities capitalized? Do you have any accidental double capitals (CAnada)?
- Formatting mistakes: Formatting refers to how the text is printed on the page. Do you have one space after commas, periods, and question marks? Do you have no spaces after apostrophes? Did you use the same font type and size through your whole document? Is your document single spaced or double spaced as required in the instructions?

While proofreading, you may find grammar mistakes that slipped by you during your editing and revising. One of the most common mistakes is missing the *-s*, *-ed*, or *-ing* on the end of a word. You may also find that you missed some subject–verb agreement, so you'll want to correct those mistakes (*We goes* to *We go*).

To proofread a text, you should read it very carefully. It's easy to miss mistakes in your text. That's why some people recommend reading your text backward, from end to beginning, or printing your text on paper or saving it as a PDF file and proofreading that instead of a Word document.

Activity A | Refer back to a paragraph or other writing activity you have completed for this unit. Follow the procedure above to proofread your writing.

Activity B | After you have finished proofreading your sentences, trade texts with a partner. Can you find any mistakes that he or she has missed?

Writing Skill

Avoiding Run-On Sentences

A bridge needs a strong structure so that it doesn't fall down. Similarly, the sentences you write must have good structure to make your texts strong. A very common structural error in many students' writing is called the run-on sentence.

Run-on sentences happen when two independent clauses (groups of words that contain a subject and a verb and a complete idea) are connected using a comma. Another name for this error is a comma splice, because *splice* means to connect together.

Look at the two examples of comma splice below. Each of the four underlined independent clauses could stand alone.

     ✗ 1. Five workers built the new bridge, the construction project lasted six weeks.

     ✗ 2. Gravel is a kind of crushed rock, it is applied after the roadway has been graded.

The most common way to correct a comma splice is to replace the comma with a period. This turns one run-on sentence into two grammatically correct sentences. It is important to remember to capitalize the first letter of the second sentence.

     ✓ 1. Five workers built the new bridge.
     ✓   The construction project lasted six weeks.
     ✓ 2. Gravel is a kind of crushed rock.
     ✓   It is applied after the roadway has been graded.

How can you recognize a run-on sentence? Look at the clauses on either side of the comma. If they both have a **subject** and a conjugated verb and neither one starts with an adverb (*after, before, while, because, since, although, unless, until,* etc.) they are independent clauses and can stand alone. If both clauses can stand alone, it is a run-on sentence.

     ✗ 1. Five **workers** built the new bridge, the **construction project** lasted six weeks.

     ✗ 2. **Gravel** is a kind of crushed rock, **it** is applied after the roadway has been graded.

Activity A | Read the following four sentences. Decide for each if it is a run-on sentence or if it is correct. Checking to see if there is a subject and conjugated verb in each clause will help you do this. Write RO or place a check mark in the space provided.

1. _____ Steel and wood are the most common building materials in Canada, they are strong and inexpensive.

2. _____ After designing a new office building, the engineering team will think about plans for parking.

3. _____ It is important that all citizens have access to safe, clean housing.

4. _____ There is a risk of earthquakes in some countries, engineers must design buildings to stay strong even if an earthquake happens.

Activity B | For each run-on sentence that you identified in Activity A, rewrite it below making the necessary corrections. Then compare your corrections with a partner.

_____

_____

_____

_____

_____

Sentence and Grammar Skill

Understanding Compound Sentences and Complex Sentences

Compound Sentences

In Unit 1 you learned about simple sentences. Simple sentences consist of a **subject** and a <u>verb</u> and express a complete thought.

The **wind** <u>blew</u> in from the sea.

In Unit 2 you learned that an independent clause is a group of words that contains a subject and a conjugated verb (and sometimes other components) and expresses a complete thought. It is able to stand alone. Another name for an independent clause is a main clause. The simple sentence above is an independent clause.

A compound sentence is made from two independent clauses of equal importance. The two independent clauses are connected by a coordinating conjunction. This chart shows the most common coordinating conjunctions and their uses and some examples.

Coordinating Conjunction (CC)	Function	Example
and	additional information	The workers compacted the graded dirt, **and** then they laid a layer of coarse gravel.
or	choice	A roadway must be graded well, **or** rainwater will not drain correctly.
so	result, consequence	The temperature fell below zero degrees, **so** the water froze.
but	contrast	Steel frame houses are strong, **but** wood is a more common construction material in Canada.
yet	contrast (more formal than *but*)	Steel frame houses are strong, **yet** wood is a more common construction material in Canada.

Punctuation Rule   In most compound sentences, there must be a comma after the first independent clause and before the coordinating conjunction.

The **workers** compacted the graded dirt, and then **they** laid a layer of coarse gravel.
independent clause   *comma + CC*   *independent clause*

Be careful! Only use a comma if the coordinating conjunction is separating two independent clauses in a compound sentence. In a simple sentence with a compound verb (discussed in Unit 1), don't use a comma. The following is a simple sentence. It has only one independent clause, so there is no comma before *and*.

The **workers** compacted the graded dirt and laid a layer of coarse gravel.
subject   *compound verb*

Activity A | In each of the four sentences below, highlight the subject(s), underline the verb(s), and draw a box around the coordinating conjunction. Then write S (simple sentence) or C (compound sentence) in the space provided. If it is a compound sentence, add a comma in the correct place.

1. _____ Beam bridges use concrete or steel beams to support the deck.

2. _____ The ends of the arms can intersect with the road leading up to the bridge or they can hook up to another truss unit to form a longer span.

3. _____ Truss bridges can carry heavy loads over long spans, so many railroad bridges are truss bridges.

4. _____ The route is cleared of obstacles such as trees or rocks, and then the roadway is graded so it will drain.

Activity B | Below you will find pairs of simple sentences and a coordinating conjunction. Combine the two simple sentences into a compound sentence using the coordinating conjunction given. You will have to change some punctuation. You will also have to change some letters from uppercase to lowercase.

1. Roman roads were very well built. They stretched for thousands of kilometres around ancient Rome. (*and*)
2. Concrete can be applied in one layer. Asphalt is applied in two layers. (*but*)
3. Igloos look difficult to build. They are easy to build. (*yet*)
4. Tunnel entries are good for blocking wind. Many igloos use tunnel entries. (*so*)

Complex Sentences

A complex sentence consists of one independent clause and one (or more) dependent clauses.

You learned in Unit 2 that a dependent clause has a subject and a verb but does not express a complete thought on its own. It depends on having another clause with it to complete the idea. A dependent clause (also known as a subordinate clause) includes a conjunction, but not a coordinating conjunction. Instead, a dependent clause includes a subordinating conjunction (SC). The most common subordinating conjunctions are listed below.

after	because	if	until
although	before	since	when
as	even though	unless	while

The clause below has a subject and a verb, but it expresses an incomplete thought and it starts with a subordinating conjunction. Therefore, it is a dependent clause.

Because the **roadway** was not graded correctly
SC   *subject*   *verb*

The clause needs an independent clause to turn it into a complete sentence.

Because the **roadway** was not graded correctly, big puddles formed.

A complex sentence is made up of one independent clause, one (or more) dependent clauses, and a subordinating conjunction. Each complex sentence expresses a complete thought.

Before workers pour the concrete, they must grade the roadway.
        dependent clause   *independent clause*

The roadway won't drain properly unless the roadway is graded properly.
    independent clause   *dependent clause*

Although suspension bridges may look like they can't support much weight, they are very strong.
                    dependent clause   *independent clause*
We don't often think about how roads are made even though we drive or walk on them almost every day.
        independent clause   *dependent clause*

Notice that either the dependent clause or the independent clause can come first:

Because the roadway was not graded correctly, the rainwater did not drain.
                dependent clause   *independent clause*

The rainwater did not drain because the roadway was not graded correctly.
        independent clause   *dependent clause*

Punctuation Rules

1. If the dependent clause comes first, use a comma to separate it from the independent clause.

    Because the roadway was not graded correctly, the rainwater did not drain.
            dependent clause   *comma*   *independent clause*

2. If the independent clause comes first, there is NO comma separating the two clauses.

The roadway did not drain because the roadway was not graded correctly.
independent clause   *no comma*   *dependent clause*

Good writing has a mix of simple, compound, and complex sentences.

Activity C | For each of the sentences below, reverse the order of the dependent and independent clauses. Add or remove the comma as necessary.

1. Until they started building modern roads in the 1700s, people were influenced by the Roman style of road building.
2. Concrete can be applied in one layer while asphalt is applied in two layers.
3. Building an igloo is actually quite easy although it looks difficult.
4. Because they prevent the wind from getting in, many igloos use tunnel entries.

Activity D | Read the following text carefully. Correct the five mistakes related to simple, compound, and complex sentences.

In some countries, there are high winds from hurricanes, tornadoes, or typhoons. Engineers and architects must build, and design houses that will not be damaged in high winds. One danger is that high winds can lift the roof off the house, roof trusses are made extra strong with something called a hurricane tie. Because doors are often a weak point builders should install wind-resistant doors. Reinforced concrete is very strong and it can protect against high winds and flying objects. Windows can be built with plastic instead of glass, covering windows with wooden storm shutters is a better option. Because this will provide more protection.

Activity E | Look back at some of the writing (either a few sentences or a paragraph) you have done for this unit. Find five sentences and label them as simple, compound, or complex. Find two cases where you have one simple sentence after another. Can you add a coordinating conjunction and make a compound sentence?

Find two more cases where you have two simple sentences together. Can you add a subordinating conjunction and make them into two complex sentences?

Check that you have used commas correctly in your new sentences. Share what you've written with a partner and discuss your answers.

Activity F | Writing Task: Simplified Paragraph | Imagine you are going to write a definition paragraph about spider webs. Carefully read the article below, then close your book and write five sentences based on what you've read: one topic sentence, three sentences that express supporting ideas, and one concluding sentence. Write your supporting ideas as compound or complex sentences. Share your paragraph with a partner and exchange feedback on each other's compound and complex sentences.

http://www.newsobserver.com/news/technology/article23721193

What Are Spider Webs Made Of?

1   Spider webs are made of silk, produced from spinnerets at the end of a spider's abdomen. Most spiders have three pairs of spinnerets. The silk for these comes from silk glands within the abdomen.

2   A spider may be able to produce as many as six different types of silk. These silks can be used and combined to spin webs, wrap prey, line their retreats, construct egg cocoons, and travel.

3   This silk has some amazing properties. It is composed of a mixture of protein crystals in a matrix of amino acids. This structure makes it one of the strongest natural fibres, about half as strong as steel. But unlike steel, spider silk can expand and stretch, so it is actually "tougher" than steel. Researchers are focusing on ways to create versions of this silk in a lab to create new fibre products.

4   Different species of spider spin different kinds of webs. These webs are adapted to their habitats, hunting styles, and prey. Spiders can be very flexible about the dimensions and outer shapes of their webs so that they fit the space the spider has chosen. However, the internal geometry of the web is usually fairly consistent for each species.

5   Spiders don't have tools, so they rely greatly on their sense of touch to guide them in web building. When building a web, a spider probably uses its legs, the tension of the threads, and the distance between anchor sites to measure and plan how to build the web.

Source: Broadfoot, M. V. (2011, October 31). What are spider webs made of? *The News and Observer*. Retrieved from http://www.newsobserver.com/news/technology/article23721193.html

Using Memorization Strategies

In post-secondary studies, you learn different types of information in different ways. You can use memorization strategies to remember some types of information, such as lists of simple facts, dates, or very simple definitions.

Creating an acronym can help you memorize strings of words. The *Oxford Advanced Learner's Dictionary* defines an acronym as "a word formed from the first letters of the words that make up the name of something." For example, an NGO is a **n**on-**g**overnmental **o**rganization.

If you were trying to remember the five types of bridges you read about on pages 97–99, you might use the acronym B-CATS:

Beam
Cantilever
Arch
Truss
Suspension

Another learning strategy involving memory is creating a link between the information you want to learn and one of your other senses, such as vision, hearing, or touch. Come up with a mental picture or image of a word you want to remember. Repeating lists of dates aloud or creating a song incorporating the information you want to remember are two ways to use sound to help you remember. Some people also create a connection between the information and certain body movements.

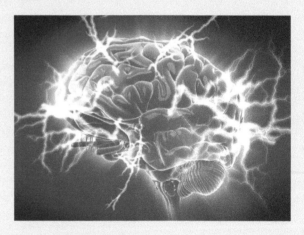

Source: Oxford, R. L. (1990). *Language learning strategies: What every teacher should know*. Boston, MA: Heinle & Heinle.

UNIT OUTCOME

Writing Assignment: Definition Paragraph

Write a definition paragraph of 150 to 250 words on a topic related to structural engineering and the built environment. (Your instructor may give you an alternative length.) You may write on a topic based on your Unit Inquiry Question, develop another topic of your choosing connected to the built environment, or choose one of the following topics:

- What are the characteristics of a skyscraper?
- What is a greenhouse?
- What are the different types of tunnels?

Use the skills you have developed in this unit to complete the assignment. Follow the steps below to practise each of the new skills you have learned to write a well-developed definition paragraph.

1. **Brainstorm and find information**: In addition to the readings and other topic-related information in this unit, your information sources may include a magazine article. You may want to do a search for more information related to your Unit Inquiry Question. Look at the notes you made during your freewriting session and your reverse thinking brainstorming session. If necessary, do another five minutes of reverse thinking to generate more ideas.

2. **Outline**: List your topic, your chosen inquiry question, and the working title of your paragraph.

   Topic: _____

   Inquiry Question: _____

   Paragraph Title: _____

   Use the template below to create an outline for your paragraph. See the outline on page 91 for more detail about the body of the paragraph.

Topic Sentence — One sentence that identifies what you will be defining:

Main Body (Supporting Ideas)

Supporting idea 1 (a description of characteristics, categories, or a synonym):

Supporting idea 2 (a description of characteristics, categories, or a synonym):

Supporting idea 3 (a description of characteristics, categories, or a synonym):

Concluding Sentence

Concluding sentence that closes the paragraph:

3. **Write a first draft**: Write the first draft of your paragraph. Use AWL and mid-frequency vocabulary from this unit if possible.

4. **Self-check**: Wait a day, then check your first draft. Remember to check the following:

    - Check that your definition paragraph has a topic sentence, supporting ideas with details, and a concluding sentence.

    - Check that you have used connecting phrases to add additional information or to introduce examples.

    - Look at your sentences that describe characteristics and categories or make comparisons. Have you used some of the language you saw on pages 110–112?

- Check the compound and complex sentences in your paragraph. Does each one have a coordinating or subordinating conjunction? Have you used commas correctly in these sentences?

- Check your paragraph for run-on sentences. Add correct punctuation or shorten your sentences if necessary.

5. **Revise**: Revise your first draft.

6. **Compose final draft**: Write a final draft of your paragraph.

7. **Proofread**: Check the final draft of your paragraph for any small errors you may have missed. In particular, look for spelling errors, typos, and punctuation mistakes.

Evaluation: Definition Paragraph Rubric

Use the following rubric to evaluate your essay. In which areas do you need to improve most?

E = **Emerging**: frequent difficulty using unit skills; needs a lot more work
D = **Developing**: some difficulty using unit skills; some improvement still required
S = **Satisfactory**: able to use unit skills most of the time; meets average expectations for this level
O = **Outstanding**: exceptional use of unit skills; exceeds expectations for this level

Skill	E	D	S	O
The definition paragraph has a topic sentence, supporting ideas, and a concluding sentence that connects to the topic.				
There is enough detail to explain each of the supporting ideas.				
AWL and mid-frequency vocabulary items from this unit are used when appropriate and with few mistakes.				
Correct language for definitions has been used, with accurate subject–verb agreement.				
The text uses connectors to add additional information or provide examples.				
The paragraph does not contain any run-on sentences.				
The paragraph includes grammatically correct simple, complex, and compound sentences with commas where necessary.				

Unit Review

Activity A | What do you know about the topic of structural engineering and the built environment that you did not know before you started this unit? Discuss with a partner or small group. Be prepared to report what you learned to the class.

Activity B | Look back at the Unit Inquiry Question you developed at the start of this unit and discuss it with a partner or small group. Then share your answers with the class. Use the following questions to help you:

1. What information did you find in this unit that helped you answer your question?
2. How would you answer your question now?

Activity C | Use the following checklist to review the skills you have learned in this unit. First decide which 10 skills you think are the most important. Circle the number beside each of these 10 skills. If you learned a skill in this unit that isn't listed below, write it in the blank row at the end of the checklist. Then put a check mark in the box beside those points you feel you have learned. Be prepared to discuss your choices with the class.

	Self-Assessment Checklist
☐	1. I can talk about structural engineering and the built environment based on what I've read in this unit.
☐	2. I can ask about categories and characteristics to help write an inquiry question to guide my learning.
☐	3. I can use connectors of additional information and examples to join my sentences together.
☐	4. I can add suffixes to adjectives and verbs to create nouns.
☐	5. I can use AWL and mid-frequency vocabulary from this unit in my writing.
☐	6. I can step outside my box to engage more critically with the texts I read.
☐	7. I can use reverse thinking as a brainstorming technique to generate ideas before writing.
☐	8. I can create an outline with key ideas before writing a paragraph.

☐	9. I can ask 5W + H questions to help come up with ideas and to help decide on the best sources of information.
☐	10. I can use magazine articles to find information on a topic.
☐	11. I can avoid plagiarism by changing the words and sentence structure when writing about another person's ideas.
☐	12. I can find appropriate details to support my ideas.
☐	13. I can use appropriate language when defining characteristics and categories or comparing things.
☐	14. I can proofread my text for errors in spelling, punctuation, capitalization, and formatting before I submit my work.
☐	15. I can avoid run-on sentences by connecting my sentences appropriately.
☐	16. I can create grammatically correct complex and compound sentences, using commas as necessary.
☐	17. I can use memorization strategies to help me learn and remember information.
☐	18. I can write a well-structured definition paragraph that contains a topic sentence, supporting ideas, detail, and a concluding sentence.
☐	19.

Activity D | Put a check mark in the box beside the vocabulary items from this unit that you feel confident using in your writing.

Vocabulary Checklist

☐ compact (v.) 4000	☐ route (n.) AWL
☐ construct (v.) AWL	☐ similar (adj.) AWL
☐ develop (v.) 2000	☐ slope (n.) 3000
☐ extend (v.) 2000	☐ structure (n.) AWL
☐ obstacle (n.) 4000	☐ transportation (n.) AWL

UNIT 4

Health Sciences

Kinesiology

EXPLORING IDEAS

Introduction

Kinesiology is the study of movement and the body. Kinesiologists study how the body responds to exercise. They care about the health and well-being of people.

Activity A | Discuss the following questions with a partner or small group.

1. What sports did you play when you were young?
2. What sports are popular in the country you are from?

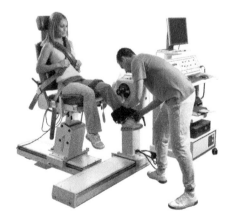

3. Have you ever suffered from a sports injury? If you have, how did it happen and how did you recover from it?
4. Do you know any ways an athlete can prevent injury?
5. Kinesiology majors might pursue a career in physical education, sports medicine, or physiotherapy. Is kinesiology a popular major in your home country? Why or why not?

Activity B | A survey is a set of questions that a researcher uses to find information about a specific topic. Surveys can be used to find out people's opinions on a topic, people's habits and preferences, or the number of people who engage in an activity.

Take a few minutes to complete the following health survey that a kinesiology student might conduct on a college or university campus. Do you agree or disagree with each statement? Then survey three different classmates. Be sure to ask your classmates for their reasons. Take notes of your classmates' reasons.

	Agree	Disagree
1. It is safe to use exercise equipment without professional instruction.		
2. The best way to lose weight is to go on a diet.		
3. Eating fast food occasionally won't harm your body.		
4. It is not necessary to take vitamins if you eat fruits and vegetables every day.		
5. Four to five hours of restful sleep every night is sufficient for a healthy lifestyle.		

Activity C | Choose one survey question to discuss with a partner. Talk about your opinions and your reasons. Use the notes you took when you surveyed your classmates to help you with ideas. When you choose your partner, find a classmate that you did not survey.

Fostering Inquiry

Expressing an Opinion

In college or university, you will be asked to express an opinion on different topics. One way to develop an educated opinion is to begin with a good inquiry question. When you begin researching your inquiry question, you will learn about the different opinions people have on the topic and their reasons for supporting their position. As you continue researching, reading information related to your inquiry question, and discussing your topic with others, you will begin to develop your own opinion about the topic and will be able to support it with ideas.

Activity A | What do you want to know more about in relation to the field of kinesiology or sports and exercise? For example:

- How do compulsory fitness classes help schoolchildren in their other subjects?
- How can university sports teams benefit from the study of sports and exercise medicine (SEM)?
- How can children who play competitive sports avoid injuries?

1. Write two or three questions you are curious about on the topic of kinesiology.
2. When you are finished, share your questions with a partner or small group.
3. Choose one question to be your inquiry question for this unit. It does not have to be the same question as your partner or group.
4. Write your inquiry question in the space provided. Look back at this question as you work through the unit. This is your Unit Inquiry Question.

My Unit Inquiry Question:

_____

_____

_____

Activity B | Writing Task: Freewriting | Write for at least five minutes on the topic of your Unit Inquiry Question. Do not stop writing during this time. After five minutes, read what you have written and circle two or three ideas that you would like to explore further to answer your Unit Inquiry Question.

Structure

Opinion Paragraph

Purpose

The purpose of an opinion paragraph is to express your opinion about a topic. In writing an opinion paragraph, you try to convince the reader to take your side or agree with your opinion. You can do this by including facts and examples to support your opinion. Another way to convince your reader is to refer to authorities or studies on the topic.

Audience

The audience for an opinion paragraph will depend on the context. For example, sometimes people write about their opinions on controversial issues in newspaper articles. In this situation, the audience includes the members of the general public who are interested in staying informed on issues that might affect their lives. If you write your opinion for a class assignment, the audience is your instructor or classmates.

Activity A | Opinion paragraphs sometimes discuss controversial issues. According to the *Oxford Advanced Learner's Dictionary, controversial* means "causing a lot of angry public discussion and disagreement." One controversial issue related to kinesiology is the use of performance-enhancing drugs in professional sports. What is another example of a controversial issue related to kinesiology, professional sports, junior sports, or physical education that you have heard about in the news recently? Discuss the news story with your partner.

Activity B | Read the sample opinion paragraph below about athletes who use performance-enhancing drugs. Then answer the questions that follow.

Performance-Enhancing Drugs

In my opinion, athletes who use performance-enhancing drugs (PEDs) are not cheating. They are not being dishonest, and they don't have an unfair advantage. First, PED use is widespread in high-level amateur and professional sports. Some coaches even encourage their athletes to use them. Athletes who use PEDs are not deceiving other athletes because everyone is aware of what is going on. Athletes who don't use them are at a disadvantage, but that is their decision. Second, competitive athletes train exceptionally hard, which is very hard on their bodies. Many PEDs are used only to assist them in recovery, not to boost their performance during competition. Finally, athletes who have health conditions like asthma or joint injuries are allowed to use certain kinds of steroids and other medicines that are classified as PEDs. If all athletes had access to the same kinds of medicinal drugs, no one would have an unfair advantage. It might be true that some PEDs are unhealthy and even dangerous. However, it has been nearly impossible to enforce bans on PEDs. Currently, all high-level athletes have the same access to them. If performance-enhancing drugs and techniques are going to be banned, they should be banned for being dangerous, but not because they give athletes who use them an unfair advantage. In conclusion, athletes who use performance-enhancing drugs are not being dishonest.

1. What is the writer's opinion?
2. What is the purpose of this paragraph?
3. Who is the audience of this paragraph?
4. What is the controversial issue?
5. Highlight the three supporting ideas in the paragraph. Underline the supporting details for each of these supporting ideas.

Structure of an Opinion Paragraph

An opinion paragraph expresses an opinion and is supported by reasons.

The topic sentence in an opinion paragraph clearly states your opinion. The topic sentence is usually the first sentence of the paragraph.

After the topic sentence, your paragraph should have one to three supporting ideas. These ideas are reasons or facts that directly support your opinion. Each supporting idea should have one to three details to support it. Supporting details can be examples, facts, statistics, or references from textbooks, journal articles, or websites.

The last sentence in your opinion paragraph is the concluding sentence. This sentence brings closure to the paragraph. It should remind the reader what your paragraph is about. You can either paraphrase the topic sentence or summarize your supporting ideas.

Figure 4.1 shows an outline of an opinion paragraph.

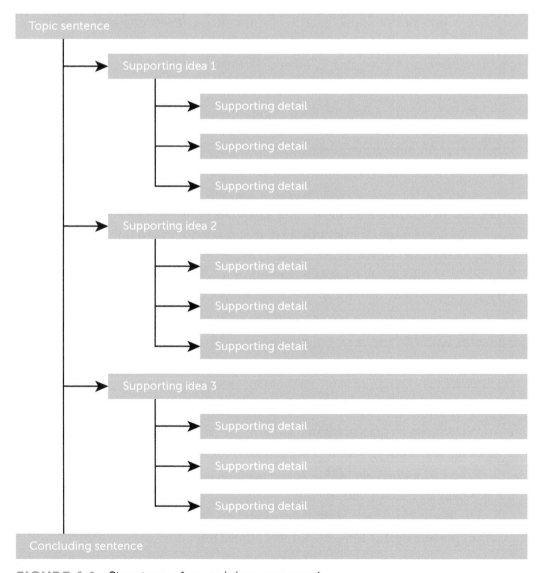

FIGURE 4.1 Structure of an opinion paragraph

Using Connectors of Contrast

Connectors of contrast are used to show the relationship of ideas in a sentence or paragraph. These connectors indicate that one idea contrasts with (or differs from) another idea in the sentence, or that one idea is unexpectedly linked to the other idea. Connectors help your writing flow smoothly by making the connections clear for the reader.

Here are some connectors of contrast.

although	in spite of
even though	despite
though	on the other hand
however	while
nevertheless	in contrast

Connectors can appear in different places in a sentence. The most common position is at the beginning of the sentence. When a connector starts a phrase at the beginning of a sentence, that phrase must be followed by a comma.

Although it was snowing, we played soccer.

Despite the snow, we played soccer.

When a connector appears in the middle of a sentence, a comma is not necessary.

We played soccer **although** it was snowing.

We played soccer **despite** the snow.

Activity C | Below you will find an example of an opinion paragraph. Read the paragraph carefully and answer the questions that follow.

Walking

In my opinion, walking is the best form of exercise. First, walking helps you burn calories. According to a Harvard Medical School website, if you walk briskly for 30 minutes, you will burn approximately 150 calories. A blogger on the same website notes that at the end of the week, this is equivalent to a fast food hamburger and French fries. Nevertheless, even if you walk briskly for 30 minutes a day, you should still eat three healthy meals a day rather than choosing fast food regularly. Second, going for a walk helps reduce the chance of serious disease and illness. According to health professionals, daily walking reduces cholesterol, which reduces the chance of heart attacks and strokes. Third, taking a leisurely stroll helps with your mood. When you walk, your body produces endorphins, which are mood elevators. After a walk in the park, you are sure to feel happy and refreshed. However, be careful not to overdo it. If you walk too quickly, you might twist your ankle. Make sure you wear sturdy walking shoes to avoid injury. In conclusion, walking as a form of exercise is an excellent way to burn calories, reduce the chance of serious disease, and keep you happy.

References

Godman, H. (2013). Think fast when kids want fast food. *Harvard Health Blog*. Retrieved from http://www.health.harvard.edu/blog/think-fast-when-kids-want-fast-food-201301315846

Harvard Health. (2004). Calories burned in 30 minutes for people of three different weights. *Harvard Health Publications—Harvard Medical School*. Retrieved from http://www.health.harvard.edu/diet-and-weight-loss/calories-burned-in-30-minutes-of-leisure-and-routine-activities

1. What is the writer's opinion?
2. What are the three supporting ideas in this paragraph?
3. What words or phrases introduce the supporting ideas?
4. What details are used to support the supporting ideas?
5. Does the writer use connectors of contrast? If so, which ones?
6. What is special about the first and last sentences in this paragraph?

Activity D | Revisit your Unit Inquiry Question on page 130. What information or new ideas have you thought of or discussed that will help you answer your question? Share your ideas with a partner or small group. At this point, you may consider revising your Unit Inquiry Question.

ACADEMIC READING

Vocabulary

Vocabulary Skill: Forming Verbs

Verbs are action words. Some verbs are formed by adding a suffix to the end of a noun or adjective. Some common verb suffixes are *-ify*, *-ize*, *-en*, and *-ate*.

See the examples in the chart on the next page. Notice that sometimes there are spelling changes when adding a suffix.

Adjective or Noun	Suffix	Verb
beauty (n.)	-ify	beautify (to make beautiful)
private (adj.)	-ize	privatize (to make private)
soft (adj.)	-en	soften (to make soft)
medical (n./adj.)	-ate	medicate (to provide medicine)

Activity A | Some verbs have a suffix that indicates that the word is a verb. For example, the verb suffix *-en* means "to make". If added to the word *hard*, the word changes to the verb *harden* which means "to make hard". Complete the verbs in the sentences below with an appropriate suffix: *-ate, -en, -ify,* or *-ize.*

1. It is easy to ident_____ the Canadian athletes, because their red and white uniforms stand out. There is also a large maple leaf on their jackets.

2. The dance teacher began to demonstr_____ the new hip-hop moves for the class.

3. A running specialist can custom_____ running shoes for athletes to improve their gait.

4. Ana decided to simpl_____ her weekly workout routine from practising yoga, going swimming, and attending boot camp to going to the gym twice a week.

5. The track and field association plans to wid_____ and length_____ the running track.

6. The cheerleading squad chose to mod_____ its routine for the Western Universities Cheerleading Competition.

7. After taking performance-enhancing drugs, the athlete began to hallucin_____. He said he could see pink elephants in the distance.

8. The indoor soccer league decided to standard_____ the practice schedules to attract more people.

9. The media always exagger_____ scandals that involve famous professional athletes.

10. To strength_____ and tone her muscles, Ryoko started weightlifting at her local sports centre.

Vocabulary Preview: The Academic Word List

Activity B | The following AWL words are taken from the academic reading "Ben Johnson," on pages 139–141. The definitions of the words are provided. Read the words and their definitions and choose the correct word to complete the sentences that follow. You might have to change the form of the word to fit the sentence.

rely (v.): depend on

achievement (n.): something a person does successfully that required some effort or skill

controversy (n.): a public debate about an issue that is usually heated and lasts a long time

status (n.): the social position of someone in relation to someone else

perceive (v.): regard as

significant (adj.): very important

1. Since the 1970s, the feminist movement in the United States has helped to improve the _____ of female athletes.

2. The _____ about Lance Armstrong was whether he took performance-enhancing drugs when he won the Tour de France.

3. Lionel Messi, considered to be the world's best soccer player, has many outstanding _____ including a 2012 Guinness World Record for most goals.

4. It is important for athletes to _____ themselves as winners.

5. The coach of the women's lacrosse team says the team members should _____ on each other for support on and off the field.

6. Ben Johnson was accused of having _____ levels of performance-enhancing drugs in his blood during his track and field career.

Vocabulary Preview: Mid-frequency Vocabulary

Activity C | Read each sentence and match the bolded word to its definition on page 138. Write the letter on the line provided.

Sentences

1. _____ The news is full of **scandalous** stories about athletes who behave badly.

2. _____ Terry Fox is a Canadian **hero**. He is admired for the movement he started when he ran across Canada to raise money for cancer research.

3. _____ My whole family watched my nephew play in his high school **championship** basketball game. It was very exciting.

4. _____ The university athletic department has issued a document listing illegal **substances** the athletes are prohibited to use.

5. _____ **Athletes** from all over the world competed at the Pan Am Games in Toronto, Canada.

6. _____ If you want to know the types of drugs that the World Anti-Doping Agency has **banned**, you should go to their web page for the full document.

Definitions

a. a competition to determine a champion
b. prohibited
c. shocking
d. a brave or admirable person
e. a person who participates in sports
f. a type of solid, liquid, or gas that has particular qualities

Reading

The following reading, "Ben Johnson," is an excerpt from the textbook *Sport in Canada: A History*. This textbook is about the history of sport in Canada. It is used in first-year kinesiology courses in Canada.

Using a Glossary

A glossary is a list of definitions for words used in a particular text. Glossaries can be found at the end of a textbook chapter (usually in alphabetical order) or in footnotes under the reading (in order of appearance). Reviewing the glossary before reading a text is a good pre-reading strategy to familiarize yourself with any unfamiliar vocabulary. The reading on pages 139–140 has a glossary at the bottom of each page.

A glossary can be used for more than just previewing a text. You can also use a glossary to review vocabulary for an exam. You can customize the glossaries in your textbooks by adding other words you want to remember from texts you are reading. Reviewing words in a glossary may help you follow lectures, and you can also highlight important words in the glossary that your instructor emphasizes in the lectures during the semester.

Activity A | You are going to read a textbook excerpt about a famous Canadian Olympic athlete. Before you read the text, look at the glossary words defined in the footnotes on pages 139–141. Choose five words you think are interesting and write a sentence for each word on the topic of sports and exercise medicine. Then share your sentences with a partner.

Activity B | Look at the glossary words defined in the footnotes on pages 139–141 again. Look at the photos that accompany the reading. What do you think this textbook excerpt is about? Write down your prediction and discuss it with a partner, then share your prediction with the whole class.

My prediction: _____

_____

Activity C | Read the textbook excerpt to review your prediction. Was it correct? How did the words in the glossary help you make your prediction? How did the photographs help you? Discuss your answers with a partner, then share your answers with the whole class.

READING

Ben Johnson

1 What distinguishes Ben Johnson's career and heroic **status** is **controversy** on the world stage of sport. The stripping of Ben Johnson's 1988 (Seoul) Olympic gold medal for the 100-metre sprint event is one of the most **scandalous** affairs in the history of modern sport. Although this distinction[1] places Johnson more toward anti-hero than **hero**, he is still **perceived** as a star.

2 Johnson was born in Jamaica, the fifth of six children. At 15, his family immigrated to Scarborough, Ontario. In 1977, Ben met Charlie Francis. He became Ben's coach through to the Olympic Games in 1988.

3 Johnson won the 100-metre Canadian junior **championship** in 10.66 seconds in 1979. After that, his national calibre[2] status rose. He was named to the Canadian Olympic team for the Moscow Games in 1980. In terms of world level sprinting **achievements**, in 1986 Johnson beat Carl Lewis three times.

_____

[1] the quality of being something that is special
[2] the quality of a person's ability

4   In 1987, Johnson set and/or re-set world indoor sprint records in the 50 metre (5.55 seconds) and 60 metre (6.41 seconds) in four major national races. He won several top **athlete** awards and was named a member of the Order of Canada. For Johnson, his crowning achievement was his 100-metre world record of 9.83 seconds, set in Rome, Italy at the World Track and Field Championships.

5   For the next year, Johnson held on to his title of world's fastest man on earth. Johnson's archrival,[3] Carl Lewis, became outspoken in his insinuation[4] about "some" track and field athletes **relying** on **banned substances** after Johnson's world record achievement in Rome. The implication[5] was that Johnson was among that group.

6   Lewis defeated Johnson in Zurich in August 1988. This was the first meeting of the two sprinters since the Rome event. People had doubts about Johnson's Olympic chances for a gold medal.

7   The Games of the 24th Olympiad opened on 17 September 1988 in Seoul, Korea. "King Carl," as the media dubbed Lewis, had publicly declared in Zurich that he would never again lose to Ben Johnson. Lewis was Johnson's nemesis.[6] Most Canadians who were alive in 1988 have some recollection of Ben Johnson speeding to Olympic gold in a world record time of 9.79 seconds on 24 September 1988. Embedded[7] in the collective memory is the image of Johnson, dressed in bright red track shorts and top, muscles rippling, leading the whole pack of runners from the start, then, almost at the finish line, raising his right arm, index finger extended to proclaim his number one status, while at the same time looking over his left shoulder to see Lewis well behind him.

8   Sixty-two hours later, the world learned that Johnson's urine samples had shown **significant** amounts of a steroid,[8] and he was disqualified for using a banned substance. The front page of the *Toronto Sun*, in bold headlines, asked, "Why

---

[3] a competitor

[4] an indirect suggestion that a bad thing is true

[5] something that is not stated directly

[6] a long-time competitor

[7] fixed firmly

[8] a chemical substance used to improve a person's performance

Ben?" and carried the caption, "Canada's shame." Canadian euphoria[9] disappeared as quickly as it had grown.

9   Ever since the Johnson scandal, many other athletes have been found guilty of using banned substances to enhance athletic performance, including Carl Lewis. Regardless of his guilt, Johnson was a world-class athlete. He returned to his career for a short time and competed in the 1992 Barcelona Olympic Games. He finished last in his semifinal heat. A year later, he was found guilty of doping in Montreal and was banned for life. He coached several athletes, developed a clothing line, and ran stunt events such as one where he ran against a horse. Johnson appeared in a series of commercials for "Cheetah Power Surge" beverages. In the ads, Johnson was asked, "Ben, when you run, do you Cheetah?" and he responded, "Absolutely, I Cheetah all the time."

Source: Morrow, D., & Wamsley, K. (2013). *Sport in Canada: A history* (3rd ed., pp. 148–153). Don Mills, ON: Oxford University Press.

---

[9] happiness and excitement that lasts a short time

Activity D | Discuss the following questions about the reading with a partner or small group.

1. Who is Ben Johnson?
2. Why do people consider Ben Johnson a Canadian hero?
3. Why was Ben Johnson criticized? What did he do?

Activity E | Writing Task: Short Paragraph | Do you think it was fair that Ben Johnson was stripped of his medal for using performance-enhancing drugs? Using information from the textbook excerpt and your own ideas, write a short paragraph to express your opinion. Give three reasons for your opinion.

Once you've finished your paragraph, read it over and see if you can introduce five words from the textbook excerpt in your paragraph. Then share your ideas in a small group. In your group, who thinks it was fair and who thinks it was not fair that Johnson was stripped of his medal? What different arguments and supporting ideas do your group members have to support their opinions?

Activity F | Compare your paragraph with the sample paragraph for Unit 4 in Appendix 2 and answer the questions that follow. Focus on the paragraph structure and the supporting ideas for the topic sentence.

1. What is the topic of the sample paragraph?
2. What is the writer's opinion on the topic?
3. What is the first supporting idea?
4. What is the second supporting idea?
5. What is the third supporting idea?
6. How is the concluding sentence written? Does the author summarize the main points or paraphrase the topic sentence?
7. How do the ideas in the sample paragraph compare with those in yours?

Critical Thinking

Examining Evidence

In Unit 2, you learned that it is important to evaluate the sources you use in your assignments. It is equally important to examine the evidence you collect. Once you have evaluated your evidence, you should examine it to check that it includes different perspectives on your topic.

A perspective is a point of view. If the evidence you have collected provides only one perspective on your topic, you might need to collect more evidence with multiple perspectives. It is important to consider different perspectives in researching your inquiry question so that you understand a range of opinions and viewpoints. For example, earlier in this unit you read a paragraph about the use of performance-enhancing drugs in sport. The paragraph was written from the point of view of someone who feels that athletes should be allowed to use them. This is not the only point of view.

A sports medicine doctor or sports psychologist might say that the use of performance-enhancing drugs causes dangerous side effects and is a risk to the athlete's health. Some athletes might hold the opinion that using performance-enhancing drugs while training is fair, but that they should not be used leading up to a competition.

Once you have collected your evidence, sort it into these different groups:

1. evidence that supports your opinion;
2. evidence that challenges your opinion; and
3. neutral evidence that doesn't support or challenge your opinion.

Source: Adapted from Watt, J., & Colyer, J. (2014). *IQ: A practical guide to inquiry-based learning*. Don Mills, ON: Oxford University Press.

PROCESS FUNDAMENTALS

Brainstorming and Outlining

Five Points of View

Five points of view is a type of brainstorming technique. Using this technique, you look at your topic from five different points of view. The purpose is to get the point of view from a variety of people. The fun part of this technique is that you can choose any person's point of view; for example, you can select your mom, your best friend, your neighbour, a co-worker, and a librarian.

In the following activities, try to think about your Unit Inquiry Question from the point of view of five different people of your choice. Thinking of each of the people you have chosen, what would you tell them about your Unit Inquiry Question?

What point of view would you expect each of these people to have? What questions would they ask you about your Unit Inquiry Question? What information about your inquiry question would each person already have? What would each person be interested to find out? What would you tell them about your Unit Inquiry Question? You should only spend a few minutes brainstorming ideas for your topic from these five points of view.

Below are examples of five different points of view on the question Do you agree or disagree that the best way to lose weight is to go on a diet?

"I think my mom, who is a nurse, would say that it's not healthy to go on a diet. If you eat three regular meals and exercise every day, you should be able to maintain a good weight. My mom might ask, *What do you mean by 'diet'?*"

"My best friend went on a no-carb, high-protein diet last year before her sister's wedding, and she lost 25 pounds. She wasn't able to keep the weight off. She would probably say that going on a crash diet to lose weight quickly is not the best solution, but if you want to lose weight in a short time, it's okay. She might ask *What are the pros and cons of popular diets on the market?* She might also ask *Why do some diets work for some people but not others?*"

"My doctor would recommend living a healthy lifestyle—eating lots of fruits and vegetables, going for a daily walk to reduce stress, and cutting out trans fat and sugar as much as possible. But she would probably tell me that it's not necessary to go on one of the popular diets advertised online that make promises about losing lots of weight quickly."

"My retired neighbour might say that diets are a waste of money and that if you want to lose weight, you should be active. My neighbour is very active. He is always repairing something on his house, making his yard look beautiful, or building something in his garage.

"I think a weight loss consultant would try to sell me meal replacement shakes or diet supplements. I've read that they also sell special diet teas that help burn fat."

Activity A | Look back at the survey you competed in the *Exploring Ideas* section. Choose one survey question and respond to it using the five-points-of-view brainstorming technique. (Do not choose the same survey question that you discussed with a partner in Activity C of the *Exploring Ideas* section.) Write down the five different points of view, agreeing or disagreeing with the statement, and share them with a partner.

Activity B | Look back at your Unit Inquiry Question on page 130. Come up with five points of view and spend a few minutes brainstorming ideas about your Unit Inquiry Question from these points of view. You might consider thinking about what your best friend, a police officer, an economist, a biologist, or a teacher might say. Write down your brainstorming ideas in your notebook.

Activity C | What are your reasons for choosing the people you chose for your five-points-of-view brainstorming? Was the five-points-of-view brainstorming technique effective in helping you generate a variety of perspectives related to your inquiry question? Discuss with a partner.

Outlining

The ideas you generate from a five-points-of-view brainstorming activity can help you in your writing. They can be used to help you create a paragraph outline.

For example, imagine your Unit Inquiry Question is related to the long-term effects on children who participate in competitive sports. You hold the opinion that there are more negative effects than positive effects on these children.

One supporting idea might be related to the emotional effects, such as the pressure children feel to win competitions and make their friends and parents proud.

One of your points of view might be from a psychologist. Since psychologists study the mind, a psychologist might be concerned about the child's sense of identity as it relates to winning and losing in competitive sports.

Another supporting idea might be related to the physical effects, such as the strain that competitive sports put on children's growing bones and muscles.

Another point of view might be from a kinesiologist. Since kinesiologists are concerned with how the body responds to exercise, they might also argue that many children who aren't taught by a professional instructor don't learn enough about safety related to the sport, not only for them but for other players.

The sample outline below shows how the ideas from a brainstorming session (page 144) are used to create an outline for an opinion paragraph.

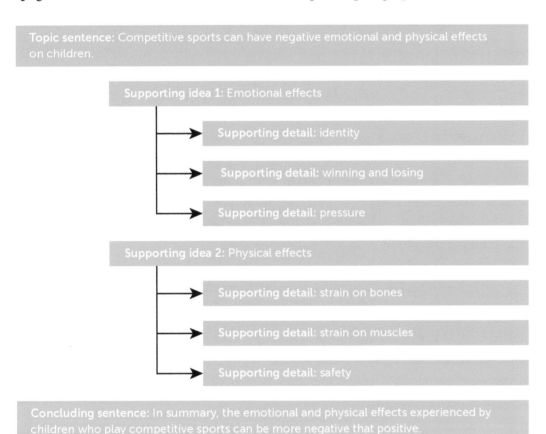

Topic sentence: Competitive sports can have negative emotional and physical effects on children.

Supporting idea 1: Emotional effects

Supporting detail: identity

Supporting detail: winning and losing

Supporting detail: pressure

Supporting idea 2: Physical effects

Supporting detail: strain on bones

Supporting detail: strain on muscles

Supporting detail: safety

Concluding sentence: In summary, the emotional and physical effects experienced by children who play competitive sports can be more negative that positive.

Activity D | Look back at the ideas you developed in Activity B for your Unit Inquiry Question through the five-points-of-view brainstorming technique. Using the outline template shown in Figure 4.1 on page 132, create an outline for your opinion paragraph. As you complete more tasks in this unit, you can use your outline to add more ideas and details to support your topic.

Before You Write

Taking Notes

Taking notes is a versatile skill—you will use it a lot in college or university and use it in different ways. When you are researching sources of information for your assignments, you should write down all the reference information. Even if you don't end up using all the sources you collect, it is a good habit to make note of the sources and where you found them.

Once you have found some sources to use in your assignment and start reading them, take simple notes of what you are reading. You can note keywords in the margins that will help remind you of what each text is about. You can also write brief notes on sticky notes and put them in your textbook or journal articles to remind you of what information you can use in your assignments.

For more on note-taking, see page 151.

Activity A | Think about the note-taking strategies you use before you begin the writing process. What types of note-taking do you do, and why? Record a few of your ideas and share them with a partner. Try to add at least one of your partner's note-taking strategies to your own list.

Activity B | In this activity, you are going to practise note-taking using the Ben Johnson reading on pages 139–141. Follow these steps:

Step 1: Look back at the Ben Johnson textbook excerpt. With a partner, find the topic sentence of paragraph 1 and rewrite the topic sentence in your own words in the space provided on page 147. If there is not one clear topic sentence in the paragraph, write your own.

Step 2: After the topic sentence that you and your partner wrote, write two or three important points from paragraph 1. Use your own words, and do not worry about writing full sentences when making notes.

Step 3: With your partner, review paragraph 1, comparing it with your notes to make sure you have not missed any important points.

Step 4: Now, divide the remaining paragraphs in the Ben Johnson reading between you and your partner. For example, one person can take notes on paragraphs 2, 3, 4, and 5, and the other person can take notes on paragraphs 6, 7, 8, and 9. For each paragraph, note the topic sentence and some important details, then check your notes against the paragraph.

Step 5: When you are finished, discuss your notes with your partner. Give each other feedback on your rewritten topic sentences and the main points you decided to write down. Would your partner have written the topic sentences differently? Would your partner have chosen different points?

Paragraph 1:

_____

_____

_____

_____

Paragraph 2:

_____

_____

_____

_____

Paragraph 3:

_____

_____

_____

_____

Paragraph 4:

_____

_____

_____

_____

Paragraph 5:

_____

_____

_____

_____

Paragraph 6:

_____

_____

_____

_____

Paragraph 7:

_____

_____

_____

_____

Paragraph 8:

_____

_____

_____

_____

Paragraph 9:

_____

_____

_____

_____

Activity C | After your discussion, think about how you identified and chose the main points in the paragraphs and prepare a brief report to share with the class.

Content Skill

Using a Report

You will use different sources of information in your post-secondary studies. The requirements of your assignments and topic will determine the types of sources that will be appropriate for your writing assignments. Original research studies, essays, and historical documents are a few examples. Reports are another possible source.

Reports are often formal. They are written in a specific structure. They come from different sources. For example, they can come from government departments, universities, private companies, think tanks, private individuals, or local or national organizations. A report can be written by one person or a team of people. Reports have different audiences (e.g., specific professional groups or the general public). You can find reports in trade journals, government publications or websites, or industry-specific websites, among other places.

Activity A | Look back at your Unit Inquiry Question on page 130. If you wanted to use information from a report to help research this question, what type of report would you use? Where would you find such a report?

Activity B | Look at the titles of the following six reports. For each title, discuss the questions that follow with a partner.

    a. Canadian Centre for Ethics in Sport Annual Report 2014–2015
    b. Faculty of Kinesiology Annual Research Report 2014–2015
    c. Public Health Agency of Canada—How Healthy are Canadians?
    d. 2015 The ParticipACTION Report Card on Physical Activity for Children and Youth
    e. What Sport Can Do: The True Sport Report
    f. The Canadian Academy of Sport Medicine Position Statement—Violence and Injuries in Ice Hockey

    1. Who do you think wrote this report?
    2. Who do you think is the intended audience?
    3. What kind of information do you think you could find in this report?
    4. How reliable do you think the information would be? Why?

Activity C | The reading on page 150, "Kids Need Room to Move," is an excerpt from a report titled "Is Canada in the Running? Short Form Report Card." It is about children's physical activity levels in Canada compared to those in other countries. Before you read, think about this title and discuss the four questions in Activity B above with a partner.

Activity D | Read the report and answer this question: Are children in Canada getting enough physical activity? As you read, highlight the information that supports your answer, then compare your highlighted information with a partner. Discuss your opinions about whether children in Canada are getting enough physical activity.

Kids Need Room to Move

1   When Canada is considered in a global context, we are a developed country. But when looking at the lifestyles of our children and youth, it might be more accurate to say we are overdeveloped.

2   Canada is among the leaders in our relatively sophisticated policies, places, and programs:

- 95% of parents report local availability of parks and outdoor spaces. 94% report local availability of public facilities and programs for physical activity, such as pools, arenas, and leagues.
- There is a physical education (PE) curriculum at schools in every province and territory. Most students have access to a gymnasium (95%), playing fields (91%), and areas with playground equipment (73%) during school hours.
- 75% of Canadian kids aged 5–19 participate in organized physical activities or sport.

3   Even though 84% of Canadian kids aged 3–4 are active enough to meet guidelines, this falls to only 7% of kids meeting guidelines at ages 5–11, and only 4% meeting guidelines at ages 12–17. The question is, if our policies, places, and programs are well developed, why is this not translating into enough activity for our kids?

- 62% of Canadian parents say their kids aged 5–17 years are always driven to and from school (by car, bus, transit, etc.).
- Canadian kids aged 3–4 spend 5.8 hours a day being sedentary. Kids aged 5–11 spend 7.6 hours. Kids aged 12–17 spend 9.3 hours.

4   Why are our kids sitting more and moving less? The answer requires a hard look at our culture of convenience. For most Canadians, the socially acceptable walking distance to school is less than 1.6 km. Distance between home and school is the single most reported reason why kids do not walk or bike to get there.

5   Our country values efficiency—doing more in less time—which may be at direct odds with promoting children's health. We have engineered opportunities for spontaneous movement (such as getting to places on foot and playing outdoors) out of our kids' daily lives. We have tried to compensate with organized activities such as dance recitals, soccer leagues, and PE classes. Canadian parents look to structured activities and schools to get their kids moving:

- 82% of parents agree that the education system should place more importance on providing quality PE.
- 79% of parents contribute financially to their kids' physical activities. Only 37% of parents often play actively with their children.

6 Organized sports may never make up for lost (active) time:

- One study shows that only 24% of kids got a full 60 minutes of moderate/vigorous activity in one session of soccer.
- Kids on hockey teams spend half of the time during practices in moderate/vigorous activity, but in an actual game, they don't move for nearly a third of the time.

7 In Canada, there is a tendency to build more and impose more structure, but perhaps these efforts are somewhat misguided. To increase daily physical activity levels for all kids, we must encourage the accumulation of physical activity throughout a child's day. We should consider a mix of opportunities (e.g., sport, active play, active transportation). In some cases, we may need to step back and do less. Developed societies such as Canada must acknowledge that children need room to move.

Source: Janson, K. (2014, May 20). *Is Canada in the running? How Canada stacks up against 14 other countries on physical activity for children and youth (Short form report card).* Retrieved from http://www.rbc.com/community-sustainability/_assets-custom/pdf/AHKC-2014-Short-Form-Report-Card-English.pdf

Preventing Plagiarism

Taking Notes

Good note-taking skills will help you with research. When you read any outside sources for your written assignments, you should take notes in your own words. You can do this by imagining that you are explaining the ideas to a classmate. Don't just copy the words you see on the page; use your own words to express the ideas. If you do copy down any parts of the text word for word, you should keep track of that. For example, highlight or mark the parts of the texts you copy word for word in a different colour than what you used to take notes in your own words.

Another strategy is to keep a separate section of direct quotations that you might use in your assignments with the full reference information. Jotting down the reference information will save you time later and will make it easier for you to check that all your references are complete and correct.

Paragraphing Skill

Writing a Concluding Sentence

The concluding sentence is the last sentence of a paragraph. It reminds the reader what the paragraph was about. It can be written in different ways. One way is to paraphrase the topic sentence. That means to rewrite the topic sentence of the paragraph in a different way. Another way is to summarize the supporting ideas in your paragraph. Which way you choose will depend on the topic and the information you include in your paragraph. Either way, a concluding sentence signals to the reader the end of the paragraph.

The phrases below can be used at the beginning of the concluding sentence.

Finally,   In conclusion,   In summary,   In short,   In brief,

Notice that a comma follows each of these phrases.

See the examples below that show the two ways you can write your concluding sentence.

Type 1: Paraphrase of the Topic Sentence

Walking

In my opinion, walking is the best form of exercise. First, walking helps you burn calories. According to a Harvard Medical School website, if you walk briskly for 30 minutes, you will burn approximately 150 calories. A blogger on the same website notes that at the end of the week, this is equivalent to a fast food hamburger and French fries. Nevertheless, even if you walk briskly for 30 minutes a day, you should still eat three healthy meals a day rather than choosing fast food regularly. Second, going for a walk helps reduce the chance of serious disease and illness. According to health professionals, daily walking reduces cholesterol, which reduces the chance of heart attacks and strokes. Third, taking a leisurely stroll helps with your mood. When you walk, your body produces endorphins, which are mood elevators. After a walk in the park, you are sure to feel happy and refreshed. However, be careful not to overdo it. If you walk too quickly, you might twist your ankle. Make sure you wear sturdy walking shoes to avoid injury. **In conclusion, walking is an excellent way to exercise.**

References

Godman, H. (2013). Think fast when kids want fast food. *Harvard Health Blog*. Retrieved from http://www.health.harvard.edu/blog/think-fast-when-kids-want-fast-food-201301315846

Harvard Health. (2004). Calories burned in 30 minutes for people of three different weights. *Harvard Health Publications—Harvard Medical School*. Retrieved from http://www.health.harvard.edu/diet-and-weight-loss/calories-burned-in-30-minutes-of-leisure-and-routine-activities

Topic sentence: In my opinion, walking is the best form of exercise.

Concluding sentence: In conclusion, walking is an excellent way to exercise.

Type 2: Summary of Supporting Ideas Mentioned in the Paragraph

Walking

In my opinion, walking is the best form of exercise. **First, walking helps you burn calories.** According to a Harvard Medical School website, if you walk briskly for 30 minutes, you will burn approximately 150 calories. A blogger on the same website notes that at the end of the week, this is equivalent to a fast food hamburger and French fries. Nevertheless, even if you walk briskly for 30 minutes a day, you should still eat three healthy meals a day rather than choosing fast food regularly. **Second, going for a walk helps reduce the chance of serious disease and illness.** According to health professionals, daily walking reduces cholesterol, which reduces the chance of heart attacks and strokes. **Third, taking a leisurely stroll helps with your mood.** When you walk, your body produces endorphins, which are mood elevators. After a walk in the park, you are sure to feel happy and refreshed. However, be careful not to overdo it. If you walk too quickly, you might twist your ankle. Make sure you wear sturdy walking shoes to avoid injury. **In conclusion, walking as a form of exercise is an excellent way to burn calories, reduce the chance of serious disease, and keep you happy.**

References

Godman, H. (2013). Think fast when kids want fast food. *Harvard Health Blog*. Retrieved from http://www.health.harvard.edu/blog/think-fast-when-kids-want-fast-food-201301315846

Harvard Health. (2004). Calories burned in 30 minutes for people of three different weights. *Harvard Health Publications—Harvard Medical School*. Retrieved from http://www.health.harvard.edu/diet-and-weight-loss/calories-burned-in-30-minutes-of-leisure-and-routine-activities

Supporting ideas: walking helps you burn calories; walking reduces the chance of serious disease and illness; walking helps keep you in a good mood

Concluding sentence: In conclusion, walking as a form of exercise is an excellent way to burn calories, reduce the chance of serious disease, and keep you happy.

Activity A | Reread the opinion paragraph "Performance-Enhancing Drugs" from page 131. In the concluding sentence, the writer used one of the two types of conclusions mentioned. Did the writer paraphrase the topic sentence or give a summary of the supporting ideas?

Performance-Enhancing Drugs

In my opinion, athletes who use performance-enhancing drugs (PEDs) and are not cheating. They are not being dishonest, and they don't have an unfair advantage. First, PED use is very widespread in high-level amateur and professional sports. Some coaches even encourage their athletes to use them. Athletes who use PEDs are not deceiving other athletes because everyone is aware of what is going on. Athletes who don't use them are at a disadvantage, but that is their decision. Second, competitive athletes train exceptionally hard, which is very hard on their bodies. Many PEDs are used only to assist them in recovery, not to boost their performance during competition. Finally, athletes who have health conditions like asthma or joint injuries are allowed to use certain kinds of steroids and other medicines that are classified as PEDs. If all athletes had access to the same kinds of medicinal drugs, no one would have an unfair advantage. It might be true that some PEDs are unhealthy and even dangerous. However, it has been nearly impossible to enforce bans on PEDs. Currently, all high-level athletes have the same access to them. If performance-enhancing drugs and techniques are going to be banned, they should be banned for being dangerous, but not because they give athletes who use them an unfair advantage. In conclusion, athletes who use performance-enhancing drugs are not being dishonest.

Activity B | For the above paragraph, rewrite the concluding sentence so that it follows the style of the other type.

_____

_____

_____

Activity C | With a partner, compare the concluding sentences you wrote in Activity B. Tell each other *how* you wrote your concluding sentence. Did you reread the paragraph? Did you look for the connectors and read the information after the connectors? Or did you use some other approach?

Activity D | Look back to the concluding sentence you wrote in your opinion paragraph outline on page 145. In your concluding sentence, did you paraphrase the topic sentence or summarize the supporting ideas?

- If you paraphrased the topic sentence, write a different concluding sentence that summarizes the supporting ideas.
- If you summarized the supporting ideas, write a different concluding sentence that paraphrases the topic sentence. Share your concluding sentences with a partner and discuss what you wrote.

Language Skill

Expressing Opinions

Certain introductory phrases can be used at the beginning of a sentence in which you express your opinion. These phrases signal to the reader that you are expressing your opinion.

Here are some common opinion phrases.

In my opinion . . .	I strongly believe (that) . . .
I think (that) . . .	I am convinced that . . .
I feel (that) . . .	From my point of view . . .
I believe (that) . . .	

In your writing, you may also want to express agreement or disagreement with another person's point of view. The chart below sets out some agreement and disagreement expressions you can use in your writing.

Agreement Expression	Example
I agree with [NAME] that . . .	I agree with Smith that it is better to allow children time to play outside than to register them in organized sports.
I believe [NAME] is correct in stating that . . .	I believe Jones is correct in stating that the use of performance-enhancing drugs in professional sports gives some athletes an unfair advantage.
I am of the same opinion as [NAME] because . . .	I am of the same opinion as the District B elementary school teachers because the children at the school where I work get only about two hours of physical activity a day.
Like [NAME], I believe that . . .	Like Johnston, I believe that children should regularly get outside for exercise.

Disagreement Expression	Example
I disagree with [NAME] that . . .	I disagree with Smith that it is better to allow children time to play outside than to register them in organized sports.
I believe [NAME] is incorrect in stating that . . .	I believe Jones is incorrect in stating that the use of performance-enhancing drugs in professional sports gives some athletes an unfair advantage.
I am of a different opinion than [NAME] because . . .	I am of a different opinion than the District B elementary school teachers because the children at the school where I work get plenty of physical activity in a day.
Unlike [NAME], I believe that . . .	Unlike Johnston, I believe that children should focus more on studying than on getting outside to exercise.

Activity A | Look back at the opinion paragraphs "Performance-Enhancing Drugs" and "Walking" in this unit on pages 131 and 134. In small groups, discuss whether you agree or disagree with the author's opinions in each one. Give reasons and examples to support your agreement or disagreement.

For example, if you agree with the author that walking is the best form of exercise, you might say, "I agree that walking is the best form of exercise because it is what's most convenient for me. As a student, I don't have time to go to the gym. However, I walk to the university every day and I usually feel refreshed when I get there."

Activity B | After your small group discussion, nominate someone in your group to give a report to the whole class. As you listen to your classmates give their reports, take notes to record their ideas.

Activity C | Writing Task: Short Opinion Paragraph | Write a short opinion paragraph based on what you and your group members discussed in Activity A. Share your paragraph with a partner and compare the agreement and disagreement expressions you used.

WRITING FUNDAMENTALS

Composition Skill

Using Checklists

When you have an assignment, one way to help you organize it is to use a checklist. Writing a checklist is useful because doing so helps you think about everything you need to include in your assignment. As you work through your assignment, the checklist will remind you of what you have completed and what you haven't completed.

Sometimes students think that if they have to write a paragraph, they should just start writing. However, taking a bit of time to put together a checklist of the things you should do or include will help you complete the writing task more successfully and completely.

For example, if you have to write a paragraph for your English class, a few things you can put on your checklist are the three main parts of a paragraph:

- ☐ topic sentence
- ☐ supporting ideas and details
- ☐ a concluding sentence

You can also include specific grammar points that you are learning in your English class or grammar points that you have difficulty with and will need to double-check in your final paper. You can do the same for connectors and vocabulary too.

Another idea to help you design a checklist for your assignments is to take the assignment rubric your instructor gives you and add specific information from the rubric to your checklist. For example, if one of the requirements of the assignment is to make reference to your course readings, add this to your checklist.

Activity A | Do you use checklists in daily life to remind you of tasks you have to do? Do you write your lists on paper or do you use your phone? Do you check back on your list or do you just write down the things you need to do and forget about the list? Discuss with a partner how you use checklists in your everyday life.

Activity B | Imagine you are preparing to write an opinion paragraph about your Unit Inquiry Question. What items would you include in your checklist? Write a checklist and compare it with a partner. Make sure it includes things that are common to opinion paragraphs, like a topic sentence with a clear opinion, supporting ideas and details, and a concluding sentence that paraphrases the topic sentence or summarizes the main ideas developed in your paragraph.

Activity C | Writing Task: First Draft | Write a first draft of an opinion paragraph based on your Unit Inquiry Question. After you write your first draft, refer to the checklist you completed in Activity B and check that your topic sentence includes a clear opinion, your supporting ideas and examples support your opinion, and your concluding sentence is appropriate.

Writing Skill

Avoiding Repetition

You want your writing to be clear, and your audience to pay attention to your message. One thing that can distract your audience from your message is unnecessary repetition of words, phrases, and grammar structures. Your reader will notice when you repeat the same words or phrases and use the same grammatical structures, and they may be distracted from what you are trying to communicate.

Compare these two sentences:

John twisted John's ankle while John was jogging because John didn't stretch before John's run.

John twisted his ankle while he was jogging because he didn't stretch before his run.

In the first sentence, it is impossible not to notice John's name being used again and again. It is hard to read because of all the repetition. The other sentence is very clear. The reader can focus on the idea and not on the words used to express it.

Using pronouns instead of repeating the same noun over and over is a good way to improve your writing. You can use possessive adjectives. For example, *John's ankle* becomes *his ankle*. You can also use synonyms to give your paragraph variety. Finally, you can avoid repetition by leaving out unnecessary information.

Read the two paragraphs below. Which one sounds better? Why?

Paragraph 1

In my opinion, having a pet dog can improve people's health. First of all, having a pet dog reduces people's stress. When you come home after a busy day at school, your pet dog is waiting for you at home. When you enter the house, your pet dog is there to greet you. If you are feeling sad about a low mark you got at school, you can talk to your pet dog about it. Your pet dog will listen to you and your pet dog won't make any judgements. Second, a pet dog provides companionship. Dogs are commonly referred to as "man's best friend." Pet dogs are loyal and pet dogs will always be there for you. Having a pet dog improves your quality of life and your general health. Third, having a pet dog will help you get outside and get exercise because you have to walk your pet dog every day. You will get exercise and will also get a lot of Vitamin D. Walking your pet dog every day for at least 30 minutes is a good way to maintain a healthy weight. In summary, having a pet dog is beneficial to your overall health and well-being.

Paragraph 2

In my opinion, having a pet dog can improve people's health. First of all, dogs can reduce stress. When you come home after a busy day at school, your dog is waiting for you, ready to greet you when you come inside. If you are feeling sad about a low mark you got at school, you can tell your dog about it. Your dog will listen to you and won't make any judgements. Second, a pet dog provides companionship. Dogs are commonly referred to as "man's best friend." Dogs are loyal and will always be there for you. Having a friend you can count on improves your quality of life and your general health. Third, walking your dog every day is a healthy habit. You will get exercise and a lot of Vitamin D. Walking your dog every day for at least 30 minutes is a good way to maintain a healthy weight. In summary, having a pet dog is beneficial to your overall health and well-being.

Activity A | What is the main topic of paragraph 1? How many times did the writer repeat the main topic? In paragraph 2, how many times does the writer make reference to the main topic? What are the different ways the writer refers to the main topic? Write them in your notebook and compare answers with a partner.

Activity B | The opinion paragraph on page 161 argues why female athletes should earn the same salary as male athletes.

- First, scan the paragraph and circle all the words and phrases the author repeats.
- Then rewrite the paragraph and compare your revisions with a partner's. In what ways is your paragraph similar to or different from your partner's? Discuss why you think the repeated words you identified should or should not be changed.

> ## Should Female Athletes Earn the Same as Male Athletes?
>
> In my opinion, female athletes should earn the same salary as male athletes. First, female athletes use a lot of effort. In golf, female athletes have to use 80 percent of their force. Male athletes have to use only 50 percent to drive the ball the same distance (Netto, 2016). Female athletes have to work harder in golf. Second, many female athletes would like to enter sport as a career. Female athletes do not receive a livable salary. Female athletes have to work. Work takes away from training time. For example, Canadian female athletes who play hockey in the Canadian Women's Hockey League may earn a maximum of $1000 if they win the Clarkson Cup at the end of the season (Mack, 2014). Most of these female athletes work. The female athletes then practise in the evenings (Mack, 2014). The message that is given when female athletes are not paid the same as male athletes is that female athletes are not as valued as male athletes. Female athletes invest a lot into training. Female athletes are put at risk of physical injury. Physical injury might end female athletes' careers. Female athletes' salaries should reflect this. Female athletes should earn the same as male athletes if sport is to advance in the future.
>
> ### References
>
> Mack, C. M. (2014, December 10). CWHL: Top female hockey players go unpaid. *Canadian Living*. Retrieved from http://www.canadianliving.com/life-and-relationships/money-and-career/article/cwhl-top-female-hockey-players-go-unpaid
>
> Netto, K. (2016, April 17). Should women athletes earn the same as men? The science says they work as hard. *The Conversation*. Retrieved from http://theconversation.com/should-women-athletes-earn-the-same-as-men-the-science-says-they-work-as-hard-57210

Sentence and Grammar Skill

Using Parallel Structure

Creating Parallel Structure

Parallel structure is an important part of good writing. Sometimes a sentence will contain a list of three things, qualities, or actions. Each of the three should be the same form—nouns, verbs, adjectives, phrases, or even clauses. Ensuring that you have parallel structure in your lists will make your sentences flow more smoothly and be more concise and readable.

Consider the example below.

Ben Johnson was a hard-working, serious athlete with a lot of talent.

Hard-working and *serious* are adjectives, but *with a lot of talent* is a prepositional phrase containing the noun *talent*. They all describe the noun *athlete*, but they are not parallel with each other: they are not all the same part of speech. One way to make the above sentence parallel is to change all the items in the series to adjectives:

Ben Johnson was a hard-working, serious, and talented athlete.

The sentence above has parallel structure because all the items in the series are adjectives.

Using Commas to Separate a Series

When you have a list of three or more things, you should separate the items with commas and add a coordinating conjunction like *and*.

Examples

Kinesiology is the scientific study of anatomy, physiology, and movement.
Ben Johnson was born in Jamaica, grew up in Toronto, and competed in Seoul.

Activity A | For the following parallel sentences, underline the items that are listed in a series.

1. Sally's weekly exercise routine includes lifting weights, jogging in the park, and taking a yoga class.
2. Mary works at the recreation centre. Her duties include planning programs for children, giving nutrition workshops, and teaching a Zumba class.
3. A good gymnast is flexible, creative, and strong.
4. Mary learned shooting drills, dribbling techniques, and passing skills at the weekend basketball camp.
5. The Running Injury Clinic helps athletes recover from injuries, train for competitions, and improve their running technique.

Activity B | Rewrite the following sentences so that they are parallel.

1. The kinesiology professor lectured about ways people can improve their performance in sports and developing their awareness of injury prevention.
2. People who graduate with a degree in kinesiology can work as physical education teachers, in physical therapy, or coordinate recreation programs.

3. The Faculty of Kinesiology summer exercise program for children has three goals: to show kids the importance of exercise, to show kids the importance of eating right, and showing kids that they have to have fun.

4. To help me with my frozen shoulder, the kinesiologist stretched my arm, my back muscles were massaged, he asked me to lift my arm above my head, and he was applying heat to my shoulder.

5. Most kinesiology students enjoy studying science, physical activity, and to work with people.

Learning Strategy

Making Inferences

An inference is a conclusion you make based on something you've read or heard. For example, in the sentence "Sally works out at the gym and does yoga twice a week," you might infer that Sally is healthy, because these activities help people keep fit. Remember, however, you can't be sure that Sally is healthy because the sentence doesn't say anything about her other habits. In addition to working out, she could be doing unhealthy things like eating only junk food and not getting enough sleep.

Making an inference is sometimes called "reading between the lines" or "filling in the gaps." When you make an inference, you use your life experiences and background knowledge to help you come to a conclusion about what you have read or heard. You can infer many things from a single sentence, but that doesn't mean that everything can be inferred.

Look at this sentence from the report "Kids Need Room to Move" on pages 150–151.

Distance between home and school is the single most reported reason why kids do not walk or bike to get there.

From this sentence, we can infer that many children live far from their schools. We can also infer that either parents do not want their children to walk or bike long distances to school or children do not want to walk or bike these distances.

UNIT OUTCOME

Writing Assignment: Opinion Paragraph

Write an opinion paragraph of 150 to 250 words on a topic related to kinesiology, sports, or exercise. (Your instructor may give you an alternative length.) You may write on a topic based on your Unit Inquiry Question, develop another topic of your choosing connected to health and kinesiology, or choose one of the following topics:

- Why should senior citizens participate in aerobic exercise?
- Why is childhood obesity on the rise?
- Why should female professional athletes earn the same salary as male professional athletes?

Use the skills you have developed in this unit to complete the assignment. Follow the steps below to practise each of the new skills you have learned to write a well-developed opinion paragraph.

1. **Brainstorm and find information**: Do a search for information related to your Unit Inquiry Question. In addition to the readings and other topic-related information in this unit, your information sources may include reports. Look back at the freewriting you did in the *Fostering Inquiry* section. If necessary, use the five-points-of-view technique to brainstorm some additional ideas related to health or kinesiology that you have been exploring in your Unit Inquiry Question.

2. **Outline**: List your topic, your chosen inquiry question, and the working title of your paragraph.

   Topic: _____

   Inquiry Question: _____

   _____

   Paragraph Title: _____

Use the template below to create an outline for your paragraph.

Topic Sentence

Topic sentence that states your opinion:

Main Body (Supporting Ideas)

Supporting idea 1 (with detail to back up your opinion):

Supporting idea 2 (with detail to back up your opinion):

Supporting idea 3 (with detail to back up your opinion):

Concluding Sentence

Concluding sentence to summarize your main points or paraphrase your topic sentence:

3. **Write a first draft**: Write a first draft of your paragraph. Use AWL and mid-frequency vocabulary from this unit if possible.

4. **Self-check**: Wait a day, then check your first draft. Remember to check the following:

   • Check that your opinion paragraph has a topic sentence, supporting sentences, and a concluding sentence.

   • Check the verbs in your paragraph. When you have used verb suffixes, are they correct? Are they spelled correctly?

- Check your paragraph for parallel structure. When you have listed things in a series, do all the items in the series have the same grammatical structure?

- Check that you have avoided unnecessary repetition in your paragraph.

- If you have used information from a report in your paragraph, check that you have used appropriate expressions to agree or disagree with the authors of the report.

5. **Revise**: Revise your first draft.

6. **Compose final draft**: Write a final draft of your opinion paragraph.

7. **Proofread**: Check the final draft of your paragraph for any small errors you may have missed. In particular, look for spelling errors, typos, and punctuation mistakes.

Evaluation: Opinion Paragraph Rubric

Use the following rubric to evaluate your essay. In which areas do you need to improve most?

E = **Emerging**: frequent difficulty using unit skills; needs a lot more work
D = **Developing**: some difficulty using unit skills; some improvement still required
S = **Satisfactory**: able to use unit skills most of the time; meets average expectations for this level
O = **Outstanding**: exceptional use of unit skills; exceeds expectations for this level

Skill	E	D	S	O
The opinion paragraph has a topic sentence, supporting sentences, and a concluding sentence that connects to the topic.				
AWL and mid-frequency vocabulary items from this unit are used when appropriate and with few mistakes.				
Opinion sentences are clearly written and use an introductory phrase.				
The paragraph uses connectors of contrast to show relationships between ideas.				
Unnecessary repetition is avoided.				
Verb suffixes are used accurately.				
Sentences with lists or series use parallel structure, and these sentences are punctuated correctly.				

Unit Review

Activity A | What do you know about the topic of kinesiology, sports, or exercise that you did not know before you started this unit? Discuss with a partner or small group. Be prepared to report what you learned to the class.

Activity B | Look back at the Unit Inquiry Question you developed at the start of this unit and discuss it with a partner or small group. Then share your answers with the class. Use the following questions to help you:

1. What information did you find in this unit that helped you answer your question?
2. How would you answer your question now?

Activity C | Use the following checklist to review the skills you have learned in this unit. First decide which 10 skills you think are the most important. Circle the number beside each of these 10 skills. If you learned a skill in this unit that isn't listed below, write it in the blank row at the end of the checklist. Then put a check mark in the box beside those points you feel you have learned. Be prepared to discuss your choices with the class.

	Self-Assessment Checklist
☐	1. I can talk about kinesiology, sports, and exercise based on what I've read in this unit.
☐	2. I can develop an inquiry question to guide my learning and to develop an opinion.
☐	3. I can use connectors of contrast to show relationships between ideas in my writing.
☐	4. I can form verbs by adding suffixes to nouns and adjectives.
☐	5. I can use AWL and mid-frequency words from this unit in my writing.
☐	6. I can use a glossary to help me generate ideas about the contents of the text.
☐	7. I can examine evidence, taking point of view into account.
☐	8. I can use the five-points-of-view brainstorming technique to generate ideas before writing.

☐	9. I can create an outline with key ideas before writing a paragraph.
☐	10. I can take notes while I read to help me during the writing process
☐	11. I can use a report to find information about a topic.
☐	12. I can avoid plagiarism by using specific note-taking techniques.
☐	13. I can write a concluding sentence.
☐	14. I can express my opinion using common introductory phrases.
☐	15. I can use checklists to ensure that I complete my writing tasks successfully.
☐	16. I can avoid unnecessary repetition in my writing.
☐	17. I can identify and write sentences containing parallel structure and punctuate them correctly.
☐	18. I can make inferences to help me with my learning.
☐	19. I can write a well-structured opinion paragraph that contains a topic sentence, supporting sentences, and a concluding sentence.
☐	20.

Activity D | Put a check mark in the box beside the vocabulary items from this unit that you feel confident using in your writing.

Vocabulary Checklist

☐	achievement (n.) AWL	☐	perceive (v.) AWL
☐	athlete (n.) 3000	☐	rely (v.) AWL
☐	banned (adj.) 3000	☐	scandalous (adj.) 4000
☐	championship (n.) 3000	☐	significant (adj.) AWL
☐	controversy (n.) AWL	☐	status (n.) AWL
☐	hero (n.) 3000	☐	substance (n.) 3000

UNIT 5

Trends in Society

Sociology

EXPLORING IDEAS

Introduction

Sociology is the study of human society. The word *society* refers to the group of people that live together in a place such as a city or country. Sociology includes the study of relationships, groups, institutions, habits, and practices; these include families, work, religion, crime, and education. Sociology is often concerned with the changes affecting society.

Studying sociology might involve discussing the types of people who make up various societies. For example, how many children are there? How many senior citizens? How many women and men? In some societies, families have many children, and in other places the families are very small. Sometimes changes happen within a society when the types of people that make up that society change.

Activity A | Look at the photos above and discuss the following questions with a partner or small group.

1. What differences do you notice about the families in these pictures?
2. Imagine if, in one place, all the families were similar to the family on the left and in another place, all the families were similar to the one on the right. How would this affect the larger population in each society?
3. Some countries have very young populations. That means there are many children and teenagers. In other places, the population is very old: there are many more older people than young people. Can you think of a country that has a very young population? Can you think of a country that has a very old population? Check your answers against Figure 5.1 on the next page, a table from *The Atlantic*, and discuss the information you see.

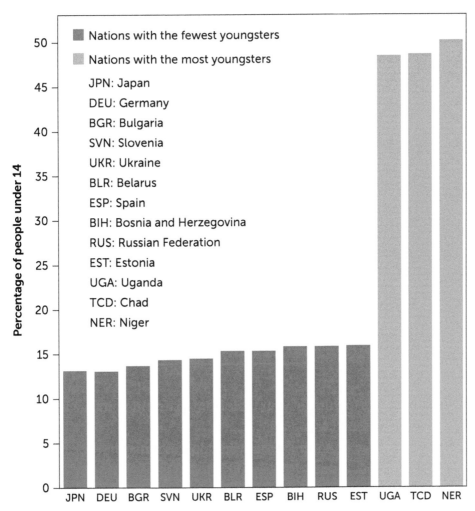

FIGURE 5.1 Percentage of people under age 14, by country

There are many possible topics related to changes to the structure or habits of society. The structure of society refers to the different groups that form our society. People can be grouped by socioeconomic class, job or occupation, region, gender, or interests. In Activity A you discussed differences related to families. You discussed some of the changes to the structure of families, in terms of the number of children families have in different countries.

The habits of society are the things people do throughout their lives, for example, their habits in education, work, forming families, and spending leisure time. Grocery shopping habits are an example: Do people in Canadian society prefer to shop at large supermarkets more than farmers' markets or small, family-run grocery stores?

Using a pyramid of perspectives is a good technique to help you explore ideas. It involves thinking about a topic in three different ways.

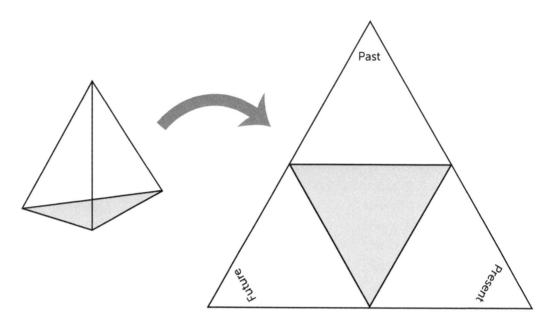

1. The first way is to think of your topic from a **current** point of view. Focus on now—the present day and time.
2. The second way is to think about your topic as it may have been in the **past** and throughout history. How would it have been different in the past? How would it have changed over time?
3. The third way (or perspective) is to use your imagination to think about the **future** as it relates to your topic. What could be different in the future?

Activity B | You have discussed how the structure of families may change depending where they live. Choose another topic related to habits, structures, or institutions in society. Think about your topic from three points of view or perspectives: past, present, and future. Make a pyramid of perspectives diagram similar to the one above, labelling the three spaces 1. Past, 2. Present, 3. Future. Write the ideas you've thought of for each of these perspectives in the spaces.

Topic: _____

Activity C | Work with two classmates. Share the three perspectives (past, present, and future) on your topic that you included in the pyramid you made in Activity B. Ask your classmates if they have any different perspectives on your topic. Then discuss each of your classmates' pyramids. Do you and your partners share any of the same ideas?

Activity D | Think about and discuss information sources with your partners. Where would you look to find information about your topic? Each partner should share one information source with the group.

Fostering Inquiry

Inquiring about Changes and Trends

It can be interesting to think about how things around you are changing. Noticing changes and trends can help guide you to ask some good questions when you're inquiring into a topic. Change can happen suddenly or slowly over time; it can be unexpected or predictable. Sometimes many people can be affected by a change, while other times, a change affects only a few people in society.

The *Oxford Advanced Learner's Dictionary* defines the word *trend* as "a general direction in which a situation is changing or developing." Trends usually affect many people at the same time in the same way. Trends can affect a society's economy, politics, and even tastes in fashion and music.

Thinking about changes and trends can guide your inquiry. For example, if you are interested in education, you might think about changes currently happening in schools. Are more young people studying at university or college than in the past? Are they studying in different programs than their parents did? Is there a trend in young people working part time while they study? Is it common for students to study abroad in another country as part of their program? What could be causing these changes?

Activity A | What do you want to know more about in relation to sociology and the changes and trends in society? For example:

- Why are more young people attending university today?
- How are families changing today?
- Why do fewer people own cars in Canadian cities than in the past?

1. Write two or three questions you are curious about on the topic of sociology and change.
2. When you are finished, compare your questions with a partner or small group.
3. Choose one question to be your inquiry question for this unit. It does not have to be the same question as your partner or group.

4. Write your inquiry question in the space provided. Look back at this question as you work through the unit. This is your Unit Inquiry Question.

My Unit Inquiry Question:

_____

_____

_____

Activity B | Writing Task: Freewriting | Freewriting can help you think of ideas related to your inquiry question and topic. Instead of setting a timer, aim to write until you fill half a page on the topic you've chosen for your inquiry question. You can write anything you think of that is related to this topic. If you finish before your classmates, go back over your text to see if any interesting ideas jump out at you. Are there any ideas that you would like to research as you work through this unit?

Structure

Graphic-Description Paragraph

Purpose
Graphs or charts are often used to communicate information about trends affecting society or the economy. This method of presenting information is quite common in fields such as economics, psychology, sociology, political science, or business. A graphic-description paragraph helps readers to better understand a graph or chart by putting into words the information communicated visually in the graphic.

Audience
A graphic-description paragraph, which presents data or summarizes background information, can have various types of audiences. In an academic context, these paragraphs are often found in research papers that address colleagues. In an exam, or as part of an in-class presentation, your audience for this type of writing would be your instructor or your fellow classmates. In a business context, a paragraph describing changes or trends in a graphic would probably be written for a manager, colleagues, or clients.

Activity A | With a partner or small group, look at the graph below and read the graphic-description paragraph that describes the information shown in the graph. Then answer the questions that follow.

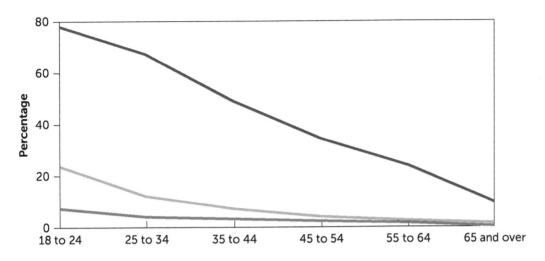

—— Watched television on the Internet, 2000

—— Used the Internet at home to download or watch television or movies, 2005

—— Used the Internet to download or watch television, movies, or video clips online, 2010

FIGURE 5.2 Canadians' use of the Internet for watching television or movies, 2000–2010

According to three different surveys carried out by Statistics Canada, Canadians' use of the Internet to watch TV and movies has increased a lot since the year 2000. In 2000, less than 20 percent of 18- to 24-year-olds watched TV on the Internet. In that same year, less than 5 percent of 35- to 44-year-olds and 55- to 64-year-olds watched TV on the Internet. Almost no Canadians 65 and over used the Internet to watch TV. In 2005, about one-quarter of 18- to 24-year-olds used the Internet to watch TV or movies. As well, more 18- to 24-year-olds and 35- to 44-year-olds used the Internet for entertainment in 2005 than in 2000. However, still almost no Canadians 65 years and over used the Internet for TV or movies. In 2010, close to 80 percent of 18- to 24-year-old Canadians used the Internet to view TV, movies, or videos. Approximately half of all 35- to 44-year-olds and 40 percent of 45- to 54-year-olds also watched these three things on the Internet. Around 10 percent of those 65 years and over watched videos, movies, or TV online in 2010. In conclusion, more Canadians used the Internet to watch TV and movies in 2010 than in 2000, and more young people used the Internet for these purposes than older Canadians.

1. What changes or trends is this paragraph describing?
2. What are the three time periods discussed in this paragraph?
3. What is the function of the last sentence in this paragraph?
4. What words (or phrase) introduce the last sentence?
5. What is missing from this piece of writing?

Structure of a Graphic-Description Paragraph

A graphic-description paragraph discusses or describes the information presented on a graph or chart.

The topic sentence in a graphic-description paragraph should contain two things: a general description of the changes and trends you will describe and a reference to where the information in your paragraph comes from. To reference your information, you can use the phrase "according to [source], . . . " This phrase can be used at the beginning or end of your topic sentence.

According to three different surveys carried out by Statistics Canada, Canadians' use of the Internet to watch TV and movies has increased a lot since the year 2000.

Canadians' use of the Internet to watch TV and movies has increased a lot since the year 2000, **according to** three different surveys carried out by Statistics Canada.

Don't forget to include a comma! If you use "According to [source]," at the beginning of the sentence, the phrase is followed by a comma. If it comes at the end of the sentence, a comma should come before it.

In this unit, you will be expected to have three points of reference (or description points) in your paragraph. To choose your description points, look at the information presented on the changes and trends you want to describe and choose three points. You may choose three different points in time, or three different groups, such as teens, adults, and senior citizens. Your choice will depend on what your topic is and the information you have.

Once you have chosen your three description points, write one to three details about each point. For example, if your three description points are three different years, your supporting detail might describe what children, teenagers, and adults were doing in each of those three years.

The concluding sentence at the end of the paragraph should summarize and close the paragraph. It should not be the same as the topic sentence. Use different words or focus on different points to conclude and summarize. Look back at the paragraph in Activity A on page 175 to see how the topic sentence and the concluding sentence differ.

Figure 5.3 illustrates the structure of a graphic-description paragraph.

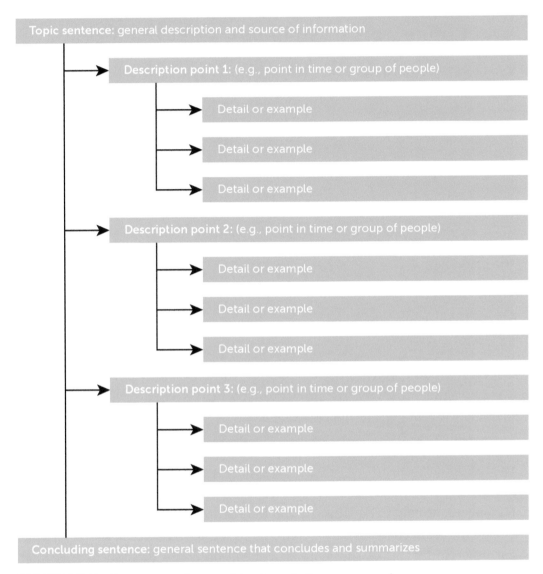

FIGURE 5.3 Structure of a graphic-description paragraph

Language Tip

Using Connectors of Summary and Conclusion

Connectors of summary and conclusion are used at the end of paragraphs.

A connector of summary is used to summarize the information that came before it in the paragraph.

In short,
To summarize,
In summary,
In sum,

A connector of conclusion is used to introduce the final concluding sentence of the paragraph.

In conclusion,
To conclude,
In closing,

Like other connectors, connectors of summary and conclusion most commonly appear at the beginning of the sentence. When a connector is at the beginning of a sentence, it must be followed by a comma.

Activity B | In Activity A on page 175, you read a short graphic-description paragraph about how Canadians use the Internet to watch TV and movies. You identified the connecting phrase that introduced the last sentence in the paragraph. What other connector of summary or conclusion could be used in that final question? Choose from the connectors of summary and conclusion in the Language Tip box. Then compare your answer with a partner or small group.

Activity C | On page 179 are two graphic-description paragraphs. Each paragraph has a topic sentence and description points, but is missing a concluding sentence. Add a concluding sentence to each paragraph, using a connector of summary or conclusion to link the sentence to the paragraph.

1. According to Statistics Canada, many Canadian young people move out and live on their own, but more are staying to live with their parents. In 1981, just over 40 percent of 25- to 29-year-olds lived at home with their parents. This number grew, and by the turn of the century, more than 50 percent of those in this age group were living with their parents. Fifty-nine percent of Canadians aged 25 to 29 were living with their parents in both 2006 and 2011.

Concluding sentence: _____

_____

2. According to Statistics Canada, many Canadian women have gaps in their eating habits. In terms of fruits and vegetables, only 62 percent of girls eat enough fruits and vegetables every day. Similarly, girls 10 to 16 do not drink enough milk every day. For adults, 66 percent of women over 61 do not eat enough bread and grain products per day. This age group also does not get enough milk and dairy products. Many adult women skip breakfast as well.

Concluding sentence: _____

_____

Activity D | Look back at Figure 5.2 on page 175. Carefully read the following graphic-description paragraph that describes the data shown in that graph and answer the questions that follow.

Canadians' Use of the Internet for Watching Television and Movies, 2000–2010

Young people use the Internet to watch TV and movies more than older people, according to three different surveys carried out by Statistics Canada. Approximately 7 percent of Canadians aged 18 to 24 used the Internet to watch TV in 2000. More than 20 percent of 18- to 24-year-olds used the Internet to watch TV or movies in 2005. In 2010, this number grew to almost 80 percent. Meanwhile, Canadians aged 45 to 54 used the Internet for the same purpose less than the younger group. Less than 10 percent of people in this age group used the Internet for watching or downloading television or movies in both 2000 and 2005. More than 30 percent of people aged 45 to 54 used the Internet for these entertainment purposes in 2010. Of the senior citizens in Canada (aged 65 and over), almost none used the Internet to watch TV or movies in 2000. By 2005, this number had not changed. However, the number grew to about 10 percent in 2010. In summary, more young Canadians than older Canadians have used the Internet to watch TV and movies.

1. What is the purpose of this paragraph?
2. Who is the audience of this paragraph: experts or non-experts? How do you know this?
3. What is the topic sentence of this paragraph?
4. What trends or changes are being described in this paragraph?
5. Find and number the three description points in the text. Are they points in time or different groups?
6. Highlight the supporting details or examples for each of these description points.
7. Compare this paragraph to the paragraph in Activity A on page 175. You may have noticed that these paragraphs are describing the same graph. What is the biggest difference in the organization of these two paragraphs?

Activity E | Think of an aspect of society that interests you, such as young people's hobbies, students' study habits, or Canadians' consumption of the news and current events. Do an Internet search for a graphic that shows a change or trend related to this aspect of society. If a computer is not available, your instructor will provide some possible graphics; choose one that interests you.

Imagine you were going to explain the trends or changes affecting this aspect of society to someone, focusing on three different points in time or three different groups, depending on the topic and the information provided.

Fill in the outline on the next page with one sentence in each box. When you have finished writing, exchange your graphic and outline with a partner. Study each other's chosen graphic and sentences and provide feedback, using the following questions to guide you.

1. What change or trend is going to be discussed? Does the topic sentence describe the changes or trends in a general way and give the source of the information?
2. Are there three description points and are they organized in a logical order?
3. Do the three points clearly explain what the graphic is showing? How would you improve these sentences?

4. What do you like most about these sentences?

5. Could these sentences be expanded into a paragraph? Why or why not?

6. Does the concluding sentence summarize the information in the three description points? Explain.

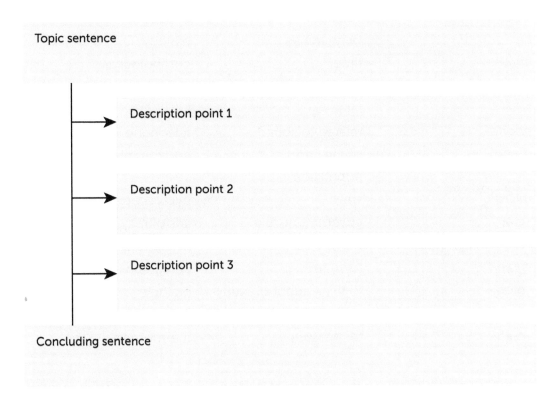

Topic sentence

Description point 1

Description point 2

Description point 3

Concluding sentence

Activity F | Revisit your Unit Inquiry Question on page 174. What information or new ideas have you thought of or discussed that will help you answer your question? Have you thought of any information sources that may contain texts or graphics related to your Unit Inquiry Question? Share your ideas with a partner or small group. At this point, you may consider revising your Unit Inquiry Question.

ACADEMIC READING

Vocabulary

Vocabulary Skill: Recognizing Latin and Greek Loanwords

English has many words that originally came from other languages. Latin and Greek are two of the most common source languages. Words that come from Latin and Greek are especially common in academic contexts.

Sometimes the Latin or Greek loanword is a root word in English; sometimes the loanword is turned into an English prefix or suffix that can be added to a root word.

Latin/Greek Loanword	Meaning/Related To	Example English Word
aqu-	water	aquatic
bio-	living things	biology
chrono-	time	chronological
therm-	hot/heat	thermometer
tele-	far away	television
phone-	related to sound	telephone
demo-	of the people/ population	demographic
micro-	small	microscope
-cracy	government/rule	aristocracy
-ous, -eous, -ious	full of	mysterious
-graph	to write	paragraph
-ology	to think about or study	biology
-scope	to see	telescope
-meter	to measure	thermometer

The relationship between the meaning of the Latin or Greek root, prefix, or suffix and the meaning of the English word is not always direct. It can be more of a general idea. For example, *telephone* is made up of *tele*, which means far away, and *phone*, which means sound. A telephone is a device that carries sound from far away.

Whether the relationship between the loanword and the English word is obvious or indirect, recognizing the Latin or Greek loanwords can help you figure out the meaning of new words you see while reading.

Activity A | The bolded words in the following definition sentences contain words with Greek or Latin parts:

In a **democracy**, the people vote to choose the government.
A **microphone** lets you hear quiet sounds.
A **microscope** is a tool that helps you see small things.
Phonology is the study of the sounds that make up languages.
A **biography** is the written story of a person's life.
A **thermos** is a bottle that keeps hot drinks warm.
Microbiology is the study of very small living things, such as cells.

Can you match the parts to their meaning in the columns below? Two have been done for you.

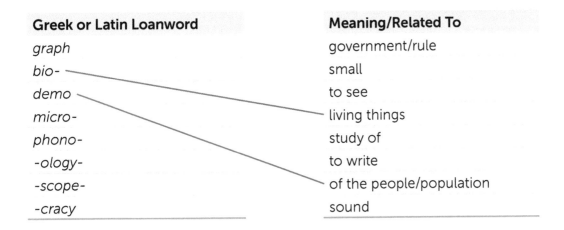

Greek or Latin Loanword	Meaning/Related To
graph	government/rule
bio-	small
demo	to see
micro-	living things
phono-	study of
-ology-	to write
-scope-	of the people/population
-cracy	sound

Vocabulary Preview: The Academic Word List

Activity B | The bolded AWL words in the sentences below are taken from the academic reading "The Greying of Canada," on pages 186–188. First read the six definitions, then read the sentences with the bolded AWL words. Match each definition to the correct AWL word in a sentence.

Definitions

    a. money provided by the government to people who need financial help because they are unemployed, ill/sick, etc. (n.)

    b. all the people who were born at about the same time (n.)

    c. covering or affecting the whole world (adj.)

    d. a person considered separately rather than as part of a group (n.)

    e. a fact or an event in nature or society, especially one that is not fully understood. (The plural form of this word is *phenomena*.) (n.)

    f. the act of communicating with somebody, especially while you work, play, or spend time together (n.)

Sentences

    1. _____ Students of the current **generation** have many more opportunities to travel and study in different countries than their parents did.

    2. _____ Although in Canadian society the average age of marriage is 30, each **individual** must decide if he or she will marry and at what age.

3. _____ More and more young people in urban areas are choosing not to buy a car, a **phenomenon** the advertising industry is working to understand.

4. _____ The **interaction** between younger people and older people in the workplace is difficult because their different opinions and values can sometimes cause conflict.

5. _____ There has been a **global** rise in the last 10 years in the number of children that can go to school.

6. _____ Some countries provide high unemployment **benefits** to citizens if they lose their job, while other countries' unemployment benefits are quite low.

Vocabulary Preview: Mid-frequency Vocabulary

Activity C | The definitions of six words are provided below. Read the words and their definitions and choose the correct word for each blank to complete the text that follows. You might have to change the form of the word to fit the sentence.

elderly (adj.): a polite or formal word for people that are old
retirement (n.): the period of your life after you have stopped work at a particular age
gap (n.): a difference that separates people, or their opinions, situation, etc. **or** a space between two things or in the middle of something
contribute (v.): to be one of the causes of something
physical (adj.): connected with a person's body rather than mind
increase (v.): to become or to make something greater in amount, number, value, etc.

The question of when to begin ___retirement___ is a big one for many workers. Generally, they try to find a balance: they have to work long enough to have money to support themselves after they've stopped working. But they also want to be in good _____ health so they can enjoy their time off. The variation in cultural values ___Contributes___ to the variation in retirement practices. In some societies, the ___elderly___ are expected to have earned enough money when they were younger to support themselves after they have finished working. There has been an _____ in the number of people working to a later age to earn enough money for their retirement, as there is often a _____ between how much money they need and how much money they've saved. In other societies, younger people are expected to help with their parents' retirement, either with money or a place to live.

Reading

The following reading, "The Greying of Canada," is an excerpt from *Introduction to Sociology*, a textbook used in some first-year sociology classes at Canadian universities.

Generating Questions

There are several strategies you can use to read more effectively. One of them is generating questions about the text before you read it. Before you read a text straight through, skim it for keywords, headings, photos, and graphics. What interests you about these aspects of the text? What are you curious to learn more about? Write some questions based on your pre-reading. As you read, try to answer these questions. Using these questions to guide your reading will help you read more effectively.

Activity A | "The Greying of Canada" discusses a changing trend in Canada's population. What do you think the word *greying* refers to in this case? With a partner or small group, brainstorm a list of the effects of having a population with more older people than younger people.

Activity B | Skim "The Greying of Canada." Different things may grab your attention as you skim: keywords, headings, photos, graphs, and so on. These things may pique your curiosity and make you want to ask questions. What are you wondering about after skimming this article? Write six 5W + H questions (*who, what, when, where, why, how*), as explained on page 102 in Unit 3

Activity C | Now read the text, keeping your list of six questions beside you as you read. Try to find answers to these questions from the reading. You may not find answers to all your questions. When you are finished, compare your questions and answers with a partner.

READING

The Greying of Canada

1   What does it mean to be **elderly**? Some define it as an issue of **physical** health, while others simply define it by chronological[1] age. The Canadian government, for example, typically classifies people aged 65 years old as elderly, at which point citizens are eligible for federal **benefits** such as Canada Pension Plan and Old Age Security payments. The World Health Organization has no standard, other than noting that 65 years old is the commonly accepted definition in most core nations,[2] but it suggests a cut-off somewhere between 50 and 55 years old for semi-peripheral nations,[3] such as those in Africa (World Health Organization, 2012). CARP (formerly the Canadian Association of Retired Persons, now just known as CARP) no longer has an eligible age of membership because they suggest that people of all ages can begin to plan for their **retirement**. It is interesting to note CARP's name change; by taking the word *retired* out of its name, the organization can broaden its base to any older Canadians, not just retirees. This is especially important now that many people are working to age 70 and beyond.

2   There is an element of social construction, both local and **global**, in the way **individuals** and nations define who is elderly; that is, the shared meaning of the concept of elderly is created through **interactions** among people in society. This is exemplified by the truism[4] that you are only as old as you feel. Demographically, the Canadian population over age 65 **increased** from 5 percent in 1901 (Novak, 1997) to 14.4 percent in 2011. Statistics Canada estimates that by 2051 the percentage will increase to 25.5 percent (Statistics Canada, 2010). This increase has been called "the greying of Canada," a term that describes the **phenomenon** of a larger and larger proportion of the population getting older and older.

3   There are several reasons why Canada is greying so rapidly. One of these is life expectancy: the average number of years a person born today may expect to live. When reviewing Statistics Canada figures that group the elderly by age, it is clear that in Canada, at least, we are living longer. Between 1983 and 2013, the number of elderly citizens over 85 increased by more than 100 percent. In 2013 the number of

---

[1] the number of years a person has lived, as opposed to his or her level of physical, mental, or emotional development

[2] countries with the strongest economic activity

[3] countries whose economies are still developing and are not as strong as the economies of core nations

[4] a statement that is clearly true and does not therefore add anything interesting or important to a discussion

centenarians (those 100 years or older) in Canada was 6900, almost 20 centenarians per 100,000 persons, compared to 11 centenarians per 100,000 persons in 2001 (Statistics Canada, 2013b).

4   Another reason for the greying of Canada is because of the aging of the baby boomers. Nearly a third of the Canadian population was born in the **generation** following World War II (between 1946 and 1964) when Canadian families averaged 3.7 children per family (compared to 1.7 today) (Statistics Canada, 2012a). Baby boomers began to reach the age of 65 in 2011. Finally, the proportion of old to young can be expected to continue to increase because of the below-replacement fertility rate (i.e., the average number of children per woman). A low birth rate[5] **contributes** to the higher percentage of older people in the population.

5   As we noted above, not all Canadians age equally. Most glaring is the difference between men and women; as Figure 5.4 shows, women have longer life expectancies than men. In 2013, there were ninety 65- to 79-year-old men per one hundred 65- to 79-year-old women. However, there were only sixty 80+ year-old men per one hundred 80+ year-old women. Nevertheless, as the graph shows, the sex ratio actually increased over time, indicating that men are closing the **gap** between their life spans and those of women (Statistics Canada, 2013c).

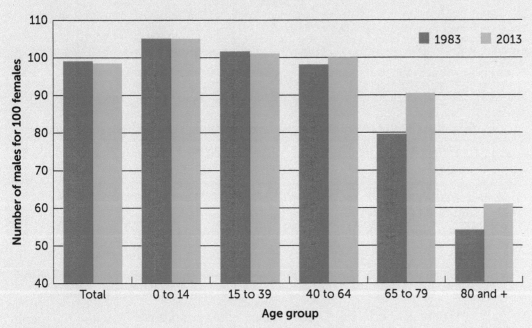

FIGURE 5.4 Sex ratio by age group, 1983 and 2013

This Statistics Canada chart shows that women live significantly longer than men. However, over the past two decades, men have been living longer than they did in the past. (Graph courtesy of Statistics Canada, 2013b.)

---

[5] the number of births every year for every 1000 people in the population of a place

References

Novak, M. (1997). Aging and society: A Canadian perspective (3rd ed.). Scarborough, ON: Nelson.

Statistics Canada. (2010, January). Life expectancy. Statistics Canada Catalogue no. 82-229-X. Retrieved from http://www.statcan.gc.ca/pub/82-229-x/2009001/demo/lif-eng.htm

Statistics Canada. (2012). Portrait of families and living arrangements in Canada: Families, households and marital status, 2011 census of population. Statistics Canada Catalogue no. 98-312-X2011001. Retrieved from http://www12.statcan.gc.ca/censusrecensement/2011/as-sa/98-312-x/98-312-x2011001-eng.pdf

Statistics Canada. (2013a, November 25). Canada's population estimates: Age and sex, 2013. *The Daily*. Retrieved from http://nationtalk.ca/story/canadas-population-estimates-age-and-sex-2013

Statistics Canada. (2013b). Chart 2.3: Sex ratio by age group, 1983 and 2013, Canada. Statistics Canada Catalogue 91-215-X. Retrieved from http://www.statcan.gc.ca/pub/91-215-x/2013002/ct008-eng.htm

World Health Organization. (2012). Definition of an older or elderly person. Retrieved from http://www.who.int/healthinfo/survey/ageingdefnolder/en/index.html

Source: Little, W., & McGivern, R. (2012). *Introduction to sociology* (2nd Canadian ed., pp. 400–402). Retrieved from https://opentextbc.ca/introductiontosociology2ndedition/

Activity D | Discuss the following questions with a partner or small group.

1. Why did the organization called CARP change its name?
2. In your own words, explain one of the reasons why Canada is "greying so rapidly."
3. What are baby boomers and how do they contribute to the aging of the Canadian population?
4. Do you agree with the phrase "you're only as old as you feel"? Why or why not?
5. What do you know about an aging population that you did not know before?

Activity E | Writing Task: Graphic Description | Look at the graph on page 189, and then at the topic sentence and concluding sentence that could be used in a paragraph to describe the graph. To complete the paragraph, choose three good description points that describe the graph well and write two sentences for each. Once you've written your sentences, go back and look at the vocabulary you've used. Try to use some of the key vocabulary from "The Greying of Canada," but make sure your sentences are your own. Use a dictionary for help if you need it.

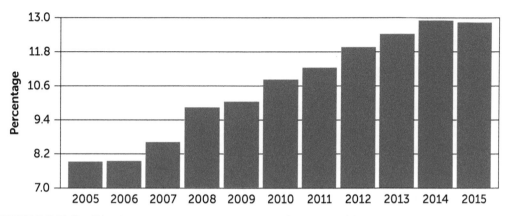

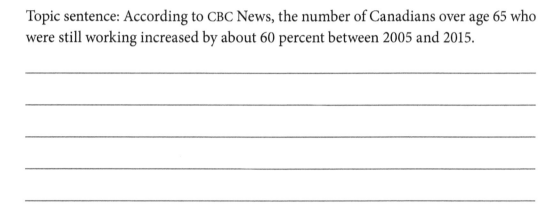

FIGURE 5.5   Employment rate for workers 65 and older

Topic sentence: According to CBC News, the number of Canadians over age 65 who were still working increased by about 60 percent between 2005 and 2015.

_____

_____

_____

_____

_____

Concluding sentence: In conclusion, the number of Canadian senior citizens still working after age 65 has increased greatly since 2005.

Activity F | Compare your sentences with the Unit 5 sample paragraph in Appendix 2 and answer these questions.

1. Is each of your sentences a complete sentence? (Does it have a subject and a conjugated verb?)
2. Does each sentence begin with a capital letter and end with a period?
3. Do your sentences include any new nouns from the reading? Are they used correctly?
4. Do your sentences include any new adjectives from the reading? Are they used correctly?
5. Do your sentences include any new verbs from the reading? Are they used correctly?
6. Have you used any punctuation in your sentences? Did you use it correctly?
7. How do the ideas in the sample sentences compare with the ideas in your sentences?

Differentiating between Fact and Opinion

When you're reading a text for class, it is important to pay close attention to whether you are reading fact or opinion.

Facts are true statements that can be confirmed or checked by finding the source of information. Consider the following statement:

In 2013, the number of centenarians (those 100 years or older) in Canada was 6900.

This is a fact that can be proven by consulting Statistics Canada, the department of the government that gathers statistical data on the Canadian population.

By contrast, consider this statement:

There were no centenarians in Canada in 2013.

If you researched the data to try to prove this statement, you would find that it is not true. Therefore, it is not a true fact.

An opinion is a feeling or belief that a person has. Different people may have different opinions. Consider the following:

The happiest time in a person's life is childhood.

This is an opinion because while some people may believe this, others may disagree. There is no way to prove whether this is true or not. Opinions sometimes include words like *think, feel, believe,* or *should.* It can sometimes be difficult to tell when you are reading an opinion. Sometimes opinions are made to sound like facts. For example, if someone says "All young people must learn to drive," it sounds like a statement that every young person will be forced to learn to drive. However, this is not true; it is simply someone's opinion. It would be more accurate if the person had said, "All young people *should* learn to drive."

PROCESS FUNDAMENTALS

Brainstorming and Outlining

Pyramid of Perspectives

In the *Exploring Ideas* section on pages 170–173, you learned to brainstorm by considering a topic from past, present, and future perspectives. You can also use the pyramid of perspectives to examine a graphic and prepare to write about it. When looking at a graphic, you may prefer to examine it using a different pyramid of perspectives, one that looks at the beginning, middle, and end of the time period covered by the graphic.

Activity A | Look at the graphic below. It shows changes and trends in immigration patterns to Canada. Every year, people immigrate to Canada from around the world. They often speak other languages in addition to English or French. This graphic shows the top ten first languages among immigrants to Canada from 2001 to 2010.

Top 10 spoken languages | The native (first) language of an individual upon entering Canada, 2001 to 2010.

Rank	2001	2002	2003	2004	2005	2006	2007	2008	2009	2010	Rank
1	Mandarin	Mandarin	Mandarin	Mandarin	Mandarin	Mandarin	English	English	English	Tagalog	1
2	English	English	English	English	English	English	Mandarin	Mandarin	Tagalog	Arabic	2
3	Arabic	Arabic	Arabic	Arabic	Arabic	Arabic	Arabic	Arabic	Mandarin	Mandarin	3
4	Urdu	Punjabi	Punjabi	Spanish	Punjabi	Punjabi	Spanish	Tagalog	Arabic	English	4
5	Punjabi	Urdu	Spanish	Punjabi	Spanish	Spanish	Tagalog	Spanish	Spanish	Punjabi	5
6	Tagalog	Tagalog	Urdu	Tagalog	Tagalog	Tagalog	Punjabi	Punjabi	Punjabi	Spanish	6
7	Spanish	Spanish	Tagalog	Urdu	Urdu	Urdu	Urdu	French	French	French	7
8	Russian	Russian	Russian	Russian	Russian	French	French	Urdu	Russian	Russian	8
9	Korean	Korean	Korean	French	French	Russian	Russian	Korean	Urdu	Creole	9
10	Chinese	Farsi	Romanian	Romanian	Gujarati	Korean	Farsi	Russian	Korean	Urdu	10

Imagine you were going to write a paragraph about the changing trends related to the first languages of immigrants to Canada between 2001 and 2010, based on this graphic. Consider the graphic in three different ways, focusing on the beginning, the middle, and then the end. Make notes about each time period in a large pyramid of perspectives diagram like the one below, then share your diagram with a partner. Ask your partner to add one idea to each face of your pyramid.

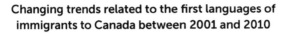

Changing trends related to the first languages of immigrants to Canada between 2001 and 2010

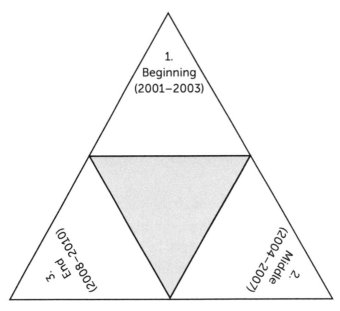

Activity B | Look back at the Unit Inquiry Question you wrote on page 174. Think about where you would find information on this topic in the form of a chart or graph. Using some graphics supplied by your instructor, choose one related to your Unit Inquiry Question. If you have access to the Internet or a library, you may find a different graphic related to your Unit Inquiry Question that you prefer to use. Think about your chosen graphic using the pyramid of perspectives. In a pyramid of perspectives diagram, write your ideas related to the beginning, middle, and end of the time period shown in your graphic.

Outlining

The ideas in your pyramid of perspectives can help you form the structure of your paragraph. Your notes about the beginning, middle, and end may be useful in developing the description points in your graphic-description paragraph.

Activity C | Writing Task: Graphic-Description Paragraph Outline | Create an outline using the template on page 181 for a graphic-descriptive paragraph based on your pyramid of perspectives brainstorm in

Activity B. Which ideas seem most useful to you as you continue to explore your Unit Inquiry Question and the related graphic? As you complete more tasks in this unit, you can use this rough outline to build on more ideas and details to support your topic.

Before You Write

Predicting Vocabulary

Before you go on vacation, you probably think about what you will need, and then pack those things into your suitcase. You should do the same thing before you write: think about what types of things you want to say in your text, then prepare the words and phrases you will need to do that. Asking yourself the following questions will get you started:

- What **nouns** will I need? What people, places, or things am I planning to describe in my paragraph? Sometimes you may know the informal word for something, but you may need to look up the formal word in the dictionary. An example of this is *car* and *vehicle*.
- What **verbs** will I need? What types of actions, movements, or states will I have to describe? What verb tense will I be writing in? What prepositions typically go with the verbs I will be using?
- What **connecting phrases** will I need at the beginning, middle, and end of my paragraph? Do I know what punctuation I need to use with these phrases?

While you're predicting vocabulary, make sure you have a dictionary nearby to look up any words you're not sure about or any collocations you don't know. Also, pay attention to the spelling and punctuation you will need to use with these words.

Activity A | Imagine you are writing a paragraph describing a graph or chart on each of the following topics. With a partner, try to predict five to ten vocabulary words you might need to write each paragraph.

1. the rise in youth unemployment in Europe in the last decade
2. the increasing average age of marriage for American men and women
3. the increase in pet ownership in China
4. the decline in church attendance in Canada
5. the move of more and more South American people from the country to the city (urbanization)

Activity B | Look back at the Unit Inquiry Question you wrote on page 174. Predict approximately 10 to 15 vocabulary words you might need to write about this topic. Write the words below. Then show your words to a partner. Can your partner add any more to your list?

_____   _____   _____

_____   _____   _____

_____   _____   _____

_____   _____   _____

_____   _____   _____

Content Skill

Using Information from a Blog Post

Have you ever read a blog? Maybe you even write one! The word *blog* is a short form of the words *web log.* The first blogs, which appeared in the 1990s, were online journals where people wrote about their personal thoughts and issues. Today, individuals still write blogs, but many news organizations, companies, universities, and political parties have blogs too. Blog posts tend to be more informal than articles you might read in a newspaper. They also include more opinions.

You can use blogs as sources of information for your academic writing, but you have to choose your sources very carefully. You want to be sure you can trust the information you are reading and that it has come from a good source. Does the information you're reading contain facts? Does the information you're reading reference a source such as an encyclopedia or book, a scientist, university, or government? Is the information on the blog supported by scientific studies? Or is it simply someone's opinion?

Activity A | Your instructor will provide you with a list of the most popular blogs in Canada. With a partner, examine the top five blogs on the list. Would you use any of these as sources for your academic writing? Why or why not?

Activity B | Quickly skim the title, blog note, and the blog post entitled "Is Ageism Common in our Health Care System?" on page 195 for answers to the following questions:

1. What type of blog is it from?
2. What is the source of the information presented?
3. Is the information made up of facts or opinions?

Is Ageism Common in Our Health Care System?

Blog note: *Behind the Scenes at the Hospital* is a blog about issues affecting the health care system in Canada.

1   Doctors and nurses like to think they provide equal care to all patients that enter the hospital. However, a recent study found that ageism is quite common in hospitals across Canada. *Ageism* refers to treating people differently because of their age. It was found that young people in Canadian hospitals received better care than older people.

2   According to Ahn et al. (2015), the treatment patients receive in hospital is influenced by their age. In this study, the researchers looked at records of more than 1000 patients. Of those, 167 patients were aged 70 years or older. The researchers noticed that older people came to the hospital with different injuries than younger people. Older people are more likely to be injured by falling. Compared to younger patients, patients over 70 were more likely to experience delays in treatment and older patients were less likely than younger ones to be offered surgery as a treatment. Older patients were much more likely to die while in hospital.

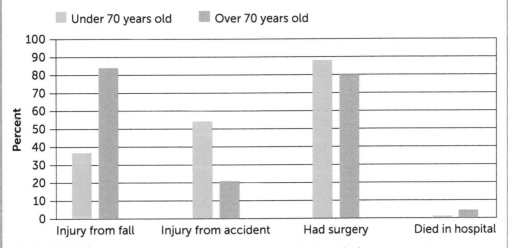

FIGURE 5.6   Older versus younger people in hospital

3   It's hard to know what to do about this problem. As Goldman (2015) put it:

> We need to debunk the many myths about seniors and health care; for example, that the age of the patient makes it more difficult to operate on them. What we need is a huge dose of empathy in health care. [. . .] And, medical schools need to recruit would-be students who love taking care of seniors.

References

Ahn, H., Bailey, C. S., Rivers, C. S., Noonan, V. K., Tsai, E. C., Fourney, D. R., . . . Rick Hansen Spinal Cord Injury Registry Network. (2015). Effect of older age on treatment decisions and outcomes among patients with traumatic spinal cord injury. *Canadian Medical Association Journal, 187*(12), 873–880.

Goldman, B. (2015, June 6). Ageism still rampant in health care. *White Coat, Black Art* [blog]. Retrieved from http://www.cbc.ca/radio/whitecoat/blog/ageism-still-rampant-in-health-scare-1.3139864

 Activity C | Writing Task: Graphic Description | Study Figure 5.6, which accompanies the blog post. Write three sentences to describe it.

1. _____

2. _____

3. _____

Preventing Plagiarism

Acknowledging Your Source

When you use others' ideas or words in your writing, you must say where these ideas or words came from. This is called acknowledging your source.

Each source must be acknowledged in two places. The first is in the text, immediately after the sentence where you include the ideas or words that were taken from another book, article, or website. In academic writing, you must include the author's last name and the year the article, book, or website was published, in parentheses.

Example

There are several reasons the Canadian population is aging. One reason is that life expectancies are longer now than before (Little, 2012).

You must also acknowledge the source of your ideas and words in a reference list. This is a list that is included at the end of your text that shows all the sources you used in your text.

References

Little, W. (2012). *Introduction to sociology* (2nd Canadian ed.). Retrieved from https://opentextbc.ca/introductiontosociology2ndedition/

Paragraphing Skill

Organizing a Paragraph

A strong academic paragraph includes a topic sentence, supporting ideas or description points, detail, and a concluding sentence. It's important to think about how the supporting ideas in your paragraph will be organized. There are several ways to organize the supporting ideas in your paragraph.

Chronological Order (by time)

Start with a discussion of what was happening at the earliest point in time and end with a discussion of what is most recent. Looking at a graphic as having a beginning, middle, and end, as you did in the pyramid of perspectives activity on page 192, may help you organize your description points chronologically.

Activity A | Read the topic sentence and concluding sentence below, along with the three supporting sentences. Number the three supporting sentences to put them in chronological order.

Topic sentence: Many young Canadians move out and live on their own, but more are staying to live with their parents.

Supporting sentence #_____: At the turn of the millennium, more than 50 percent of Canadians in this age group were living with their parents.

Supporting sentence #_____: Fifty-nine percent of Canadians aged 25 to 29 were living with their parents in 2011.

Supporting sentence #_____: In 1981, more than 40 percent of 25- to 29-year-olds lived with their parents.

Concluding sentence: To conclude, more young people in Canada are living with their parents through their twenties.

Order of Importance or Interest

Put the idea that you think is the most important or interesting first. Follow this with the other ideas, ending with the sentence you find least important or interesting.

Activity B | Figure 5.7 on page 198 shows the numbers of men and women who graduated in the fields of science, technology, engineering, mathematics, and computer science in 2011. Read the topic sentence based on the information in this graph. Write three supporting ideas for the topic sentence and order them in terms of importance or interest.

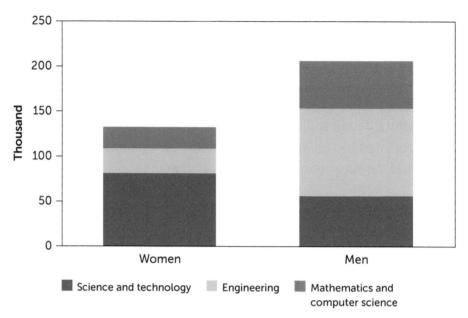

Source: Statistics Canada, National Household Survey, 2011.

FIGURE 5.7   Number of STEM university graduates aged 25 to 35, by sex, 2011

Topic Sentence: There are more men than women who graduated from the STEM fields in Canada in 2011.

Supporting Idea 1	Supporting Idea 2	Supporting Idea 3

Activity C | Share your sentences with a partner and explain why you put the ideas in the order that you did. Do you and your partner agree on which idea you've rated most important or interesting? If not, discuss your reasons.

Keep in mind that whether you choose to organize your paragraph chronologically or in terms of importance or interest, there is not always just one right way to organize a paragraph. Look back at the graph and sample paragraph for Activity A in the *Structure* section on page 175. The paragraph is organized chronologically. The three supporting ideas in the paragraph relate to three different points in time, represented by the red line (2000), the light blue line (2005), and the purple line (2010). The detail for each of these supporting ideas is the description of the different habits of different age groups in each of these years.

However, that paragraph could be structured in a different way. Different age groups can be chosen as the supporting ideas. In that case, the detail for each supporting idea would describe the habits of different age groups in different years, as you can see in the sample graphic-description paragraph in Activity D in the *Structure* section on page 179.

Activity D | Look back at your Unit Inquiry Question. What are some supporting ideas that you might use when you write about it? How will you order those supporting ideas? Will you organize them chronologically (by time) or in order of importance or interest? Once you decide how to organize your paragraph, you might want to add this information to the outline you began on page 192.

Language Skill

Using the Language of Changes and Trends

In academic writing, students and researchers often describe trends in research data. To describe that data, writers use quantifying language, language of approximation, language of comparison, and language of contrast.

Quantifying Language

Quantifying language describes quantities; in other words, how much or many of something there is.

> Seventy percent of youth in Canada own a smartphone.

There are four things to remember about describing percentages:

- If a percentage comes at the beginning of a sentence, write it using words, not numbers.

  Seventy percent of youth in Canada own a smartphone.
  However, 70 percent of youth in Canada own a smartphone.

- To refer to a group using percentages, use *they* for the group. Make sure the verb in your sentence has the correct conjugation for *they*.

  Seventy percent of youth in Canada own a smartphone, and they use it every day.
  Seventy percent of youth in Canada ~~owns~~ a smartphone, and they use it every day.

- Do not use *of* when writing a number and not a percentage.

  Forty thousand ~~of~~ youth own smartphones.

- Use *the majority of* only if the quantity is more than 50 percent.

  The majority of the youth in Canada own a smartphone.

Language of Approximation

The word *approximate* means almost. The following are a variety of words and phrases that can be used to give an approximation rather than providing an exact number.

Almost 40 percent of youth in Canada own a smartphone.
Approximately 40 percent of youth in Canada own a smartphone.
Close to 40 percent of youth in Canada own a smartphone.
Over 40 percent of youth in Canada own a smartphone.
Just under 40 percent of youth in Canada own a smartphone.
Less than 40 percent of youth in Canada own a smartphone.

Activity A | Look back at Figure 5.7 "Number of STEM university graduates aged 25 to 34, by sex, 2011" in the *Organizing a Paragraph* section on page 198. Write two sentences about women using percentages and approximations. Then write two sentences about men using percentages and approximations. You will add more sentences in the next activities, as you continue to build your graphic description. Because the chart doesn't give exact numbers, it is okay in this instance to make an educated guess about percentages based on what you see.

Language of Comparison

In descriptions of trends, you can often compare two or more groups to each other. Use the words *more . . . than* to compare. The placement of the word *more* varies depending on what you are comparing.

1. Comparing numbers of people in a group:

   More men study engineering **than** women study engineering.
   More men study engineering **than** women do.
   More men **than** women study engineering.

2. Comparing verbs or actions:

   In Canada, women drive **more than** men do.
   Younger people use cellphones **more than** senior citizens do.
   Those who live in the city eat in restaurants **more than** people who live in the country do.

3. Comparing the object of a verb or action:

Young people watch **more** TV shows online **than** on television sets.
Students buy **more** books **than** video games.

Activity B | Using the same graph as in Activity A (Figure 5.7), write two sentences comparing men to women.

_____

_____

Language of Contrast

You can also compare groups using two sentences linked by a connector of contrast. You learned about some of these words on page 133 of Unit 4. Phrases such as *however, in contrast,* and *on the other hand* work well for this. Remember to use a comma after the connector.

Over 80 percent of young people own a smartphone. **However,** only 20 percent of older people own a smartphone.
Over 80 percent of young people own a smartphone. **In contrast,** only 20 percent of older people own a smartphone.
Over 80 percent of young people own a smartphone. **On the other hand,** only 20 percent of older people own a smartphone.

Activity C | Look back at Figure 5.7 again and write two pairs of sentences contrasting women and men. Link each pair of sentences with a connector of contrast.

_____

_____

Activity D | Writing Task: Graphic-Description Paragraph | Write a paragraph to describe Figure 5.7 using the four sentences you wrote in Activity A, the two sentences you wrote for Activity B, and the four sentences you wrote for Activity C. These sentences make up the body of your paragraph. You may have to reorder these sentences.

Put the sentences about women together and the sentences about men together. Then add a topic sentence and a concluding sentence to your paragraph. Remember that the concluding sentence should not be exactly the same as the topic sentence. It should conclude or summarize in a different way, focusing on different points. Refer back to page 181 if you need to.

WRITING FUNDAMENTALS

Composition Skill

Asking for Peer Review

Your peers are people like you: your friends or classmates. Peer review, or getting your classmates to review your writing, can be a valuable way to improve your skills. It can be helpful to have someone else read your assignments before you submit them to your instructor.

Here are some ways to make sure your peer review goes smoothly:

- Choose a peer reviewer who will be able to give you useful comments on your writing. A classmate in your writing class will be able to give you more helpful comments than someone whose writing is at a lower level.
- Tell your peer reviewer what you would like him or her to look for. Are you concerned about spelling mistakes? Verb tense errors? Telling peer reviewers what to look for will help them know where to focus their attention.
- Before the peer review session, talk with your reviewer about the difference between error and preference. Errors are mistakes where a rule is being broken and what you've written is incorrect. However, when there is more than one way to say something, and your reviewer likes one way better than the other, that is just a preference. *Yesterday I went to the store* and *I went to the store yesterday* are both correct, although you may prefer one or the other.
- Don't forget that writing isn't just about grammar. Ask your reviewer what they think about the content and ideas of your writing. If you are describing a graphic, is your description accurate? Has your peer reviewer learned anything from reading your text?
- It can be helpful if the reviewer phrases suggestions with the word *I*. For example, saying *I don't understand this paragraph* or *I would use the simple past in this sentence* may be more helpful than saying things like *This sentence is wrong* or *You should do this*.

Activity A | Refer back to a paragraph or other writing activity you have completed for this unit. Following the procedure above, have a friend or classmate carry out a peer review. Meet with your classmate or friend to talk about your text. What were its strengths and weaknesses? What could you do to improve it?

Writing Skill

Achieving Cohesion Using Pronouns

A paragraph is not just a group of separate sentences. The sentences must have a connection to each other in order to give your paragraph meaning. This connection in writing is called *cohesion*.

One way to achieve cohesion in your writing is to use pronouns. They will help you avoid repetition and ensure your sentences flow together properly. The most common pronouns you will use in writing a description of a change or trend are the third person plural pronouns *they* and *them*. *They* is the pronoun used as the subject in a sentence, and *them* is used as the object in a sentence.

Use a pronoun to refer to a group of people in one sentence as in the following.

Older patients were more likely to have surgery to stabilize the spine. **They** were also much more likely to die during their initial stay in hospital.

As Canada's population ages, **our doctors** are spending more of their time with older patients. And according to a troubling new Canadian study, ageism is alive and well among many of **them**.

You can also use the pronoun *this* to refer to a general idea expressed in the previous sentence.

It is interesting to note CARP's name change; by **taking the word *retired* out of its name, the organization can broaden its base to any older Canadians, not just retirees. This** is especially important now that many people are working to age 70 and beyond.

This refers to a general idea: CARP's name change and the fact that by taking the word *retired* out of its name, the organization can broaden its base to any older Canadians, not just retirees.

Activity A | Look at the following pairs of sentences. For each of the pronouns *they*, *them*, or *this*, highlight the group or idea in the first sentence it is referring to.

1. According to a recent market survey, 90 percent of Canadians aged 18 to 34 own a smartphone. However, only 66 percent of them own a video game console.
2. Canadian adults used the Internet approximately 400 minutes per week in 2000. In 2015, they used the Internet more than 1000 minutes per week.
3. More and more Canadians are choosing to access the Internet with their car computer instead of with a smartphone. This is a new phenomenon that has smartphone companies worried.

4. <u>Nineteen percent of adults</u> in Canada are cord cutters. <u>They</u> do not watch cable television and watch shows using the Internet instead.

5. Many Internet users have <u>installed ad blockers</u>. They are software programs that block advertisements when you are surfing the Internet.

Activity B | Read the following pairs of sentences. These sentences do not use pronouns to show cohesion. Substitute *they*, *them*, or *this* into the second sentence in each pair where possible.

1. Many smartphone users must frequently replace their devices. Smartphone users tend to buy a new phone every one to three years.

2. Small screen size is a source of frustration for many smartphone users. The frustration caused by small screen size causes them to move to a computer to do certain tasks.

3. People under 30 are the heaviest users of smartphones. Any parent, teacher, or anyone with friends under 30 will not be surprised by the fact that people under 30 are the heaviest users of smartphones.

4. Canadian senior citizens used an average of three cellphone apps per month. The majority of Canadian senior citizens used apps for banking and surfing the Internet.

Sentence and Grammar Skill

Using Simple Present, Simple Past, and Present Perfect

When describing changes and trends, the most common verb tenses used are simple present and simple past; however, present perfect may also be used.

Simple Present

In Unit 1, you learned about the simple present tense. It is used to describe a habit, routine, or repeated action. In a paragraph describing trends or changes, you use the simple present to describe behaviour that is happening now.

Simple Past

The simple past tense is used to describe actions or states that started and ended at a specific time in the past. When describing changes and trends, you'll often look back at points in the past and describe people's behaviour at that time.

Some verbs have a regular past tense. This means that the past tense is formed by adding an -*ed* to the present tense. Sometimes there are spelling changes:

chang**ed**, increas**ed**, stop**ped**, stud**ied**

Other verbs have an irregular past tense, which means that the past tense is not formed by adding -ed. Often the past tense form is quite different from the present tense.

go → went
become → became
grow → grew
rise → rose
cost → cost

Present Perfect

To describe actions or states that started at a specific point in the past and continue into the present, use the present perfect tense.

The present perfect is formed by combining the auxiliary verb *have/has* with the past participle of a verb. For regular verbs, the past participle is the same as the simple past form.

For 20 years, I **have walked** to work every morning.
Since the 1990s, the percentage of students who complete their schoolwork on a typewriter **has decreased** to zero.

Irregular verbs may have a different form:

The size of cities **has grown** since governments stopped encouraging the agricultural sector.

Time Expressions

Time expressions help indicate whether to use the simple present, simple past, or present perfect. The three lists below contain time expressions associated with the simple present, simple past, and present perfect tenses.

Present	Past	Present Perfect
Now	Then	Since [moment that action began],
Currently,	At that time,	For [duration of time],
Nowadays,*	In [past year or time period],	
Presently,	Before [past year, time period, or event],	
	[duration of time] ago	
	For [duration of time],	

---

* Try not to overuse this word in your academic writing.

Read the following paragraph, which contains some examples of these expressions in context.

The Canadian Broadcasting Corporation

The Canadian Broadcasting Corporation, or CBC, has been the country's public radio and television broadcaster **for more than 70 years. In the 1920s,** radio started to become popular across the country. However, **before the CBC began,** many Canadians listened to American radio stations. **In 1936,** the public broadcaster was born, with CBC providing programming in English, and Radio-Canada in French. **At that time,** radio was more common, but **then** in the 1950s television became popular. **Since the 1950s,** sports have been a big part of the CBC. **For more than 50 years,** from 1952 until 2014, a program called *Hockey Night in Canada* was the most popular sports show in the country. **More than 20 years ago,** the CBC started a website with news, entertainment, and sports. **Presently,** the CBC employs thousands of people across the country, and they **currently** have radio, television, podcasts, apps, streaming, and online programs. Millions of Canadians **now** enjoy the CBC's programming every month.

Notice that *for* can be used with the simple past or the present perfect. If the action started and ended in the past, the simple past is used.

She **studied** biology **for** three years. (from 2010 to 2013)

If the action started in the past but continues in the present, the present perfect is used.

She **has studied** biology **for** three years. (She started three years ago and is still studying biology in the present.)

Activity A | In each of the six sentences in the following chart, highlight the time expression. Then underline the main verb. Decide if the verb is in simple present, simple past, or present perfect form and write the tense beside the sentence. For each sentence, think about why the tense was used. Discuss your answers with a partner.

	Tense
1. Women now live longer than men.	

2. In the early twentieth century, families had large families with multiple children.

3. Families have become much smaller since the early twentieth century.

4. The Canadian Association of Retired People has had a new name for 10 years.

5. The age of retirement in Canada is currently 66.

6. Workers aged 50 in the late 1990s expected to work 13 more years before retirement.

Activity B | The following sentences compare two different time periods. Highlight the time expression used in each sentence. Then fill in the missing verb that best fits in each sentence. Make sure it is in the correct tense.

1. In 1991–92, an undergraduate student in Canada paid an average of $1706 in tuition fees, while an undergraduate now _____ $5772.

2. Currently, 586,101 people _____ in full-time college programs in Canada; however, in 1999 only 436,035 studied in full-time college programs.

3. In the mid-nineties, 17.7 percent of youth aged 18 to 24 attended university, in contrast to today when approximately 26 percent of those in this age group _____ university.

4. For the last 20 years, equal numbers of men and women _____ to university. Today, 56.3 percent of women and 43.7 percent of men _____ to university.

Activity C | Choose some of the writing (either a few sentences or a paragraph) you have done for this unit. For each sentence, determine if you are referring to an action that started and finished in the past, one that started in the past but continues in the present, or one that occurs in the present. Circle the time expressions that indicate this. Look at the verb and make sure it is the correct tense. Have you used the simple present, simple past, and present perfect correctly?

Using Affective Strategies

The word *affective* refers to emotions, such as happiness, sadness, nervousness, anxiety, or excitement. Emotions can affect how you learn. Some emotions, especially positive ones, can help you learn. Negative emotions, on the other hand, can sometimes prevent you from learning.

One affective strategy for language learning is "taking your emotional temperature." This means thinking about your mood and how you feel, especially if you are stressed or anxious. Some learners do this by keeping a language learning journal or discussing their emotions with classmates.

Another affective strategy involves reducing negative emotions such as anxiety about learning. Learning to express yourself in another language can be stressful. Cohen, Weaver, and Li (1998) note that some learners use relaxation techniques such as deep breathing or listening to relaxing music before class or before a stressful exam (as cited in Rossiter, 2003).

Others practise positive self-talk. This means saying encouraging things about yourself, to yourself. For example, instead of saying to yourself, "My writing has so many grammar mistakes!" you could say, "My writing has fewer grammar mistakes than it did last year." It could also involve picturing yourself successfully completing an in-class presentation.

Source: Rossiter, M. J. (2003). The effects of affective strategy training in the ESL classroom. Tesl-Ej, 7(2), 1-20. Retrieved from: http://www.tesl-ej.org/wordpress/issues/volume7/ej26/ej26a2/

UNIT OUTCOME

Writing Assignment: Graphic-Description Paragraph

Write a descriptive paragraph of 150 to 250 words about a graphic that shows changes or trends in society. (Your instructor may give you an alternative length.) You may write about a graphic related to a topic based on your Unit Inquiry Question or related to another topic of your choosing connected to changes or trends in society. You may also choose one of the following topics and search for a related chart or graph:

- How are young Canadians changing the way they commute to work or school?
- What are some trends related to volunteer work in Canada?
- What are some trends in Canadians' frequency of physical exercise?

Use the skills you have developed in this unit to complete the assignment. Follow the steps below to practise each of the new skills you have learned to write a well-developed descriptive paragraph.

1. **Brainstorm and find information**: Do a search for information related to your Unit Inquiry Question. In addition to the readings and other topic-related information in this unit, your information sources may include blog posts, newspaper or magazine articles, or government websites. Choose a graph or chart from one of these sources that is related to your Unit Inquiry Question. Carry out a pyramid of perspectives brainstorming session on the graphic you've chosen. Your notes from the pyramid of perspectives activities on pages 172 and 192 may be helpful.

2. **Outline**: List your topic, your chosen inquiry question and graphic, and the working title of your paragraph.

   Topic: _____

   Inquiry Question/Title of Graphic: _____

   Paragraph Title: _____

   Use the template below to create an outline for your paragraph. Use the notes and outline from the activities you completed on page 192 to help you.

Topic Sentence

Topic sentence that identifies what the paragraph will describe:

Main Body (Descriptive Points)

Descriptive point 1 (plus detail):

Descriptive point 2 (plus detail):

Descriptive point 3 (plus detail):

Concluding Sentence

Concluding sentence to summarize your main points or paraphrase your topic sentence:

3. **Write a first draft**: Write the first draft of your paragraph. Use AWL and mid-frequency vocabulary from this unit if possible.

4. **Self-check**: Wait a day, then check your first draft. Remember to check the following:

- Check that your paragraph has a topic sentence, description points, details, and a concluding sentence.

- Check that you have used connecting phrases of summary or conclusion to lead to your concluding sentence.

- Look at your sentences that describe changes or trends. Have you used the correct language for quantifying, approximating, comparing, and contrasting?

- Check your sentences to make sure they contain facts and not opinions. Replace any opinions with facts.

- Check the verb tenses in your sentences. Have you used the simple present, the simple past, and the present perfect correctly, and with appropriate time markers? Are the simple past forms spelled correctly?

- Check your paragraph for cohesion. Add pronouns or other phrases if necessary.

5. **Revise**: Revise your first draft and write a second draft.

6. **Ask for a peer review**: Exchange paragraphs with a classmate and carry out a peer review for each other. Take note of the changes your classmates suggest.

7. **Compose final draft**: Write a final draft of your paragraph.

8. **Proofread**: Check the final draft of your paragraph for any small errors you may have missed. In particular, look for spelling errors, typos, and punctuation mistakes.

Evaluation: Graphic-Description Paragraph Rubric

Use the following rubric to evaluate your essay. In which areas do you need to improve most?

E = Emerging: frequent difficulty using unit skills; needs a lot more work
D = Developing: some difficulty using unit skills; some improvement still required
S = Satisfactory: able to use unit skills most of the time; meets average expectations for this level
O = Outstanding: exceptional use of unit skills; exceeds expectations for this level

Skill	E	D	S	O
The paragraph has a topic sentence, description points, details, and a concluding sentence that connects to the topic.				
AWL and mid-frequency vocabulary items from this unit are used when appropriate and with few mistakes.				
The paragraph contains correct and accurate language for describing changes and trends.				
The paragraph is organized either chronologically or by importance or interest.				

The text uses connectors of summary and conclusion to link the concluding sentence to the paragraph.			
The paragraph uses pronouns for cohesion.			
There is acknowledgement of the sources of words or ideas used to write the paragraph.			
The paragraph includes correct use of simple present, simple past, and present perfect verb tenses, with correct spelling of past tense and past participle forms and correct use of time expressions.			

Unit Review

Activity A | What do you know about the topic of trends in society that you did not know before you started this unit? Discuss with a partner or small group. Be prepared to report what you learned to the class.

Activity B | Look back at the Unit Inquiry Question you developed at the start of this unit and discuss it with a partner or small group. Then share your answers with the class. Use the following questions to help you:

1. What information did you find in this unit that helped you answer your question?
2. How would you answer your question now?

Activity C | Use the following checklist to review the skills you have learned in this unit. First decide which 10 skills you think are the most important. Circle the number beside each of these 10 skills. If you learned a skill in this unit that isn't listed below, write it in the blank row at the end of the checklist. Then put a check mark in the box beside those points you feel you have learned. Be prepared to discuss your choices with the class.

Self-Assessment Checklist	
☐	1. I can talk about trends in society and the study of sociology based on what I've read in this unit.
☐	2. I can ask about changes and trends in society in developing an inquiry question to guide my learning.

☐	3. I can use connectors of summary and conclusion to lead to my concluding sentence.
☐	4. I can identify Latin and Greek loanwords to help understand the meaning of unfamiliar words.
☐	5. I can use AWL and mid-frequency vocabulary from this unit in my writing.
☐	6. I can make predictions about a text by asking questions before I read.
☐	7. I can tell the difference between fact and opinion when I am reading.
☐	8. I can use the pyramid of perspectives brainstorming technique to generate ideas for my writing.
☐	9. I can prepare myself for writing by predicting vocabulary I might need.
☐	10. I can use blog posts to find appropriate information on an academic topic.
☐	11. I can avoid plagiarism by acknowledging my sources when using others' ideas in my writing.
☐	12. I can organize a paragraph chronologically or in order of importance or interest.
☐	13. I can use appropriate language when writing about quantities, approximations, comparisons, and contrasts.
☐	14. I can carry out a peer review of my work with classmates.
☐	15. I can connect my sentences by using pronouns to create cohesion.
☐	16. I can use the simple present, simple past, and present perfect tenses correctly, using time expressions that signal each tense.
☐	17. I can use affective learning strategies to improve my academic performance.
☐	18. I can write a well-structured graphic-description paragraph that contains a topic sentence, description points, detail, and a concluding sentence.
☐	19.

Activity D | Put a check mark in the box beside the vocabulary items from this unit that you feel confident using in your writing.

Vocabulary Checklist

☐ benefit (n.) AWL

☐ contribute (v.) 2000

☐ elderly (adj.) 2000

☐ gap (n.) 3000

☐ generation (n.) AWL

☐ increase (v./n.) 2000

☐ individual (n.) AWL

☐ interaction (n.) AWL

☐ phenomenon (n.) AWL

☐ retirement (n.) 2000

UNIT 6

Business

Business Practices

EXPLORING IDEAS

Introduction

A job candidate usually has to do an interview before being hired.

Many jobs involve working together with other people in teams.

Activity A | Discuss the following questions with a partner or small group.

1. Have you ever had a job? What is your dream job?

2. Restaurants, retail stores, and law firms are examples of businesses. What other kinds of businesses can you think of? Are there any businesses unique to Canada that you do not see in other parts of the world? Are there any businesses that are common elsewhere that you do not see in Canada?

3. Business practices are the ways people and companies do business. Examples of these practices include holding meetings, conducting interviews, writing a document in teams, and providing customer service. Business practices involve people interacting with each other. This interaction could be between employees, between employees and their supervisors, or between employees and the public. Look at the two photos above. What business practices do you see in these photos? In each photo, what are the people doing and why?

4. How do the business practices shown in the photos compare to the business practices in another country you are familiar with?

5. Would you prefer to start your own business or work for a company? Explain.

Using a Chart

A chart is an example of a graphic organizer that may be used to organize information. A Gantt chart, invented by Henry Gantt, shows the whole plan for a complex group project (http://www.gantt.com/). By recording all the tasks, the people responsible for each task, and when each task should be completed, all members in the group can easily visualize the project plan as a whole. Organizing your projects in this way may help you complete them in a timely manner.

Below is an example of a Gantt chart created by three business students: Alice, Betty, and Chuck.

They are writing a report about dress codes for Canadian business professionals. They have made a plan so that they can work together to complete their report on time. They have made a list of what needs to be done, by whom, and when.

1. Create an inquiry question—Everyone—Saturday, Oct. 7
2. Do research—Everyone (individually)—Sunday, Oct. 8 to Thursday, Oct. 12
3. Discuss research and plan the sections of the report, including three main sections, introduction, and conclusion—Everyone—Friday, Oct. 13
4. Write the sections:
   • first two main sections—Alice—Sunday, Oct. 15 to Wednesday, Oct. 18
   • third main section—Chuck—Sunday, Oct. 15 to Tuesday, Oct. 17
   • introduction and conclusion—Betty and Chuck—Wednesday, Oct. 18 to Friday, Oct. 20
5. Combine all sections including introduction and conclusion into one document—Betty—Saturday, Oct. 21 to Sunday, Oct. 22
6. Proofread the document—Everyone—Monday, Oct. 23
7. Prepare the document for submission—Alice—Tuesday, Oct. 24
8. Submit the document—Alice—Wednesday, Oct. 25

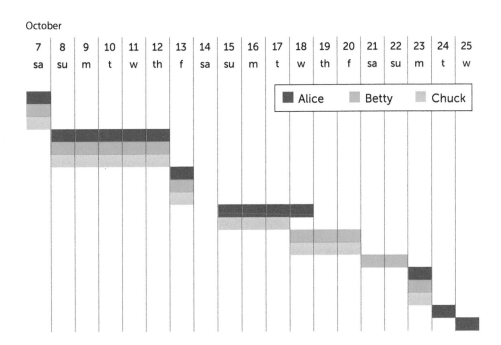

Activity B | Imagine your final assignment in a business class is a group project. Your group must write a report on a topic related to Canadian business, such as procedures related to business communication or meetings.

In a small group, create a Gantt chart to help you organize your project. Discuss how you would plan your project. Which tasks should be completed first? Which tasks should be completed last? Who should do what and when should each task be completed by?

Create a Gantt chart similar to the example on page 217. Be ready to share your plan and Gantt chart with the whole class.

Activity C | Reflect on how your group answered the questions in Activity B. Share your reflections with a partner and then report your ideas to the whole class.

These three questions may help in your reflection:

1. What are the important steps in writing a report?
2. What are some possible difficulties someone might encounter when writing a report?
3. How did you decide who should do which task and when each task should be completed by?

Fostering Inquiry

Inquiring into Business Practices

Inquiring into business practices is an important skill. Business practices in Canada may be different from what you are used to. The process of finding a job and being interviewed for a job may be unfamiliar. As well, the expectations of the employer and co-workers may be new to you. Business practices may differ depending on the industry. Inquiring into business practices will help you learn about business in Canada.

You can begin your inquiry by developing an inquiry question that guides your investigation into business practices. For example, you might be curious about the skills Canadian employers are looking for in employees. If you are already working in Canada, you might wonder why Canadians value a work–life balance. If you would like to work in Canada, you might want to know how many hours Canadians typically work in a day. As you look at information related to your inquiry question, you may come across other topics related to business such as socializing, training, or addressing superiors. As an added benefit of inquiring into business practices, you may also learn more about business practices in other countries.

Activity A | What do you want to know more about in relation to Canadian business practices? For example:

- How do people find employment in Canada?
- What should people do to prepare for a job interview?
- What are some key cultural practices people should know when they participate in an interview?

1. Write two or three questions you are curious about on the topic of Canadian business practices.
2. When you are finished, compare your questions with a partner or small group.
3. Choose one question to be your inquiry question for this unit. It does not have to be the same question as your partner or group.
4. Write your inquiry question in the space provided. Look back at this question as you work through the unit. This is your Unit Inquiry Question.

My Unit Inquiry Question:

_____

_____

_____

Activity B | Writing Task: Freewriting | Write for at least five minutes on the topic of your Unit Inquiry Question. Do not stop writing during this time. After five minutes, read what you have written and circle two or three ideas that you would like to explore further to answer your Unit Inquiry Question.

Structure

Report

Purpose

A report is a type of text written to communicate information in a clear way. The information communicated is usually based on some kind of research. It could be research you've carried out yourself, such as a survey or an experiment in a lab. Some reports communicate research or information from articles written by someone else.

In a report, you often combine information from several different sources. You must understand this information, think about it, and present it in a way that is easy to understand. Reports are not usually about details, but instead focus on the trends in the themes or ideas that are repeated in the research information or data. Sometimes you have to find ideas that are presented in a number of different sources, as opposed to focusing on the details from one particular source of information.

Audience

It is important to know who your intended audience is when you write a report. A report written for a class at college or university may have the instructor or your classmates as the audience. A report produced on the job may have your supervisor or colleagues as an audience.

Activity A | For each of the reports below, identify the purpose and audience. Then compare your ideas with your partner.

1. You are a university student doing an internship at an engineering firm. Your graduate supervisor at the university has asked you to write a report about your internship experience for the students and faculty in your engineering program.

   Purpose: _____

   Audience: _____

2. You work as a lab assistant. As part of a national research study, you do an experiment that tests the water quality of the main river in your city. You have to provide your boss, who is managing the entire research study, with a report on your research.

   Purpose: _____

   Audience: _____

3. Your supervisor has asked you to review your company's website and provide a report on it. Your supervisor wants to know what changes should be made to the website.

   Purpose: _____

   Audience: _____

Structure of a Report

Reports are very common in academic writing, but also in work and business writing. Reports in different areas of study or work may be similar in some ways and different in other ways. A biology lab report is quite different from a report for a business class, for example.

A business report has a minimum of three sections: introduction, findings and discussion, and conclusion.

Title

Introduction
(2–5 sentences long)

Findings and Discussion
(5–7 sentences long)

Conclusion
(2–5 sentences long)

FIGURE 6.1 Business report

Introduction   In this section, give general information about your topic. It is also important to state the purpose or aim of your report. Why are you writing the report? Who is the intended audience? You may also give some background information on this topic, such as past research that has been done in this area. You should aim to write two to five sentences in this section.

Findings and Discussion   The middle section of the report is where you share the major findings of your research. What are the most important ideas and themes from the research? What are the unexpected findings, if any? Summarize these important ideas and themes in your report. After summarizing the findings, discuss why they are important or interesting. This section should contain five to seven sentences.

Conclusion   The conclusion summarizes and interprets your findings. The conclusion should relate directly to the topic of your report and should not include any new information. You may give a "big picture" view as to why your findings are important or unexpected and offer some recommendations or suggestions related to the topic of your report. You may also propose future research. Aim to make this section two to five sentences long.

Note that if you use outside sources in your report, you need to include a references page at the end of your report. There are different ways of formatting your in-text citations and references page. Ask your instructor for advice.

All reports in all disciplines have these three sections, although they may have different names. Other types of reports may have more sections as well.

What a report looks like is as important as the words that it contains. A report must contain a title, headings, and sometimes subheadings. There are two main styles that can be followed. The discussion below is based on APA (American Psychological Association) style.

A report's title describes the topic of the report. It should be centred and not bolded.

Each section in a report has a heading. Headings should be centred and bolded. Some sections, especially the findings and discussion section, may have subheadings that identify major themes. They should be bolded and left-aligned.

All reports in all different disciplines have headings. Some may have more or fewer subheadings.

Review the following example of a report.

Are Soft Skills Outranking Technical Skills?

Introduction

New graduates in Edmonton, Alberta, begin their first jobs equipped with good technical skills. However, a report by Canada West Foundation entitled "Talent Is Not Enough: Closing The Skills Gap" found some new hires lack soft skills, including people skills.

Findings and Discussion

The report found that entry-level employees in the hospitality, logistics, and manufacturing sectors have good technical skills, but lack soft skills, such as communication and interpersonal skills (Harder, Jackson, & Lane, 2014). Employers also noted that initiative and accountability are important skills that some new hires are missing (Harder et al., 2014).

Many employers are willing to invest in training employees in leadership and management skills. However, employers in Edmonton believe new hires should already have soft skills like communication, interpersonal skills, initiative, and accountability when they enter the workforce and that it is not the company's responsibility to invest in this type of training (Harder et al., 2014). Stronger communication between industry and post-secondary institutions is recommended.

Conclusion

The solution to the skills gap facing the Canadian labour market is not simple. To narrow the skills gap, the researchers recommend six pathways, which are detailed in the report. The researchers also claim that as more Albertans retire, the skills gap will widen if it is not addressed in the near future (Harder et al., 2014).

Reference

Harder, C., Jackson, G., & Lane, J. (2014). *Talent is not enough: Closing the skills gap.* Calgary, AB: Canada West Foundation. Retrieved from http://cwf.ca/wp-content/uploads/2015/10/CWF_HCP_TalentNotEnough_Report_SEP2014.pdf

Language Tip

...of Importance

...the sentences and ideas in a paragraph. They help
...flows smoothly and make the connections clear
...connectors of importance to show the order of

> most of all/mostly
> mainly
> (most) especially
> particularly
> generally

...for connectors of importance is at the beginning
...nector of importance is at the beginning of a
...y a comma.

...taking inventory and stocking the warehouse.

...sumé before sending it to human resources.

...osed on the weekend, but faculty members
...tration.

...eager to speak to her supervisor about her

...t below and answer the questions that follow.

...s Shoe Company Online Store

...troduction

...ncreasing numbers and the shoe industry is no
...oe Company started selling footwear online in
...y's website was done in 2013 to make the site
...gnificant changes have happened since. This is
a re... St. John's Shoe Company describing the state
o... ...store and giving recommendations for improvements to the
website based on a survey of 100 customers.

Podcast Response

Amos.

we all spelling → unclear ideas

Instruction:
Followed multistep instructions correctly   1   2   3
(e.g. summarized in own words, posted correct information, +100 words, English name in the Subject line)

Content:
Includes information with a clear overall focus.   1   2   3
(e.g. includes relevant information in summary and opinion)

Language focus:
Use and underline at least one new sentence structure and one new vocabulary collocation   1   2   3

Total: /9

1. Not there yet   2. Meets standard for EAP 135   3. Exceeds standard

Findings and Discussion

One hundred customers were sent a survey, which asked them questions about the St. John's Shoe Company website. The questions asked about the appearance of the site, how easy the site was to use, and if they had any suggestions for improving the site.

Appearance

Generally, the customers surveyed said they liked the appearance of the site. Eighty percent of the customers said the site looked modern and professional.

Ease of Use

Ninety percent of the customers who responded to the survey found the website easy to use. They had no trouble finding the products they needed. Most importantly, they had no trouble making payments. However, some people found it difficult to shop on the site using their phones or tablets.

Conclusion

The majority of the customers who responded to the survey found the company's website well designed and easy to use. We recommend that improvements be made to the site to make it easier to use on small smartphone screens. Investment in the website is necessary if the company wants to continue to grow.

Reference

Wright, E. (2015). *E-commerce in the Canadian footwear industry: A report*. Ottawa, ON: Statistics Canada.

1. What are the purpose and audience of this report?
2. What are the three headings in this report? What are the two subheadings?
3. What two connectors of importance are used in this text?
4. What information is included in the conclusion of this report?

Activity C | Writing Task: Report Introduction | Revisit your Unit Inquiry Question in the *Fostering Inquiry* section on page 219. Write an introduction of two to five sentences for a report on this topic. Before you write, consult one source of information. How can you incorporate ideas from that source into the introduction of a report? To help plan your introduction, reflect on these questions, jotting down notes as you go:

1. Who is the audience for this report?
2. What is the purpose of this report?
3. Where will you find information for your report?

Activity D | Exchange your introduction with a partner. Read your partner's sentences and write down feedback to give to your partner. Use the following questions to help you structure your feedback.

1. Does the writer state the topic of the report?
2. Does the introduction contain the aim or purpose of the report and the audience of the report?
3. Does the introduction include some background information on the topic?
4. Does the writer organize the information using connectors of importance?
5. Does the writer use clear language?
6. Are there any spelling errors?
7. Are there any grammar errors?
8. Does the writer use a variety of sentence structures?
9. Are there any punctuation errors?

Activity E | Revisit your Unit Inquiry Question on page 219. What information or new ideas have you thought of or discussed that will help you answer your question? Share your ideas with a partner or small group. At this point, you may consider revising your Unit Inquiry Question.

ACADEMIC READING

Vocabulary

Vocabulary Skill: Recognizing Collocation

Words do not work alone. They both influence and depend on the words that come before and after them. Certain pairs or groups of words are almost always found together. These common word combinations are called *collocations*.

For example, what word would you use to fill the blank in the following sentence?

She _____ photos with her camera.

The verb *take* collocates with the noun *photo*. You don't *do a photo* or *make a photo*; you *take a photo*. The verb + noun combination [*take* + *photo*] is commonly found together. Note that [*do* + *photo*] and [*make* + *photo*] are not common combinations; in other words, the noun *photo* does not collocate with the verbs *make* or *do*.

When you learn a new vocabulary word, it is important to learn the words it collocates with. A good learner's dictionary, such as the *Oxford Advanced Learner's Dictionary*, will tell you the common collocations of a word. The *Oxford Collocations Dictionary for Students of English* is another helpful resource.

Collocations include more than just verb + noun combinations. See the chart below for the most common types of collocation:

verb + noun	**take** photos
	make observations
	make an argument
	make a decision
	do research
adjective + preposition	(to be) interested **in** something
	(to be) familiar **with** something
	(to be) successful **at** something
verb + preposition	dream **of/about** something or someone
	invest **in** something
	focus **on** something

Activity A | Each of the following sentences has a word missing. First determine which word in the sentence the missing word collocates with. Then guess which word goes in the blank. Check your answers with a dictionary. Some sentences have more than one correct answer.

1. She started her own business to _____ money and to have a more flexible schedule.

2. Before starting a new business, it is important to _____ research on the market.

3. Entrepreneurs are usually good _____ taking risks.

4. When opening a new store, it can be hard to know what to spend money _____.

5. Being a successful student means always _____ your homework.

6. The website is capable _____ handling 10,000 customers per hour.

Vocabulary Preview: The Academic Word List

Activity B | Read the list of definitions on page 227, then the sentences that follow. Match each definition to one of the bolded AWL words in each sentence. The AWL words are taken from the academic reading "Booster Juice: Business in a Blender," on pages 229–230.

Definitions

    a. a part of the economy

    b. to use something, especially fuel, energy, time, or food

    c. something that you can choose to do or have out of two or more possibilities

    d. place

    e. an idea or picture in your imagination

    f. to be an important or necessary part or result of a situation or event

Sentences

1. _____ The **location** of a store is important, as fewer customers will shop there if it's difficult to get to on foot, by transit, or by car.

2. _____ The hotel and restaurant **sector** provides many jobs for Canadians, especially during tourist season.

3. _____ Running your own business successfully **involves** good research, planning and organization, and a lot of hard work.

4. _____ Studies have shown that in many countries, the more money people earn, the more they **consume**.

5. _____ Many new companies started as nothing more than a **vision** in the founder's head.

6. _____ An **alternative** to working a double shift is working until 4:00 PM and then doing overtime from 5:00 to 10:00 PM.

Vocabulary Preview: Mid-frequency Vocabulary

Activity C | Read the words and definitions below, then complete the sentences that follow, choosing the best word to fill each of the blanks. You might have to change the form of the word to fit the sentence.

expertise (n.): expert knowledge or skill in a particular subject, activity, or job

barely (adv.): in a way that almost does not happen or exist

challenge (n): a new or difficult task that tests somebody's ability and skill

recognize (v.): to admit or to be aware that something exists or is true

competitor (n.): a person or an organization that competes against others, especially in business

succeed (v.): to be successful in your job, earning money, power, respect, etc.

For new university or college graduates, moving from the role of student to the role of employee can be a big _____. One difficulty is related to a lack of knowledge. New graduates often have a lot of general knowledge that they've gained in their studies. However, they may not have _____ in specific industries or sectors. Employers must _____ this fact and provide on-the-job training to new employees.

Some new graduates must take low-level jobs that _____ pay their bills.

Having employees of many different ages can help a company _____. Different generations bring different points of view and abilities to a workplace. Newer and older employees in a company are not _____, but rather teammates who must work together and collaborate for success.

Reading

The reading on page 229, "Booster Juice: Business in a Blender," is an excerpt from the textbook *Business Communication: Process and Product*. This textbook is used in commerce and business courses in Canadian universities. The reading tells the story of a Canadian juice company's beginnings and about its current successes.

Using the KWL Method

To help develop your reading skills, you can use the KWL method (Ogle, 1986). KWL stands for **Know–Want to Know–Learned**. Before you begin reading a text, create a KWL chart (like the one below) in your notebook and use it to make notes about the reading topic. Fill in the **K** column in the table by asking yourself *What do I already know about this topic?* To fill in the **W** column, consider if there is anything you noted in the **K** column that you'd like to learn more about. You may also make predictions about what you think you will learn in the reading. Finally, the **L** column can be filled in with notes about what you've learned after you've finished reading the text.

Know	Want to Know	Learned

Source: Ogle, D.M. (1986). K-W-L: A teaching model that develops active reading of expository text. *Reading Teacher* 39: 564-570.

Activity A | This unit's reading is about a Canadian entrepreneur who started a specialized food service company. With a partner, brainstorm a list of what you know about business, starting a company, entrepreneurship, or the food industry. Take notes during your brainstorming session.

Activity B | Using your notes from Activity A above, fill in the **K** column of your KWL chart with the things you know about the topic. Then think about any ideas in the **K** column you'd like to learn more about and add these to the **W** column. Ask yourself what you want to know about entrepreneurship and the food industry. You may also predict what you think you might learn from the text you're about to read. Compare what you've written in the first two columns of your chart with a partner.

Activity C | Now read "Booster Juice: Business in a Blender." As you read, pay attention to whether any of the points you wrote in the **W** column are discussed in the reading. Underline these points if you find them while reading. When you've finished reading, write what you learned about the topic in the **L** column. You may have answered some of the questions in the W column, or you may have learned some completely new information. Circle the ideas you found especially interesting. Compare what you've written in the **L** column with a partner.

READING

Booter Juice: Business in a Blender

1   Not only is Booster Juice in the Guinness World Records for making the world's largest smoothie, the company also claims to be the fastest growing juice bar in all of Canada. Because of the growing trend for healthier food, the juice and smoothie bar **sector** is growing at an annual rate of 30 percent. The fast food sector is growing at a rate of 3 percent. Booster Juice is meeting the need for healthy **alternatives** to fast food.
2   Booster Juice opened its first store in Edmonton in 1999. It has grown to over 170 **locations** worldwide across North America from Victoria to St. John's, and from Los Angeles to New York. Internationally, there are Booster Juice locations in India, Saudi Arabia, the Netherlands, and the United Arab Emirates (UAE).
3   All this began when two university students, Canadian Dale Wishewan and American Jon Amack, met at a school in Oregon. Wishewan, who calls himself "a plain old jock,"[1] was attending school on an athletic scholarship, and he and Amack began discussing trends in the business world.

---

[1] an informal term for someone who plays a lot of sports

4   Wishewan and Amack did not know much about the restaurant or franchise[2] business. They saw their lack of experience as an asset since they wouldn't be restrained by past history. Both were engineers. They had enough business **expertise** to **recognize** that if the juice and smoothie bar market was growing in the United States, it was only a matter of time until it popped open its lid in Canada. They wanted to be the first **involved**. That way, they felt they could grow the business according to the values they believed in. One of their most important beliefs was that quality was more important than profit. They felt this wasn't always the case with US stores. Wishewan believes that the best way to grow a business for the long run is to focus on quality. This is something the store feels proud of achieving.

5   But bringing a concept that was **succeeding** in the United States to Canada had its **challenges**. This wasn't California! How would juices fit into a colder climate? Were Canadians going to be interested in quaffing[3] down such a concept? Wishewan and Amack studied the American model, researched the Canadian market, and tested hundreds of recipes. They knew that what worked in the United States wouldn't necessarily work in Canada. They were determined to create a product suited to the Canadian climate and tempting to the Canadian appetite. They were sustained by their **vision** that Canadians are health-conscious people who want alternatives to the high-sugar, high-fat beverages offered by most fast food chains.

6   Since they began, juice and smoothie bars have quickly become an important segment of Canada's competitive beverage sector. While the fast food segment is growing at **barely** 3 percent each year, juice and smoothie bars are growing at 30 percent. In the US, American juice bar giant Jamba Juice has over 700 stores nationwide and is a healthy contributor in an industry that has already topped $1 billion in the US.

7   In Canada, other juice and smoothie **competitors** are bubbling up everywhere. Jugo Juice, a Calgary-based company, opened its first store in 1998 and continues to grow. Although originally against offering franchises, Jugo Juice joined the franchise competition in 2002 and has grown by more than double, with stores spread from Victoria to Halifax. Another Canadian juice bar company, Euphoria Smoothies, based in North Bay, Ontario, was started in 2004. According to Euphoria, more smoothies are **consumed** per capita in North Bay than anywhere else in Canada. Euphoria Smoothies has licensees in Canada and the United States as well as the United Kingdom, the UAE, and India.

Source: Guffey, M., Rhodes, K., & Rogin, P. (2011). *Business communication: Process and product* (6th Canadian ed., pp. 175–176). Toronto, ON. Nelson.

---

[2] formal permission given by a company to somebody who wants to sell its goods or services in a particular area using that company's name, logo, etc.

[3] drinking a large amount of something quickly

Activity D | Discuss the following questions with a partner or small group.

1. In what ways were the two men who founded Booster Juice not typical businessmen?
2. Why did Wishewan and Amack think Booster Juice would be successful in Canada?
3. What were the challenges of bringing an American business idea to Canada? What did the pair of men do to adapt their idea to the Canadian market?

 Activity E | Writing Task: Conclusion | Write an appropriate conclusion to the Booster Juice reading. Compare your conclusion with a partner.

Activity F | Compare your conclusion with the sample conclusion in Appendix 2. Then exchange your conclusion with a partner and offer feedback, using the following questions to guide you.

1. Does the conclusion summarize the main points or paraphrase the thesis statement?
2. Does the conclusion begin with a concluding paragraph signal word?
3. Does the conclusion relate the topic to the future?
4. Does the conclusion propose ideas for future research, or make suggestions or recommendations for future action?
5. Are there any spelling, grammar, or punctuation errors?

Critical Thinking

Playing the Contrarian

Do you know the expression "to play the contrarian"? It refers to taking the opposite point of view of the person you are speaking with in a discussion or debate. You might not agree with the point of view you are taking. However, it may help make your discussion more interesting and logically stronger.

When reading, writing, or speaking about an academic topic, it's important to play the contrarian. When reading, try to take the opposite point of view of the author. Are there problems with what the author is proposing? Is the author forgetting to mention important information? When having a discussion with someone, the phrase "I see what you mean, but . . ." is one way to understand the point of view of the person you are speaking with and to introduce an opposing point of view. Asking questions from the other point of view will make your academic work stronger.

PROCESS FUNDAMENTALS

Brainstorming and Outlining

Working in Groups

Brainstorming is a technique to generate ideas. Brainstorming can be done individually or in a group. When you brainstorm in a group, it is recommended that you structure the brainstorming session so that all people in the group are given a chance to share their ideas. There are different ways to organize a group brainstorming session. One way to organize a group brainstorming session is described below.

- Nominate a group leader. This person will take charge of the brainstorming session and make sure it is productive and fast moving.
- All group members decide on a topic to brainstorm. For example, one topic related to Canadian business practices that all group members might be interested in learning more about is the process of finding a summer job.
- Once the group members have agreed on a topic to brainstorm, each group member writes his or her ideas on individual sticky notes within a time limit of between 5 and 10 minutes.
- After they have done so, the leader asks the group members for their sticky notes and groups all similar ideas together, with the help of the group.
- Then the leader divides the group into two smaller groups. The smaller groups quietly decide on the best ideas, then the whole group comes back together to discuss what they chose and why. Use the top two or three ideas chosen by each smaller group to develop your writing.

Be sure to keep the brainstorming session moving along. Since you are working in a group, you will generate a lot of ideas. Your goal is to come up with two or three of the best ones to use in your writing.

Activity A | In a small group, discuss the advantages and disadvantages of brainstorming in a group. Write down as many advantages and disadvantages as you can think of in five minutes. Then share your ideas with the whole class. Which group came up with the most ideas? What is each group's top advantage and top disadvantage for brainstorming in a group?

Activity B | What is another way a group brainstorming session can be organized to make sure that it is productive? Reflect on your past brainstorming experiences and write down three different ideas. Then share them with a partner and combine your lists. Cross out any of the same ideas, then share your new list with the whole class.

Activity C | In a small group, try out the group brainstorming process described on page 232, choosing one of the situations below to brainstorm. You may also choose to come up with your own idea related to business practices.

1. You work at your uncle's coffee shop. It is a family business. A large coffee chain moves in across the street. Your uncle is worried he might have to close his business. Brainstorm some ideas to help your uncle respond to this new business challenge.
2. You and your classmates want to be job ready when you graduate from college or university. Brainstorm skills you will need to be successful in business and ways you can learn them.
3. The student union at your university is having a competition for the best entrepreneurial idea that will benefit the greatest number of people on campus. Brainstorm ideas for the competition.

Outlining

Writing an outline is a useful strategy for organizing your report. Here is a sample outline you can use to write your report.

Introduction

Write a sentence describing what your report is about and why that topic is important or interesting.

Findings and Discussion

Sub-theme 1

Write a sentence about one major finding.

Sub-theme 2

Write a sentence about a second major finding.

Conclusion

Write a concluding sentence and a recommendation for the future.

Reference

Include the source or sources of the information discussed in your report.

Activity D | Look back at the introduction you wrote in Activity C on page 224. Review the feedback your partner gave you and revise your introduction to improve it.

Activity E | Now imagine you are going to write the findings and discussion section to follow that introduction. With a partner, brainstorm ideas for each person's findings and discussion section. Using these ideas, write an outline for the findings and discussion section. Use the sample report outline on page 233.

Activity F | Writing Task: Findings and Discussion | Write a first draft of your findings and discussion section. Use the information you and your partner brainstormed in Activity E above. After you have written a first draft, ask your partner to look at it and provide you with feedback on structure, vocabulary, connectors, grammar, and punctuation.

Before You Write

Reflecting on Your Topic

Reflection is responding personally to experiences, new information, ideas, feelings, and beliefs. Reflection involves making connections to what you are learning. As a result, deeper learning takes place, which allows you to make better decisions about what you should do next to achieve your learning goals.

Before you write, you can improve your focus on the topic by reflecting on what you already know about your topic, reflecting on what interests you about the topic, and reflecting on what you want to learn more about in relation to your topic. Then, with a strong focus, you will have a clearer idea of what you need to look for in your sources of information and a better understanding of the arguments presented in the sources.

Spending some time reflecting on your topic before you write may help you discover aspects of your topic that you hadn't considered before.

Activity A | Look back at your Unit Inquiry Question in the *Fostering Inquiry* section on page 219. Spend some time reflecting on the questions below in relation to your Unit Inquiry Question. Take notes, so you can share your ideas with a partner in the next activity.

1. What is your inquiry question?
2. Why did you choose this topic?
3. Why are you interested in this topic?
4. What do you already know about this topic?
5. What do you want to know more about in relation to this topic?
6. How are you going to find out?
7. What assumptions do you have about this topic?

Activity B | Share the ideas you wrote in Activity A with your partner. Your partner may ask you more questions about your Unit Inquiry Question. After your discussion, spend about five minutes writing down the questions your partner asked, along with your answers to them. You may be able to use this information in answering your Unit Inquiry Question.

Content Skill

Using Survey Data and Reports

One research tool is the survey. As you learned in Unit 4, a survey involves asking a number of people the same questions. The answers they give provide data that can be analyzed to find information about that group of people. Survey data is not used to find out information about one particular person, but rather the trends revealed in the responses of the whole group—the big picture.

Surveys are very common and used in many different contexts. Companies give surveys to their customers to discover products they like or ways to improve their customer service. A company may also give a survey to its employees to determine how they like their jobs. Your school, college, or university may give you a survey, often called a course evaluation, to find out about your experience in your classes.

A government may conduct a survey to get information about its population. This particular kind of survey is called a census. The data collected is called demographic information and may include data about habits and behaviours, economic activity, or even voting intention. Statistics Canada is the national agency that administers and publishes survey results and other data from research done on the population. This agency often publishes the results of its surveys in reports.

Activity A | On page 236 is an example of the results of a survey conducted in Canada. People responsible for hiring new employees at large Canadian companies were asked questions about the most important skills they look for in job candidates. The survey asked about the most important skills for two types of candidates: entry-level (workers with less experience looking for low-level jobs) and mid-level (workers with three to eight years' experience looking for jobs above the entry level).

With your partner, look at the information and discuss the results of the survey. First, analyze the results. Look at all the different types of skills and which skills are important for the two types of candidates. What is interesting about these results? Then choose three job skills that you think are worth discussing. For example, is there a job skill on this list that surprises you? Is there a job skill that is important for entry-level candidates, but not for mid-level candidates? Is there a skill that is very important for all candidates?

Write a short summary of the results and be prepared to share it with the class.

FIGURE 6.1   Important skills and capabilities for mid-level and entry-level candidates

Writing Your Own Survey

You may choose to design and carry out a simple survey to gather information for a research project. Keep the following in mind as you do this:

- **Research Question**: It is important to know what big picture research question you are trying to find answers to. The questions on the survey will gather information that will help answer that research question.
- **Survey Questions**: It is important to write the survey questions carefully so that the answers will give you the information you are looking for. It is also important that the questions are written carefully so that people responding to the question won't favour one answer or another. Also, think about what type of answers you want to get. Should you ask yes/no questions or 5W + H questions that will require more detailed answers? Would you like the people responding to your questions to give something a score or rating (e.g., from 1 to 5)?
- **Who to Ask**: What group of people (or population) are you interested in studying? Is it a large group, such as all senior citizens in your city, or all second-year students at your college or university? Perhaps it's a smaller group, such as your class. Once you have determined the population you

want to survey, choose a small number of people that belong to this group to answer your questions; this small group is called a sample.

- **Collecting Responses**: How will you ask your questions and collect people's answers? Will you ask them in person and write their answers on paper? Will you send them an online survey via email? Will you give them the questions on a piece of paper and have them write their answers? Think carefully about the method you will use and how it will affect the answers you will get.

Activity B | Writing Task: Survey | Look back at your Unit Inquiry Question on page 219. Prepare to conduct your own survey to help answer this question. Design a simple survey of 5 to 10 questions. Think carefully about what questions to use, who to ask, and how best to collect their responses.

Activity C | The graph below comes from the same survey of Canadian companies discussed earlier in this section. In this question, employers were asked if they thought recent graduates were prepared for the workforce. The researchers asked about graduates from two types of institutions: colleges and polytechnic schools (which often have shorter programs more closely focused on preparing for a specific job) and universities (which have longer programs, in which students take a wide variety of courses). First, analyze the results. Are there any results that surprise you? If so, which ones? Next, respond to the results of this survey by expressing an opinion. Discuss your opinions with a partner, and be ready to share your ideas with the whole class.

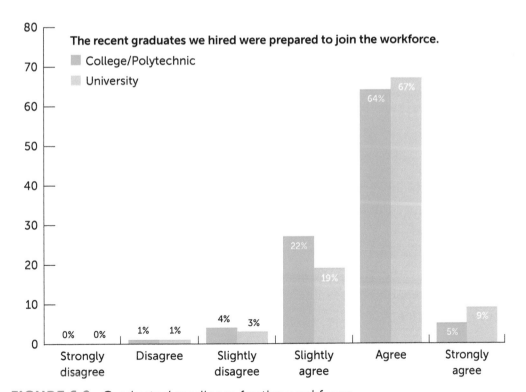

FIGURE 6.2 Graduates' readiness for the workforce

Preventing Plagiarism

Checking against the Original

When you use sources of information such as textbooks, newspaper articles, or websites to support your topic, you must check what you write against the original sources. This is a useful skill that can help you prevent plagiarism in your assignments.

Checking your work against the original will ensure that the ideas and information you use from other sources are accurately paraphrased and properly cited. You must also check that the sources you use are properly referenced and included in your references page at the end of your assignment.

There are different strategies for keeping track of the sources you use for your assignments, which makes it easier when you need to go back and check your work against an original source. You can make a chart and copy and paste the titles of the articles with the correct reference details for each of them. You can also highlight useful ideas with different colours and take notes of the information directly on the articles or in the textbook. You may also consider using bibliographic management software, such as RefWorks, Mendeley, or Zotero. The important thing is to track your sources in a systematic way.

Before you hand in an assignment to your instructor, be sure to check it against the original. You will need to plan for this, so give yourself enough time to double-check your work. You can rest easy if you always make this the last step before submitting your assignment.

Paragraphing Skill

Using Headings and Subheadings

Use headings and subheadings in your reports. Headings and subheadings will help your reader identify the information in your report. Headings and subheadings function like titles—they tell your reader what that section is going to be about—so they should be concise and informative. Headings tend to be made up of nouns or noun phrases, rather than sentences or clauses. Use headings to show the main sections of your report and use subheadings to show points of discussion that relate to your main section.

Activity A | Look at the pairs of headings below. In each pair, which heading—the first or the second—is better? Why? What do you expect to find in each section? Discuss your answers with a partner.

1. a. Findings and Discussion
   b. This is what we think about the findings.

   _____

   _____

2. a. Recommendations
   b. It doesn't work.

   _____

   _____

3. a. Methodology
   b. A system of methods used in an investigation

   _____

   _____

Activity B | Look back at the report about St. John's Shoe Company online store on pages 223–224 and discuss the following questions with a partner.

1. How many headings and subheadings are there?
2. What is the purpose of each?
3. How do they help you read the report?
4. Would you have been able to read and understand the report just as easily if it *did not* have headings and subheadings?

Activity C | Look back at the academic reading "Booster Juice: Business in a Blender" on pages 229–230. The reading does not include headings. Here is a list of possible headings. Where would you put each of them in the academic reading? Discuss your answers with a partner.

- History
- Challenges
- Industry Growth
- A Healthy Alternative
- Founders

Language Skill

Using the Language of Reports

Reports are formal. Many types of reports are considered official documents. Reports are read by a variety of people, including managers, senior employees, and administrators, so the language and the way in which they are written need to be carefully considered. In writing reports, you should avoid contractions, idioms, and colloquial language, use a formal tone or register, and use appropriate reporting verbs.

Avoid Contractions, Idioms, and Colloquial Language

When writing formally, avoid contractions. Contractions are considered informal.

> Informal: The client won't know until the third quarter.
> Formal: The client will not know until the third quarter.

Colloquial language is used in casual conversations. An idiom is a phrase whose meaning cannot be understood by simply knowing the individual words in the phrase. People understand idioms only through hearing and using them many times. When writing formally, avoid colloquial language and idioms because both are considered informal.

> Informal: It turned out that the results didn't matter.
> Formal: The results of the study showed that more research must be done.

> Informal: The new hire took a stab at solving the problem.
> Formal: The new hire attempted to solve the problem.

> Informal: The supervisor cut corners and, as a result, the product was lacking in quality.
> Formal: The supervisor chose the cheapest approach to dealing with the issue and, as a result, the product was lacking in quality.

> Informal: The research team established a game plan to survey groups of IT professionals.
> Formal: The research team established a strategy to achieve their objective of surveying IT professionals.

Use a Formal Register and Tone

Register refers to the use of language and tone, formal or informal. Business writing tends to use a formal tone rather than informal.

In formal business writing, avoid using personal pronouns such as *I, you,* and *we.* Use *the report* or *the findings* or *the recommendations* as the subject of your sentence instead.

Use general nouns such as *researchers* or *clients* or *study participants* rather than *he, she,* or *they.*

Informal: I think that companies should offer better training in this area to new hires

Formal: The recommendation is that companies should offer better training in this area to new hires.

Informal: We put the information in the graph to show the technical aspects of the research.

Formal: The graphs illustrate the technical aspects of the research.

Informal: She says the findings are unexpected and significant.

Formal: The researcher claims that the findings are unexpected and significant.

Use Reporting Verbs

In a report, you might need to make reference to studies done by other researchers. A reporting verb is used to refer to studies done by other people.

In his report based on the latest survey, Macdonald (2016) **discusses** gift giving in the Canadian workplace.

Macdonald (2016) **recommends** observing senior employees' business habits.

Note the following reporting verbs; each has its own meaning and use.

Purpose	Examples
to present facts	find
	report
	discuss
to make a suggestion	recommend
	propose
	suggest
to show agreement/disagreement	agree
	disagree
	challenge

Activity A | Read the sentences below. Each sentence contains an idiom, a group of words that has a particular meaning. An example of an idiom is "barking up the wrong tree," which means looking for something in the wrong place. Replace the idiom with a word from the list. It may be necessary to make other changes to the sentence to make the new word fit. Discuss your answers with a partner.

agree   key   estimate   efficiently   effectively   wait

1. The research team reported that they would <u>kill time</u> until the results of the main study came in.
2. The clients applauded the organization for operating <u>like a well-oiled machine</u>.
3. Macdonald (2016) and Tanaka (2015) <u>are on the same wave length</u>.
4. The research team was unsure of the total budget, but gave a <u>ballpark figure</u> of $50,000.
5. <u>The bottom line</u> to learning how to manage interpersonal communication in the workplace is careful observation of those around you.

WRITING FUNDAMENTALS

Composition Skill

Incorporating Feedback

If you submit a piece of your writing to your instructor or participate in a peer review session, you may receive a lot of feedback, including comments or suggestions on how to improve your writing. This feedback might focus on spelling, grammar, vocabulary, sentence structure, paragraph organization, or other aspects of your writing. It might also be related to your topic or ideas and how they are structured.

Your instructor's and classmates' comments can be useful in improving your writing. Use the notes below to help you incorporate this feedback into a revised draft.

- Read every mark, symbol, or comment that is written on your text.
- Some marks, symbols, or comments will refer to one thing: a word or punctuation mark. It could be a misspelled word, missing or incorrect punctuation, or the wrong word or verb tense. Usually this can be fixed by changing a single word or punctuation mark.
- Sometimes the same mistake is made many times. Your instructor or classmate may mark this mistake the first time it happens in a text, but not every time. For each type of error, you should read the rest of your text carefully to make sure you don't repeat the mistake.
- Some comments will refer to a whole sentence. For example, if you have written an incomplete or run-on sentence, you may have to change several words to incorporate this feedback.
- Some feedback may be about structure and organization. You may have to move sentences or put them in a new order.
- Sometimes feedback may be global. This means that it concerns the whole text or your writing in general. Read these comments and reflect on them. You will have to decide how they connect to your writing.

When you have finished incorporating feedback, read your text again to make sure it sounds good to you. You may even try reading it aloud.

Activity A | Refer to the feedback you received on your introduction in Activities C and D on page 224. Follow the steps above to incorporate the feedback you were given. Based on that feedback, jot down three things you would like to focus on in your final writing assignment for this unit.

Writing Skill

Varying Sentence Structure

Using a variety of sentence structures will prevent your writing from being boring. It can make your writing more interesting to the reader. Varying the length and structure of your sentences is one way to get and keep your reader's attention. Discussed on page 244 are three grammatical considerations to add variety to your writing.

Simple, Compound, and Complex Sentences

In Unit 3, you learned about three types of sentences that can be used to add variety to your writing. You learned the punctuation rules for these structures and how important commas are in compound and complex sentences.

Types of Sentence Structure

Simple—one independent clause:

Gabriela has owned a bakery in downtown Halifax for 15 years.

Compound—two independent clauses connected by a coordinating conjunction (CC).

Gabriela owns a bakery in downtown Halifax **and** her brother works there on weekends.
     independent clause   *CC*   *independent clause*

Complex—one dependent clause and one independent clause, connected by a subordinating conjunction (SC).

1. Gabriela employs 15 workers **because** her bakery is very successful.
     independent clause   *SC*   *dependent clause*

2. **Because** Gabriela's bakery is very successful, she employs 15 workers.
    SC   *dependent clause*   *independent clause*

Notice that when the SC begins the sentence, a comma is placed after the dependent clause.

Conjunctive Adverbs

Conjunctive adverbs can help ideas flow by connecting one sentence to the next. You've learned about many of these connectors in the previous units. Examples of conjunctive adverbs are *furthermore, however, in addition, in contrast, similarly,* and *next*. They can be used to show sequence, location, additional information, or order of importance. Connectors can also signal a summary or conclusion.

Conjunctive Adverb	Function	Example
Similarly,	to give additional information	Gabriela owns a bakery. **Similarly,** her brother owns a café.
However,	to contrast	Gabriela's bakery serves a variety of cakes, pastries, breads, and coffee. **However,** it does not serve hot meals.
There,	to signal location	Gabriela's bakery is located in Halifax. **There,** 15 employees serve hundreds of customers each day.

For example,	to give an example	Gabriela's bakery is very successful. **For example,** her cakes have won several awards.
Next,	to show sequence	Gabriela opened her bakery 15 years ago. **Next,** she hopes to start a delivery service for her cakes.
(Most) importantly,	to show importance	Gabriela had to keep many things in mind when she started her company. **Most importantly,** she had to follow the government's health and safety regulations.
To summarize,	to signal a conclusion	**To summarize,** Gabriela owns a successful small business that the community enjoys.

The conjunctive adverb often comes at the beginning of a simple, compound, or complex sentence. Remember that if you put the conjunctive adverb at the beginning of the sentence, you must use a comma after the conjunctive adverb.

Introductory Phrases

Introductory phrases add extra information about time, place, mood, or manner to the beginning of a sentence. One type of introductory phrase begins with a preposition and is called a prepositional phrase. The prepositional phrase is followed by a comma.

> Time: **At the job interview,** Oksana answered questions about her qualifications and work experience.
> Place: **In the laboratory,** Jakob is responsible for cleaning and preparing all lab equipment.
> Mood or manner: **With a smile on his face,** Ali arrived at the office.

If a sentence contains a prepositional phrase at the end, it can be moved to the beginning of the sentence to make it an introductory phrase. Notice that it's followed by a comma.

> Duration: Gabriela has owned a bakery in Halifax **for 15 years.**
> **For 15 years,** Gabriela has owned a bakery in downtown Halifax.

Activity A | Compare the paragraphs below. Which is more interesting? Why? Discuss your ideas with your partner.

Paragraph 1

My first job was babysitting little kids. My family moved to a new community. I was 13 years old. There were a lot of young families. The families had little kids. I was the only teenager on my street. I babysat the little kids several times a week. I babysat for almost five years. It was a good job. I played with the kids, watched TV, and did my homework. I also made some money. I learned a lot while doing this job. I applied what I learned while babysitting to my next job. This was my first job.

Paragraph 2

When I was 13 years old, I got my first job. My family moved to a new community, where there were a lot of young families with little kids. On my street, I was the only teenager. Therefore, I babysat the little kids several times a week for almost five years. It was a good job because I got to do a lot of the same things I would do at home, such as watch TV and do my homework, but I also made money while doing it. I learned a lot while doing this job. Later, I applied what I had learned while babysitting to other jobs. It has been interesting for me to see the kids I babysat grow up. I have fond memories of my first job.

Activity B | Read the paragraphs in Activity A again. Notice how the writer combined sentences and ideas in the second paragraph. Underline three examples of compound or complex sentences and discuss with a partner how the writer combined them. Notice that the writer added some information at the end of the paragraph. What kind of sentence is the final sentence?

Activity C | Read paragraph 1 on page 247. There is not a lot of variety in the sentences in this text. Paragraph 2 is an improved version of this text. It has varying sentence types and grammatical structures. However, there are some phrases missing. Find the phrases from paragraph 1 and fill in the blanks in paragraph 2. The first one has been done for you as an example.

Paragraph 1

I still remember my first job interview in English. It was several years ago. I wanted to prepare for the interview. I studied the company's website. I thought about the questions they would ask me. I talked to a friend who worked at the company. I practised talking about myself and my work experience in English. I arrived early on the day of the interview. The interview went very well. I was well prepared. I answered every question. They called and offered me the job!

Paragraph 2

Although it was several years ago, _____ *I still remember my first job interview in English* _____.
I wanted to prepare for the interview, **so** _____
_____. I thought about the questions they would
ask me **and** _____.
Then I practised talking about myself and my work experience in English. **On the day of the interview,** _____.
The interview went very well **because** _____
_____. I answered every question. **Afterwards,**
_____!

Activity D | Think about the first time you did something (e.g., the first time you got a job, the first time you volunteered, or the first time you travelled to a different country). How old were you? How did you feel? What are some things that went well or went wrong?

In a short paragraph, write about your experience. You may need to start by writing a draft similar to paragraph 1 first, then vary your sentence structure in a second draft. Connect some of your sentences with conjunctions or add more information to some sentences to indicates time, place, mood, or manner.

Exchange your second draft with a partner and check your partner's sentences. You can use the checklist below to help you give your partner feedback:

- Do the simple sentences include at least one subject and one verb?
- Find the compound sentences. Identify the coordinating conjunction used in each. Do the compound sentences include two independent clauses?
- Find the complex sentences. Do the complex sentences include subordinating conjunctions?
- Find the introductory phrases. Has your partner remembered to put a comma after each introductory phrase?
- Are the sentences written in a logical order?

Sentence and Grammar Skill

Using Noun Phrases

A noun phrase includes a noun and a modifier. Modifiers describe the meaning of a noun.

Modifiers can be adjectives or determiners. They come before the noun.

Adjectives	Determiners
friendly doctors	those factory workers
reliable colleagues	my teacher

Modifiers can also be more complex and generally go after the noun. Three common types of modifiers are listed in the table below, along with example sentences.

Type of Modifier	Examples
prepositional phrase	The factory in the middle of the city will close next month.
	John is an expert in the field of software engineering.
participial (-ing) adjective	The factory worker wearing the blue overalls rides his bike to work every day.
	The cakes baking in the kitchen made the whole restaurant smell wonderful.
adjective clause	The factory where I used to work was demolished.
	The workers who were laid off have entered training programs designed to help them integrate into the new economy.

Activity A | Underline the noun phrase in each of the following sentences. Then highlight the modifier for each noun and identify its type (determiner, adjective, prepositional phrase, participial adjective, or adjective clause).

1. These safety goggles are old.
2. Our manager works late every day.
3. The broken computer in the hallway will be recycled for parts.
4. I accidentally spilled my coffee on the resumés on the desk.
5. Rising housing prices make it difficult for students to live in the city.

Activity B | Unscramble these phrases to make a complete sentence. Underline the noun phrases in each sentence. Compare your answers with a partner.

1. is closing / The old doughnut shop / is moving in / because / one of the big doughnut franchises

   _____

2. for his expertise / in industrial design / They hired him

   _____

3. by herself / Her co-worker / every day / eats lunch

   _____

4. Kathy sold / and bought a fast food franchise / her failing shoe store / in the mall

   _____

5. to 3:00 PM / which was scheduled for 2:00 PM, / has been moved / The meeting,

   _____

Learning Strategy

Using Social Learning Strategies

Social learning strategies involve concentrating not only on the information you are trying to learn, but also on other people at the same time: your classmates, instructors, or other users of the language you are learning. Oxford (1990) suggests social learning strategies such as asking your classmates or instructors questions or asking for help with a language task. Studying in groups or doing homework or assignments together are also social learning strategies.

Focusing on the people and culture associated with the language you are learning could also help you. A user of the language you are learning (whose learning is more advanced than yours) can be a great resource. One idea is to meet with that person for conversation practice and to ask questions about the language and how it is used in real-life situations. He or she may also share information about culture such as music, books, or films associated with the language.

Source: Oxford, R. L. (1990). *Language learning strategies: What every teacher should know.* Boston, MA: Heinle & Heinle.

UNIT OUTCOME

Writing Assignment: Report

Write a report of 150 to 250 words on a topic related to Canadian business practices. (Your instructor may give you an alternative length.) You may write on a topic based on your Unit Inquiry Question, develop another topic of your choosing connected to Canadian business, or choose one of the following topics:

- What courses at Canadian colleges and universities prepare students for the business world?
- Other than technical skills, what do employers desire in their new employees?
- What kind of training beyond a university or college degree do employers recommend for new hires, and why?

Use the skills you have developed in this unit to complete the assignment. Follow the steps below to practise each of the new skills you have learned to write a well-developed report.

1. **Brainstorm and find information**: To brainstorm ideas for your paragraph, look at your notes from Activity B in the *Fostering Inquiry* section page 219. If necessary, do a group brainstorming session with some classmates about your Unit Inquiry Question or spend some time reflecting on your topic to generate more ideas.

   Then do a search for information related to your Unit Inquiry Question. In addition to the readings and other topic-related information in this unit, your information sources may include a report on survey data, a blog post, a newspaper or magazine article, or a website. You may also consider carrying out your own survey.

2. **Outline**: List your topic, your chosen inquiry question, and the working title of your report.

   Topic: _____

   Inquiry Question: _____

   Paragraph Title: _____

   Use the template on page 251 to create an outline for your report. See the outline on page 233 for more detail about the body of the report.

Introduction

Topic sentence (describing what your report is about and why that topic is important or interesting):

Findings and Discussion

Major finding 1:

Major finding 2:

Conclusion

Concluding sentence and a recommendation for the future:

References

Your source or sources of information for your report:

3. **Write a first draft**: Write the first draft of your report. Use AWL and mid-frequency vocabulary from this unit if possible.

4. **Self-check**: Wait a day, then check your first draft. Remember to check the following:

   - Check that your report has a title, an introduction, findings and discussion, and a conclusion. Does your report have headings and subheadings?

   - Look carefully at the language in your report. Have you used formal language and avoided idioms and colloquial language? Have you used reporting verbs correctly?

   - Have you used connecting phrases of importance to emphasize certain ideas?

   - Check for noun phrases in your report. When you have used noun phrases, do they include a modifier?

   - Have you used a variety of sentence structures? Do some of your sentences contain conjunctive adverbs or introductory phrases? Have you punctuated these correctly?

5. **Revise:** Revise your first draft and write a second draft.

6. **Ask for a peer review**: Carry out a peer review of your report with a classmate. Take note of the changes your classmates suggest.

7. **Compose final draft**: Write a final draft of your report.

8. **Proofread**: Check the final draft of your report for any small errors you may have missed. In particular, look for spelling errors, typos, and punctuation mistakes.

Evaluation: Report Rubric

Use the following rubric to evaluate your essay. In which areas do you need to improve most?

E = **Emerging**: frequent difficulty using unit skills; needs a lot more work
D = **Developing**: some difficulty using unit skills; some improvement still required
S = **Satisfactory**: able to use unit skills most of the time; meets average expectations for this level
O = **Outstanding**: exceptional use of unit skills; exceeds expectations for this level

Skill	E	D	S	O
The introduction and conclusion of my report are connected.				
The text has effective use of connectors of importance to emphasize ideas.				
Headings are centred and bolded and subheadings are left-aligned and bolded.				
The paragraph includes varied sentence types and grammatical structures.				
The report contains well-structured noun phrases, and modifiers are used accurately.				
The tone is formal and contractions, idioms, and colloquialisms are avoided.				
Appropriate reporting verbs are used to refer to other people's findings.				
If included, collocations are accurate.				

Unit Review

Activity A | What do you know about the topic of Canadian business practices that you did not know before you started this unit? Discuss with a partner or small group. Be prepared to report what you learned to the class.

Activity B | Look back at the Unit Inquiry Question you developed at the start of this unit and discuss it with a partner or small group. Then share your answers with the class. Use the following questions to help you:

1. What information did you find in this unit that helped you answer your question?
2. How would you answer your question now?

Activity C | Use the following checklist to review the skills you have learned in this unit. First decide which 10 skills you think are the most important. Circle the number beside each of these 10 skills. If you learned a skill in this unit that isn't listed below, write it in the blank row at the end of the checklist. Then put a check mark in the box beside those points you feel you have learned. Be prepared to discuss your choices with the class.

	Self-Assessment Checklist
☐	1. I can talk about Canadian business practices based on what I've learned in this unit.
☐	2. I can develop an inquiry question to guide my learning in a unit of study.
☐	3. I can correctly use connectors of importance in a report.
☐	4. I can recognize collocations in my reading and use them in my writing.
☐	5. I can use AWL and mid-frequency vocabulary from this unit in my writing.
☐	6. I can use the KWL method to help myself engage with a text.
☐	7. I can play the contrarian to help inquire into a writing topic.
☐	8. I can work in a group to generate ideas for a writing topic.
☐	9. I can reflect on my topic before beginning to write a report.

☐	10. I can use survey data and information from reports in my writing.
☐	11. I can avoid plagiarism by checking my writing against the original source of information.
☐	12. I can identify the difference between a heading and subheading in a report.
☐	13. I can use the language of reports and ensure a formal tone in my writing.
☐	14. I can incorporate feedback from others to improve my writing.
☐	15. I can use varied sentence and grammatical structures.
☐	16. I can use noun phrases correctly in my writing.
☐	17. I can apply social learning strategies to help me with my academic skills.
☐	18. I can write a well-structured report that contains a title, introduction, findings and discussion, conclusion, and references.
☐	19.

Activity D | Put a check mark in the box beside the vocabulary items from this unit that you feel confident using in your writing.

Vocabulary Checklist

☐	alternative (adj.) AWL	☐	involve (v.) AWL
☐	barely (adv.) 2000	☐	location (n.) AWL
☐	challenge (n.) 2000	☐	recognize (v.) 2000
☐	competitor (n.) 3000	☐	sector (n.) AWL
☐	consume (v.) AWL	☐	succeed (v.) 3000
☐	expertise (n.) 4000	☐	vision (n.) AWL

Appendix 1: Vocabulary

Unit 1

AWL Vocabulary

eventually (adv.)
expand (v.)
intense (adj.)
mature (adj.)
release (v.)
source (n.)

Mid-frequency Vocabulary

attractive (adj.)
destructive (adj.)
extreme (adj.)
peak (n.)
rapidly (adv.)
surrounding (adj.)

Unit 2

AWL Vocabulary

capable (adj.)
conceive (v.)
device (n.)
indicate (v.)
version (n.)
visible (adj.)

Mid-frequency Vocabulary

endeavour (n.)
explorer (n.)
launch (n./v.)
planet (n.)
telescope (n.)
universe (n.)

Unit 3

AWL Vocabulary

construct (v.)
route (n.)
similar (adj.)
structure (n)
transportation (n.)
vehicle (n.)

Mid-frequency Vocabulary

compact (v.)
develop (v.)
extend (v.)
obstacle (n.)
path (n.)
slope (n.)

Unit 4

AWL Vocabulary

achievement (n.)
controversy (n.)
perceive (v.)
rely (v.)
significant (adj.)
status (n.)

Mid-frequency Vocabulary

athlete (n.)
banned (adj.)
championship (n.)
hero (n.)
scandalous (adj.)
substance (n.)

Unit 5

AWL Vocabulary

benefit (n.)
generation (n.)
global (adj.)
individual (n.)
interaction (n.)
phenomenon (n.)

Mid-frequency Vocabulary

contribute (v.)
elderly (adj.)
gap (n.)
increase (v.)
physical (adj.)
retirement (n.)

Unit 6

AWL Vocabulary

alternative (adj.)
consume (v.)
involve (v.)
location (n.)
sector (n.)
vision (n.)

Mid-frequency Vocabulary

barely (adv.)
challenge (n.)
competitor (n.)
expertise (n.)
recognize (v.)
succeed (v.)

Appendix 2: Sample Writing

Unit 1

Three Stages of a Thunderstorm

Stage 1

Warm air rises quickly.
The sun heats the ground and convection begins.
A cold front makes cumulus clouds.

Stage 2

Water droplets move and hit each other inside the cloud.
Rain makes the air cool and pulls it down.
Electricity in the cloud causes lightning.

Stage 3

The updraft stops.
It rains until there is no more moisture left in the cloud.

Unit 2

Descriptive Sentences

1. snowmobile:
   a. The snowmobile driver **explores** the snowy mountain.
   b. The snowmobile driver flies over the snow.
   c. The snowmobile carries the driver over the packed snow.
   d. The snowmobile makes a whirring noise as it lifts off the ground.

2. walkie-talkies:
   a. The small black and white walkie-talkies look like toys.
   b. The black and white walkie-talkies are handy **devices**.
   c. The cute, pocket-sized, Canadian-made walkie-talkies run on batteries.
   d. The flashing light on the oval walkie-talkies **indicates** that a call is coming in.

3. Uno Cycle:
   a. The Uno Cycle looks like a high-tech unicycle.
   b. The shiny, red, aerodynamic Uno Cycle is as fast as a **launched** rocket.
   c. The Uno Cycle at top speed looks like a bright red bullet.
   d. The shiny, red, orange, and black Uno Cycle balances on one wheel.

4. caulking gun:
   a. The man carefully squeezes the silver steel trigger of the caulking gun.
   b. Like toothpaste squeezed from the tube, a perfect line of caulk oozes from the nozzle.
   c. The man dabs the white caulk so that none is **visible**.
   d. The caulking gun trigger gives off a short, sharp, shooting noise when released.

5. snow blower:
   a. The compact snow blower is approximately two feet tall.
   b. In freezing cold temperatures, the mighty snow blower is **capable** of removing snow in minutes.
   c. The red snow blower clears a path through the snow.
   d. The expensive, quiet, red snow blower blows snow through the chute.

Unit 3

What Is a Bridge?

1. Bridges provide a way for cars and people to move over water, roads, or other objects.
2. Fixed bridges do not have parts that move, while movable bridges can move to let boats pass.
3. The superstructure of a bridge is the top part where the people and vehicles move across.
4. The substructure of a bridge connects the top of the bridge with the ground.
5. There are five types of bridges.
6. The five types of bridges are beam, truss, arch, cantilever, and suspension.
7. The different bridges have different shapes, but they all move people and vehicles across a river or other space.

Unit 4

Fair or Not?

In my opinion, Ben Johnson should not have been stripped of his gold medal at the Seoul Olympics. First, Ben Johnson came in first place. Whether or not he took steroids, he still won gold. Regardless of the results of the drug test after his victory, he still ran the 100 metres in under 10 seconds. In fact, he set a world record time of 9.79 seconds. Second, although steroids were found in his urine, the results of his drug test were announced three days after he was awarded the gold medal. We don't know for sure when the drugs were taken. Ben Johnson could have taken the steroids weeks before the Seoul Olympics, so the substance might not have enhanced his performance. Third, sports fans love scandalous stories, and Ben Johnson was just unlucky that the media picked up his story. If he was actually taking these drugs, everyone would have known and he would not have been allowed to compete in the Olympics. In summary, I believe Ben Johnson was unfairly stripped of his gold medal.

Unit 5

Employment Rate Trends for Workers 65 and Older

Topic sentence: According to CBC News, the number of Canadians over age 65 who were still working increased by about 60 percent between 2005 and 2015.

In 2005, approximately 8 percent of senior citizens were employed. Similarly, in 2006, around 8 percent of Canadians over 65 had jobs. By 2010, that number increased to just over 10.6 percent. In 2011, it rose slightly higher than that. The employment rate for workers aged 65 and older was at its peak in 2014. It went down just slightly in 2015, when it was just below 13 percent.

Concluding sentence: In conclusion, the number of Canadian senior citizens still working after age 65 has increased greatly since 2005.

Unit 6

Booster Juice: Business in a Blender

Concluding paragraph: In conclusion, the juice and smoothie business continues to grow in Canada and around the world. Booster Juice has been satisfying the taste buds of health-conscious Canadian and international consumers alike since the late 90s. Following behind the popularity of Booster Juice, other Canadian juice and smoothie businesses have also opened stores in Canada and internationally. With the continued trend for a healthier life style and healthier food options, there is no stopping the juice and smoothie bar business from continuing to grow in the future.

Credits

Literary Credits

Dictionary definitions in *Academic Inquiry* were taken or adapted from Oxford Advanced Learner's Dictionary 8th Edition by. A.S. Hornby © 2010 Oxford University Press and Oxford Online Learner's Dictionary © 2017 Oxford University Press (http://www.oxfordlearnersdictionaries.com/us). Reproduced by permission.

4 Watt, J., & Colyer, J. (2014). *IQ: a practical guide to inquiry-based learning.* Don Mills, Ontario: Oxford University Press; 14 Excerpted from Science Power 10, Atlantic Edition. (2000). Toronto: McGraw-Hill Ryerson; 21 Adapted from: http://www.universetoday.com/85349/how-does-fog-form/; 24 Adapted from Science Power 10, Atlantic Edition. (2000). Toronto: McGraw-Hill Ryerson, pp.507-509; 36 Canadian Association of University Teachers. (2015). 2014–2015 CAUT almanac of post-secondary education in Canada. Ottawa, ON: Canadian Association of University Teachers. 58 Breakthrough!: Canada's Greatest Inventions and Innovations by John Melady @ 2013 by permission of Dundurn Press Limited; 67 Adapted from Yang. J. (2015, October 5). From Toronto Star, October 5 © 2015 Toronto Star Newspapers Limited. All rights reserved. Used by permission and protected by the Copyright Laws of the United States. The printing, copying redistribution, or retransmission of this Content without express written permission is prohibited; 71 Adapted from: http://www.bobsweep.com/; 77 Adapted from Source: Oxford, R. L. (1990). *Language learning strategies: What every teacher should know.* Boston, MA: Heinle & Heinle; 96. Wright, R.T. (2012) *Technology and Engineering* (6th ed).Tinley Park: Goodheart-Wilcox; 104 Adapted from Patel, N. V. (2016, February 10). Why igloos work: Catenoids, crystal structures, and the 61-degree melt point. *Inverse Magazine.* Retrieved from https://www.inverse.com/article/11327-why-igloos-work-catenoids-crystal-structures-and-the-61-degree-melt-point; 106 Retrieved from: http://www.popularmechanics.com/technology/design/a7555/how-to-build-an-igloo/) Author: Jeff Wise, Feb. 24, 2012; 109 Science with Kids. (2016) Facts about concrete. Science with Kids. Retrieved from http://sciencewithkids.com/science-facts/facts-about-concrete.html; 120 Marla Vacek Broadfoot. "What are spider webs made of?" *The News & Observer*; 139 Excerpted from: Morrow, D. & Wamsley, K. (2013). *Sport in Canada: A History* (3rd ed.). Don Mills, ON: Oxford University Press; 142 Adapted from: Watt, J., & Colyer, J. (2014). *IQ: A Practical Guide to Inquiry-based Learning.* Don Mills, Ontario: Oxford University Press; 150 Active Healthy Kids Canada (2014). Is Canada in the Running? The 2014 Report Card on Physical Activity for Children and Youth; 161 Mack, C.M. (2016). CWHL: Top female hockey players go unpaid. Retrieved from http://goo.gl/J1KC82; Netto, K. (2016, April 17). Should women athletes earn the same as men? The science says they work as hard. Retrieved from http://goo.gl/YbSJIK; 186 Little, W. et al. (2012). Introduction to Sociology–2nd Canadian Edition. pp. 400-402. Retrieved from: https://opentextbc.ca/introductiontosociology2ndedition/; 195 Garriguet, D. (2007). Canadians' Eating Habits. Health Reports, 18 (2). Ottawa, ON: Statistics Canada; Young, R. (2015). Canada's Media Landscape. Toronto, ON: IAB Canada; 206 Information adapted from http://www.cbc.radio-canada.ca/en/explore/our-history/; 207 Canadian Association of University Teachers.

(2015). 2014–2015 CAUT almanac of post-secondary education in Canada. Ottawa, ON: Canadian Association of University Teachers; **232** Based on ideas found at http://contentmarketinginstitute.com/2014/10/sticky-note-approach-to-brainstorms/; **236** Aon Hewitt (March, 2013). Developing Canada's future workforce: a survey of large private-sector employers. Report. p. 4. Retrieved from: http://thebusinesscouncil.ca/wp-content/uploads/2016/02/Developing-Canadas-Workforce-March.pdf; **237** Aon Hewitt (March, 2013). Developing Canada's future workforce: a survey of large private-sector employers. Report. p. 4. Retrieved from: http://thebusinesscouncil.ca/wp-content/uploads/2016/02/Developing-Canadas-Workforce-March.pdf; **249** Oxford, R. (1990). Language learning strategies: What every teacher should know. Boston, MA: Newbury House Publishers.

Photo Credits

Index